Grammar and the Language Teacher

Other titles in this series include

NEWMARK, Peter
Approaches to translation

NUNAN, David
Language teaching methodology: a textbook for teachers

ROBINSON, Pauline
ESP Today: a practitioner's guide

SUNDERLAND, Jane (ed.)
*Exploring gender: questions and implications for
English language education*

WEIR, Cyril
Communicative language testing

WENDEN, Anita and RUBIN, Joan
Learner strategies in language learning

WENDEN, Anita
Learner strategies and learner autonomy

Other titles of interest

AARTS, F. and AARTS, J.
English syntactic structures

ALLSOP, Jake
Student's English grammar

DOWNING, A. and LOCKE, P.
A university course in English grammar

WOODS, E. and McLEOD, N.
Using basic English grammar: form and function

WOODS, E. and McLEOD, N.
Using English grammar: meaning and form

Grammar and the Language Teacher

Edited by
Martin Bygate, Alan Tonkyn and Eddie Williams

Centre for Applied Language Studies,
University of Reading

Prentice Hall
New York London Toronto Sydney Tokyo Singapore

PRENTICE HALL INTERNATIONAL ENGLISH LANGUAGE TEACHING

First published 1994 by
Prentice Hall International (UK) Ltd
Campus 400, Maylands Avenue
Hemel Hempstead
Hertfordshire HP2 7EZ
A division of
Simon & Schuster International Group

Typeset in 10/12 Times by
Fakenham Photosetting Ltd

Printed and bound in Great Britain by
Redwood Books, Trowbridge, Wiltshire

Library of Congress Cataloging-in-Publication Data

Grammar and the language teacher / edited by Martin Bygate, Alan
   Tonkyn, and Eddie Williams.
      p.   cm. – (Prentice Hall international English language
  teaching)
    ISBN 0–13–474610–4 : £26.25 (U.K.)
    1. English language – Study and teaching – Foreign speakers.
2. English language – Grammar – Study and teaching. I. Bygate,
Martin. II. Tonkyn, Alan. III. Williams, Eddie. IV. Series:
English language teaching (Englewood Cliffs, N.J.)
PE1128.A2G77 1994
428′.007 – dc20   94–7268
                                      CIP

British Library Cataloguing in Publication Data

A catalogue record for this book is available from
the British Library

ISBN 0–13–042532–X

1 2 3 4 5 98 97 96 95 94

Contents

General Editor's Preface

If this exciting book were only a charting of the recent vicissitudes of the place and role of grammar and grammar teaching within language education, it might stand as a salutary warning of how in all fields, but perhaps especially in ours, fashion can override the dictates of sense. The recent headline 'Grammar is back!' opens Alan Tonkyn's introduction to this excellent and coherent collection of papers. It is interesting to speculate, and this book does so, whether grammar really did disappear off the edge of the language teacher's map, and if so (and I suspect that in the classroom it was always more alive and well than we think), what can be done to avoid such a manifest absurdity ever happening again. This book offers some ways in which the central place of grammar in language teaching and learning can be reaffirmed and maintained.

What are the core conditions? Firstly, as teachers and learners, we need to see grammar not primarily as a unitary object, something whose component parts have to be learned, but, rather, as a metaphor, a vehicle to encode our experiences to others in an interpersonally sensitive way, and a device to decode, in return, *their* experiences and beliefs. In doing so, we revalue grammar as an enabling device, not one which shackles and constrains. Secondly, we need to emphasise the systemic nature of grammar, showing how the internal organisation of written and spoken text conventionally realises, through the possibilities afforded by the lexicogrammar, particular semantic and pragmatic choices, functionally and economically. Thirdly, we need to see the conditions for the teaching and learning of grammar as not alien to the essence of grammar but inherent in our definition of it. If grammar is an organising metaphor to be explored, if grammar is systemic and functional, then our approach to teaching and learning should be equally creative, equally systematic and equally targeted on the achievement of functional and personal goals. In sum, as teachers we need to alter our stance towards grammar and encourage a similar change among our learners, and as consumers we need to insist on a corresponding shift in those published materials with which we work in our classrooms.

If we achieve these changes of attitude, we can begin to be receptive to some of the many intriguing questions and exciting practical possibilities offered by the papers in this book, such as the relationship between our descriptions of grammar and the use of grammar in real time, and the relationships between task design and the processing of grammar in learning and in use. The papers encourage us to examine how learners capture the prototypical essence of particular grammatical forms and learn to accommodate to their natural and constant variation. This collection also takes account of increasingly available corpora and suggests how, through these, learners can be trained to discover the conventions of grammar for themselves and understand their generic variability. In this volume we also find the influence of the contemporary focus on raising the learner's consciousness of grammatical processes and forms, through which second language acquisition can be enhanced. Finally, we are made aware that perspectives on the nature of grammar and the choice of modes of grammar teaching are never ideologically neutral and therefore always have to be critically explained in particular historical and social contexts and conditions.

If we can achieve the three conditions mentioned above, we can prepare ourselves against, not so much a second loss of grammar from language education, but what is nowadays much more likely: a narrow, debilitating and ultimately enslaving interpretation of what grammar can be made to mean.

Professor Christopher N. Candlin
Macquarie University
Sydney

Acknowledgements

We would like to acknowledge the support given by the British Association for Applied Linguistics and the Centre for Applied Language Studies, University of Reading, for the conference on 'Grammar for the Second Language Classroom', held at the University of Reading in July 1991, which led to the compilation of this volume.

We are grateful to the following publishers for permission to reproduce extracts of copyright material: Oxford University Press for the extract from Soars, J. and Soars, L. 1986, *Headway Intermediate*; Cambridge University Press for the illustration from Johnson, K. 1982, *Now for English Workbook 1* and Nelson for the extracts from Johnson, K. and Morrow, K. 1979, *Approaches*.

List of Contributors

Stephen Andrews	University of Hong Kong
Rob Batstone	Institute of Education, University of London
Mike Beaumont	University of Manchester
Martin Bygate	University of Reading
Sylvia Chalker	Freelance author and teacher trainer
Clare Gallaway	University of Manchester
Carl James	University College of Wales, Bangor
Keith Johnson	University of Lancaster
Geoffrey Leech	University of Lancaster
Rosamond Mitchell	University of Southampton
Margaret Rogers	University of Surrey
Peter Skehan	Thames Valley University
Michael Swan	Freelance author and teacher trainer
Alan Tonkyn	University of Reading
Eddie Williams	University of Reading
Dave Willis	University of Birmingham

Introduction: Grammar and the Language Teacher

ALAN TONKYN

1. The grammar revival

'Grammar is back!' This was the newspaper headline with which David Crystal prefaced one of his *English Now* radio programmes a few years ago. In recent years in Britain, there has certainly been ample evidence to support the assertion, at least with regard to English. In the realm of the teaching of English as a mother tongue, there have been a number of publications aimed at improving teachers' and trainees' grasp of updated grammatical descriptions of the language (e.g. Leech *et al.*, 1982; Jackson, 1982; Young, 1984; Freeborn, 1987; Greenbaum, 1991). There has been government pressure for a return to the formal study of grammar, which has found expression – though not always in a fashion to the government's liking – in the Kingman and Cox reports and the Language in the National Curriculum (LINC) project. In the realm of the teaching of English as a second or foreign language, there has also been a flurry of publishing activity, with the appearance of a number of new pedagogical grammars, grammar practice books, and methodology guides for teachers (e.g. Chalker, 1984, 1990; Harmer, 1987; Hall and Shepheard, 1991; Murphy, 1985, 1990; Frank and Rinvolucri, 1987; Ur, 1988; Wajnryb, 1990; Woods and McLeod, 1990; Willis, 1991).

Before proceeding further, it is important to examine the scope of what we mean by 'grammar', for, as Batstone (this volume) has remarked, grammar is 'multidimensional'. For a start, grammar can be seen as descriptive – the stuff of reference grammars and linguistic theory – or pedagogical – the stuff of lessons and textbooks. Beyond both of these lies the learner/user's own 'psycholinguistic' grammar, and the connection between descriptive and pedagogical grammars and the learner's grammatical system could be said to be the main theme of this volume. When we turn to the substance of grammar, we note that, in formal terms, grammar comprises both syntax and morphology, though it is common for apologists for a particular point of view to fasten on one or the other to represent grammar as a whole. In addition, grammar operates both within the sentence and also beyond it, where it is involved in text building and text interpretation. Furthermore, grammar learning may involve the learning of quasi-lexical items, such as pronouns or prepositions, or of interconnected systems, such as assertive and non-assertive forms or mass and count. Finally, one must also remember that distinctions of grammatical form can have very different degrees of functional meaning: some forms, such as the English present tense third person singular -*s* ending, are rules of formal correctness with little functional import; others, such as tense and aspect forms, may signal important meaning distinctions and do so in ways which are difficult to describe without detailed reference to context. (See also Williams, this volume, and Ellis, 1990: 166–8.) Grammar, like beauty, is in the eye of the beholder, and beholders must beware lest their view of the subject be limited by habit or predilection.

Returning to Crystal's newspaper headline, we are moved to ask: 'Where has grammar been? Why did it go away? Why has it now come back?' Answering these questions requires a brief historical overview of the role and status of grammar in language learning.

2. A historical overview

The original supremacy of grammar

Until fairly recently, the idea of singling out grammar for special attention in relation to foreign language teaching would have seemed odd. Within the centuries-old tradition of language learning dominated by Latin and Greek, the study of a language meant primarily the study of its grammar, both as an end in itself and also to enable the learner to read, and perhaps write, the language in question as a tool of scholarship. It was not surprising that this method of language teaching and learning was subsequently dubbed the 'grammar–translation method'.

The successors to this method in the first half of the twentieth century may have spurned grammatical knowledge as a focus and translation as a means, but they nonetheless saw their task as the transmission of the grammatical system. Thus Palmer may have used functional labels such as 'How to teach Place and Position' (Palmer, 1940) but assembled under them homogeneous sets of structural patterns. Brooks, writing largely within the American structuralist/audiolingual tradition, saw 'control of the structures of sound, form and order in the new language' as a vital underlying objective (Brooks, 1964: 111). A 1971 British guide to would-be teachers of EFL had no separate section on grammar: grammar simply occupied a key position in nearly all the chapters (Wilson and Wilson, 1971).

The centrality of grammar in language teaching mirrored the centrality of grammar in structural linguistics, which was increasingly called on to validate language teaching methods. Wilkins (1972: 68) writes: 'It is the aim of the linguist to reveal the system of the language, the *langue*, and of the language teacher to enable people to learn it'. The taxonomic and behaviourist-influenced approaches of the early structural linguists were echoed in early forms of contrastive analysis, which suggested that a relatively straightforward comparison of the structural systems of first and target language would reveal the discrepancies which would in turn form the main focus of teaching and testing. Although it disputed the adequacy of the early structuralist approach, the Chomskyan revolution in linguistics kept grammar at the centre of linguistic interest. Chomsky's ideas did not have a direct or straight-forward effect on language teaching, but they may be said to have created a climate in which a revival of mentalist or cognitive approaches to language pedagogy was easier. The name of one of these approaches, the 'cognitive code method', reflects continuing concern with language system, and it is significant that Carroll saw this method as a kind of updated grammar–translation approach (Carroll, 1966).

The decline of grammar

However, though in the late 1950s and early 1960s linguistics appeared to be about to offer a revitalised and scientific approach to grammar which would be of service to language teachers, the actual failure of linguists to agree among themselves as to the best method of grammatical analysis, and their inability to deliver the *langue* to language teachers in an accessible form, probably led to increasing scepticism amongst the latter about the relevance of modern grammatical studies to the business of language teaching. Language teachers found themselves, as Allen and Widdowson have noted, in a dilemma:

> On the one hand, traditional grammar was supposed to be 'unscientific' and therefore unworthy of serious consideration, while linguistics seemed to be a highly esoteric subject beyond the comprehension of any but the most dedicated of University scholars. ... As a result many teachers became disillusioned, not only about modern linguistics, but about linguistics in general, including traditional grammar, and there was a widespread reaction against grammar-teaching in the schools. (Allen and Widdowson, 1975: 45)

'Applied linguistics' became a rather vague cover term for a range of academic interests, with the application of pure linguistics not particularly prominent among them.

If mainstream linguistics had a somewhat equivocal effect on the status of gram-mar within language teaching, sociolinguistics may be said to have been a major influence in its dethronement. Structural linguists had long rejected prescriptivism in favour of descriptive approaches, and also asserted the primacy of speech. In the realm of sociolinguistics this led to the questioning of the pre-eminent status of standard dialects and forms of pronunciation and of the written language, and hence to a blurring of the notion of 'correctness' on which the old school grammars were based (e.g. Trudgill, 1974: 54–6). In many British schools these ideas, coupled with a humanistic emphasis on self-expression and discovery learning, led, in mother tongue teaching, to the abandonment of traditional grammar lessons and form-focused correction of written work in favour of creative writing and the development of fluent, effective speaking.

At the same time, the sociolinguist Hymes was arguing for the broadening of the notion of competence beyond its narrow Chomskyan boundaries to become 'com-municative competence', a concept with not only a linguistic dimension, but also a sociolinguistic one, seen especially in the ability to use and interpret language *appropriately* in specific contexts (Hymes, 1972).

This notion of communicative competence was also appealed to by those, such as van Ek, Richterich and Wilkins, who sought to express foreign language teaching syllabuses in terms that reflected language-in-use (e.g. Wilkins, 1976: 11). The ensuing 'functional/notional' approach to syllabus and methodology often appeared to go beyond the wishes of the original prime movers in its setting up of 'structures' and 'functions' as a simple dichotomy, and in its tendency to see the former as somehow superseded by the latter. The Communicative Language Teaching movement, which aimed to replicate in the classroom important contextual and purposive features of real communication, tended also to play down the value of grammar teaching. Communicative success, it was suggested, did not necessarily require accurate grammar. In Communicative Language Testing, grammatical accuracy was but one of several criteria set up for the assessment of effective speaking and writing.

The Language for Specific Purposes movement began under a strong structural influence (e.g. Ewer and Latorre, 1969; Swales, 1971), seeking to answer the question: 'What selection from the grammar and lexicon of the target language will be of most use to, say, a scientist?' It soon fell under the sway of the functional/ notional approach, however, and began to ask: 'What types of communicative event will our students engage in?' Munby's work in the area of syllabus design for ESP courses (Munby, 1978) can be seen to be a full-blown expression of this development: what had been of paramount importance, namely language forms, seems to become for Munby almost an afterthought, worth little detailed attention compared with the nature of the student and his/her prospective language roles, domains, functions and skills.

If sociolinguistic awareness contributed to the decline of the importance of grammar in foreign language course design and methodology, psycholinguistics also played an important part. Chomsky's conception of the child learning its mother tongue as being equipped with some form of partly 'wired-up' language acquisition device, coupled with research by Brown revealing the regularities in the order of children's acquisition of morphological features of their L1, was very influential in second language acquisition research in the United States. Evidence from morpheme acquisition studies (e.g. Dulay and Burt, 1973, 1974) of acquisitional regularities similar to those revealed by the L1 researchers was an important plank in the construction of Krashen's Input Hypothesis (Krashen, 1985). Krashen's view of the second language acquisition process, according to which an inbuilt acquisitional mechanism would operate under the right conditions of comprehensible input and low affective filter, marginalised the role of form-focused instruction.

Thus by the early 1980s, in mother tongue and foreign language teaching, especially in Britain and the United States, there were a number of reasons why grammar had lost the central position it had once held. Grammatical competence was but one component of communicative competence, and weaknesses in that area could be compensated for by strengths in, say, strategic or discourse competence. Grammatical description and instruction were seen, using Chomsky's terms, as belonging to the world of externalised (or E-) language, while what was more important was the learner's internalised (or I-) language, a language system which developed 'automatically', uninfluenced by the well-meant corrections of a parent, or by tidy-minded syllabus writers and teachers (Chomsky, 1987, cited in Cook, 1988).

The rediscovery of grammar

The second half of the 1980s saw the partial reinstatement of grammar in Britain, both in mother-tongue teaching and in the teaching of English as a second or foreign language. This, of course, is an over-simplification in that, for many teachers, grammar had never gone away: the conservatism of some and the canny eclecticism of many others maintained the tradition of explicit teaching of grammar even when such teaching was officially out of fashion. However, there is no doubt that Crystal's pronouncement reflected a noticeable swing back of the pendulum.

For the British government, a return to some form of traditional school grammar was seen as a means of halting an apparent decline in standards of written English amongst school leavers. Some educationalists (e.g. Edwards and Mercer, 1987, cited in Mitchell, this volume) argued in favour of explicit teaching of concepts and against excessive use of discovery learning. Although the linguists' syntactic theory had proved largely unassimilable by teachers in the 1960s and 1970s, the 1980s saw a revival of interest in an updated study of the language system based on the grammars of Quirk and his colleagues (e.g. Quirk *et al.*, 1972, 1985), which were a continuation of the great tradition of English grammar writing and yet bore clear evidence of linguistic influence in their approach.

The development of a grammar based on the massive COBUILD database (Sinclair, 1990) has given further impetus to the growth of interest in modern grammatical description. The computer, with its ability to reveal with much greater ease the detail of the grammatical behaviour of particular words in actual use, has stimulated interest in 'lexical' approaches to grammar, reflected in Willis (this volume), though the wisdom of relying entirely on the database rather than on native-speaker intuition in the formulation of grammatical rules has recently been questioned (Owen, 1993).

In the area of second language acquisition research, there was a widespread reaction against the strong form of the I-language approach espoused by Krashen and his colleagues. Though research (e.g. the work of Pienemann and Felix and their co-workers in Germany) continued to show that aspects of the acquisition process could be resistant to the effects of formal teaching, many champions of the importance of E-language in general, and instruction in particular, emerged. Scholars like McLaughlin and Schmidt questioned Krashen's contention that what had been formally 'learned' could not pass into the 'acquired' system and be available for spontaneous use (McLaughlin, 1987; Schmidt, 1990). An alternative view of second language acquisition as the acquisition of a cognitive skill, proposed particularly by McLaughlin and drawing on work in skill theory, appeared to give support to more traditional language teaching approaches, with its emphasis on the automatisation of language items through practice in context (e.g. McLaughlin, 1987).

Rather than simply arguing for or against the value of formal instruction, researchers now began to investigate the situations in which instruction was most likely to be of benefit, and Ellis has suggested that dimensions such as the complexity of processing operations and of form–function relationships may explain the degree of teachability of different grammatical forms (Ellis, 1990: 166–8). Many scholars have also pointed out the particular benefits of formal instruction, which make it a necessary complement to informal learning if high levels of proficiency are aimed at: instruction is much more likely than informal interaction to provide useful negative feedback; instruction can make formal features of the language salient; instruction can provide a context for extensive practice of particular forms. Because of these characteristics, instruction, it is widely believed, can help to prevent the premature fossilisation which an excessive emphasis on the performance of communicative tasks may bring, and can assist learners, especially adults, to learn more rapidly and efficiently. The period when the value of formal instruction was strongly doubted now seems to be over and, in retrospect, as Spolsky has remarked, 'does certainly seem like one of those aberrations that sometimes afflict academic minds' (Spolsky, 1989: 193).

Along with this subtler approach to the effects and benefits of instruction has come a renewed and subtler interest in contrastive analysis. Under the aegis of behaviourism, contrastive analysis (CA) had posited the transfer of language habits as a major factor in second language learning, but had failed to deliver the goods in the form of valid predictions of problematic areas for particular groups of learners. With cognitive psychology in the ascendant, CA now focuses more on the importance of L1 schemata in the mind of the learner, and the effect thereof both on the kind of hypotheses learners would put forward about the target language and on the rate of acquisition of certain features of that language. Those who have argued for an approach to grammar teaching based on 'consciousness-raising' (CR) (e.g. Rutherford, 1987) have speculated that CR may be particularly valuable in helping learners to 'reset' their L1 parameters to the form required by the L2.

It must not, of course, be assumed that the pronouncements of the mandarins of applied linguistics have immediately and directly affected language teachers and their approach to their work. However, the influence of university-based language teaching specialists on publishers, course designers and teacher trainers has been considerable, and has contributed greatly to the atmosphere in which decisions are taken in the world of practical language teaching. Thus in the 1970s and 1980s a multitude of English language coursebooks appeared in which lesson headings and objectives were stated in functional terms, with grammar relegated to a special (and often brief) language study section at the end of the lesson or unit. More recently, though the functional-communicative emphasis has remained, general courses have often given a clearer indication of the grammatical underpinning of each unit, and a large number of grammar reference and practice books have appeared to supplement the general courses, as has been noted at the beginning of this introduction.

3. This volume: an outline

Overview: different approaches to grammar

Ten of the articles included in this volume are based on papers given at the BAAL conference on 'Grammar for the Second Language Classroom', held at the University of Reading in July 1991. The present volume, and the conference which initially inspired it, reflect the revival of interest in grammar in second language teaching, but also the varied fortunes of grammar in the world of language teaching over the last thirty years.

In broad terms it can be said that the first two sections focus on grammar as an *object* for learners and teachers. Section 1, entitled 'Grammar and Grammars', attempts to answer the questions: 'What does, or should, pedagogical grammar look and sound like?' and 'How close is its relationship to descriptive grammar?'. Section 2, entitled 'Teachers' Knowledge of Grammar', reports on research into the state of language teachers' knowledge of grammar and attitudes to it. The third and fourth sections emphasise grammar as a *process*. Section 3, 'Grammar and Learning', examines the ways in which learners acquire the grammar of a foreign or second language, while Section 4, 'Grammar and Teaching', reflects current thinking on the ways in which teachers can work with, rather than against, the complex processes of language acquisition. However, the divisions of the volume reflect differences of emphasis rather than watertight compartments of content: pedagogical grammar as object, whether in the form of a printed page of a reference book or a teacher's simple grammar rule, cannot easily be kept apart from pedagogical grammar as process, whether in the form of a student's perception of part of the grammatical system, or a teacher's day-by-day monitoring of his/her students' grammatical development.

Section 1: grammar and grammars

In the first section, four authors of grammars or grammar practice books look at the question of what makes grammar pedagogical, or, in other words, how grammar can be made compatible with the needs of learners. All appear to accept what Carl James (this volume) refers to as 'the teacher's conviction that there is a relationship between what is describable and what is learnable', but all also acknowledge, in one way or another, that successful pedagogical description involves seeing grammar with the eyes of the learner.

Geoffrey Leech sees a teacher's grammar as Janus-like: facing towards academic descriptive grammar on the one hand and towards selective, sequenced, activity-based grammar for learners on the other. The terms 'mature' and 'systematic' occur several times in Leech's account of an ideal teacher's grammar, emphasising the responsibilities of the teacher as mediator and knower which set him/her apart from the learner. The picture of teacher-as-grammarian which emerges from Leech's discussion is one which emphasises relevance to the learner at all points: the teacher's understanding of grammar should be strongly meaning- and communication-related; it should be alert to awkward reality rather than merely governed by over-simplified prescriptive rule; it should be sensitive to L1/L2 contrasts; it should be aware of the need for simplicity. The conflict between descriptive truth and pedagogical simplicity becomes Leech's theme for the second part of his article, and he proposes a prototype view of grammar, with learners moving from central prototypes of categories and rules outwards towards the periphery of 'problem cases' as they develop in knowledge.

Sylvia Chalker also raises the problem of the conflict of truth and descriptive adequacy on the one hand and necessary simplification and the needs of teachers and learners on the other. She makes a special plea for grammar to make sense – a deeper sense – to the learner, rather than to be merely a collection of *ad hoc* rules. She also notes, with an author's experience, the way in which grammar tends to impose its own organisational constraints, even when grammar writers try to get away from them by such devices as functional labelling in reference grammars and courses.

Chalker sees the learner's view of grammar as being 'grammar = rules'. Michael Swan then probes the desirable qualities of these rules in more detail. He provides six criteria according to which the success of a pedagogical rule can be judged: truth, demarcation, clarity, simplicity, conceptual parsimony and relevance. Swan's realistic assessment of the learner's needs is evident in his discussion of all six: most language learners, he notes, are non-specialists in the area of grammar, and he observes: 'A little truth goes a long way when one is off one's own ground'.

In arguing for a quasi-lexical approach to grammar, David Willis is also attempting to reconstruct grammatical description from a learner's viewpoint, and to achieve that more all-embracing sense which Chalker seeks in a pedagogical grammar. In a direct challenge to the tenets of structural linguistics, Willis proposes that key grammatical words or forms, such as the modal verb *would* and the 'past participle', should be freed from bondage within certain grammatical patterns, such as conditional sentences and the passive, to allow students to make more far-reaching generalisations about them. Willis's approach reflects those of the grammar 'dictionaries' (e.g. Chalker, 1990) and of researchers into the behaviour of words as revealed so powerfully by computer-based corpora.

Section 2: teachers' knowledge of grammar

The second section examines what teachers know about grammar and how they view it. In so doing, it provides an insight into the effects of the neglect of grammar, or 'knowledge about language', in mother tongue and second language classrooms in the 1960s and 1970s, especially in Britain and the United States.

Stephen Andrews's research into teacher trainers' views of the adequacy of the grammatical knowledge of native-speaker trainees on a preliminary certification course for teachers of EFL reveals that the trainees' earlier education had poorly equipped them for the content aspect of their new profession. The fact that such trainees could continue in the profession with a number of serious weaknesses in their ability to explain grammatical points, to identify student errors correctly and to demonstrate understanding of grammatical concepts and terminology, is a mark of the extent to which the ELT profession has become deprofessionalised in the area of grammatical knowledge through a combination of simple neglect and misguided principle.

Rosamond Mitchell's account, based on British data, of National Curriculum syllabus writers' and language teachers' views of grammar reveals the uncertainties of these two groups concerning the role of grammar in language teaching. Some foreign language syllabuses appear to oscillate awkwardly between a traditional and incomplete grammatical specification, based on parts of speech, and a separate section for language functions.

Andrews's trainers and Mitchell (see also Section 4) have clear ideas about what teachers *should* know in the area of grammar, and in both cases it may be said to embrace a more descriptive aspect, which may help particularly in matters of planning, and a more pedagogical aspect, which will show itself in the ability to deal with students' problems and to make students aware of language as a system in an accessible form.

Eddie Williams begins by making explicit what is implicit in many of the other articles in this volume: grammar rules cannot be regarded as one homogeneous phenomenon. Some, like the addition of *-s* to third person singular present simple verbs in English, can be seen as purely formal (or in Williams's terms, 'constitutive') rules; others, such as the contrast between present and past tense, can be seen as more strongly meaning-related or 'communicative' rules. Williams's report on research into attitudes to grammar amongst the experienced teachers on an MA(TEFL) course reflects the uncertainties surrounding the status of grammar revealed by Mitchell in her articles in this and the final section. Most of Williams's questionnaire respondents valued an explicit knowledge of grammar for themselves, but were less confident about advocating it for their students, preferring a more covert approach. Their seeming preference for grammatical explanations to be *post hoc* and remedial exactly conforms to the finding of Faerch's Danish study (Faerch, 1986, cited in Mitchell, this volume).

Section 3: grammar and learning

The first two articles in the third section of this volume reflect the battle between I-language and E-language theories in the realm of second language acquisition. The former, as has been mentioned above, emphasise the importance of the learner's inbuilt predispositions to learn language in a particular sequence, unaffected by the precise nature of the data presented (including formal grammar instruction). The latter emphasise the importance of the external data presented to the learner and the way in which he/she processes that data. The former will tend to favour a teaching approach which allows the natural acquisition process to work. The latter will look for ways to drive the acquisition process forward.

The second two articles in this section also raise the issues of the relative merits of a more holistic or 'lexicalised' approach to grammar learning, as against a more analytical approach. For Mike Beaumont and Clare Gallaway the former approach is seen to be possibly necessary with regard to certain *parts* of the grammatical system; for Peter Skehan, it is a first *stage* in all language learning, and will be complemented by an analytical phase.

Keith Johnson's discussion of the teaching of declarative and procedural knowledge can be seen to be clearly located in the E-language camp. He accepts the value of declarative knowledge, for example in the form of explicit presentation of grammatical structure, seeing it as both a continuing generative reference point and the necessary beginning of a process which will culminate in proceduralisation, or automatisation, of that knowledge by the learner in a form available for skilled performance with minimal attention. Johnson accepts that the learner's internal representation of declarative knowledge will necessarily differ from the external form, and sees pedagogical grammar as being 'a science of hints' to aid the development in the learner of a form of that external knowledge which can readily be automatised. Johnson subtly rewrites one of the mantras of communicative language teaching by suggesting that this automatisation will be aided by teaching procedures which are not so much meaning-focused as 'form-defocused'.

By contrast, Margaret Rogers's proposals for the teaching of German word order rules take an I-language position as their starting point. They are based on a Chomskyan parameter-setting view of language according to which the child, in learning his/her mother tongue, is equipped with a number of 'switches' which will be 'set' in one way or another depending on the type of language the child is learning. Learning a foreign language will involve resetting some of these switches to fit the new data. Rogers also draws heavily on the work of Pienemann, whose findings about the seemingly unalterable sequence in which learners of German as a second language acquire word order rules also reflect an I-language stance. Rogers, following the views of the proponents of grammatical consciousness-raising, sees external intervention by the teacher as being of most value when it takes account of differences between L1 and L2 and remedies the lack of certain kinds of evidence about those differences available to learners.

Mike Beaumont and Clare Gallaway's discussion of the learning of the English article system can be seen to exemplify some of the difficulties associated with meeting Leech's criteria for pedagogic grammar. They note that, in this area, linguistic grammars are not found to be particularly helpful in forming a workable pedagogical grammar, which, in turn, finds it difficult to cope with the pragmatic complexities of the article system as actually used by native speakers. Beaumont and Gallaway's account of the process of article acquisition by L1 and L2 learners appears to highlight the importance of what Skehan (this volume) has termed the initial 'lexicalisation' (or chunk-learning) stage of acquisition. It also provides further evidence of what Rogers wishes to emphasise: the existence of sequences of acquisition which instruction will find difficult to alter, but which it may assist.

Peter Skehan's wide-ranging article can be seen as an attempt to achieve a balance between task-based and analytical approaches. Like Johnson, Skehan accepts a clear distinction between the analyst's (external, descriptive) model of a language and the user's (internal) model. The user will usually acquire language in a 'lexical' way, as unanalysed chunks. Full development will require further processes of syntacticisation, in which the lexical chunks are analysed, and relexicalisation (equivalent to Johnson's proceduralisation or 'automisation') in which the language is then made accessible for spontaneous use. Skehan points out the dangers of teaching approaches which allow learners to get stuck at the first stage and to use communication strategies to cope with language tasks – strategies which will not cause the learner's interlanguage to develop. While accepting that there is some kind of natural acquisition process, Skehan countenances a fairly wide range of intervention options in a task-based methodology: pre-emptive language work, task control approaches (similar in effect to Johnson's form-defocus gradient), and the use of a post-task product to focus learners' attention on accuracy.

Section 4: grammar and teaching

In the final section, learning theory remains to the fore, but the main focus of attention is now the teacher's role in assisting the learning process. Important issues which dominate the section are the respective roles of deductive, explicit and product-oriented approaches on the one hand and inductive, implicit and process-oriented approaches on the other. It could be said that, after a period in which language teachers in the West have tended to be wary of intervening too much in the language learning process, this section reflects a move back towards a greater degree of intervention. However, it is intervention which is influenced by the thinking and research of the last decade. It is very selective intervention, designed to complement the natural acquisition process by making evidence available which will be difficult to infer from natural input and designed also to prevent fossilisation. It is unlikely to claim for itself too great or immediate an influence on student performance, and it will often be at work almost surreptitiously, in the sequencing of tasks or the setting of particular problems for the students.

The section can be seen to fall into two parts. The first two articles, by Carl James and Rosamond Mitchell, focus on the value of knowledge about language in the teacher and for the learner. The second two, by Rob Batstone and Martin Bygate, look at ways in which, in a process- and task-oriented approach, the teacher can helpfully intervene to regulate learning.

James echoes many of the concerns of the contributors to Sections 1 and 3. He gives further detail on the key distinctions between a linguistic grammar and a grammar for teaching, and probes the issue of positive and negative evidence for the learner raised by Rogers. For James, the teacher's role as explainer involves the provision to the learner of necessary positive and negative evidence about the language being learned, but he notes a key problem for teachers which recent research has highlighted: that which is the most difficult to learn, and is therefore most in need of teaching, tends to be the most difficult to describe and therefore to teach. In this situation, James advocates a grammar-teaching strategy which takes the learner's L1 as its starting point: heightened awareness of the rules of his/her L1 will make the learner more aware of what he/she needs to know in the L2.

Mitchell's article in this section gives evidence of trends in the 1970s and 1980s mentioned in the historical overview above. She highlights L1 and L2 teachers' wariness about direct grammar teaching, and also the relative lack of interest in the teacher-as-explainer amongst researchers. Mitchell emphasises that the precise effect of explicit talk about language is still not fully understood, but makes a strong plea for such consciousness-raising on grounds very similar to those appealed to by James, namely (*inter alia*) the need for provision to learners of negative evidence and, in L2 teaching, the need for an awareness of L1/L2 contrasts.

Batstone's article deals, in effect, with the age-old and central problem of how to achieve a transfer of desired grammatical information into a learner's actual language use under the conditions of normal communication. He sets up the dilemma which teachers face: do too much for the learner by way of a highly structured and analytical approach, and the learner is unlikely to be able to mobilise the grammar when faced with the unpredictability of normal communication; do too little, and the learner, as Skehan has pointed out, is likely to automatise a fossilised and limited form of the grammar. Batstone proposes a solution to the dilemma in which learners are faced with the need to 'grammaticise' lexical items in order to communicate.

Bygate reformulates Batstone's manipulation–abdication dilemma in terms of the progression in recent times from a teacher-based to a task-based approach. Like Batstone, Bygate is concerned with the ways in which tasks can be manipulated to practise grammar or, to put it less strongly, to promote helpful generalisations. Bygate's discussion of the ways in which tasks can be varied to affect learner performance recalls both Johnson's advocacy of a progressively form-defocused approach and Skehan's anatomisation of task characteristics. Bygate's detailed exemplification of the kind of language which different task variants will produce is perhaps a sign of things to come as a more interventionist style of teaching tackles the problem of grammar *within* task-based learning.

If this volume celebrates the return of grammar to the centre stage of language teaching and learning, it must also be acknowledged that it is now a more crowded stage. The research and teaching experience of the last two decades have left their mark in the form of such things as subtler approaches to contrastive analysis, a more selective and cautious application of explicit grammatical explanation, and a desire to embed grammar teaching within tasks rather than see tasks as mere practice vehicles for particular grammatical items. Though the 'natural acquisition' movement's attempt to devalue formal grammatical instruction can now be seen to be theoretically flawed, it nonetheless served the very useful purpose of forcing apologists for instruction to examine its value more closely, leading to the kind of insights and approaches evident in this volume. If this book encourages further development and questioning of currently emerging orthodoxies related to the role of grammar and grammar instruction within language teaching, it will have served its purpose.

References

Allen, J.P.B. and Widdowson, H.G. 1975. 'Grammar and language teaching', in Allen, J.P.B. and Corder, S. Pit (eds.), *The Edinburgh Course in Applied Linguistics*, vol. 2, OUP, Oxford.

Brooks, N. 1964. *Language and Language Learning*, Harcourt, Brace, Jovanovich, New York.

Carroll, J.B. 1966. 'Psychology, research and language teaching', in Valdman, A. (ed.), *Trends in Language Teaching*, McGraw-Hill, New York.

Chalker, S. 1984. *Current English Grammar*, Macmillan, London.

Chalker, S. 1990. *English Grammar Word by Word*, Nelson, Walton-on-Thames.

Cook, V.J. 1988. *Chomsky's Universal Grammar*, Blackwell, Oxford.

Dulay, H.C. and Burt, M.K. 1973. 'Should we teach children syntax?', *Language Learning*, vol. 23, no. 2: 245–57.

Dulay, H.C. and Burt, M.K. 1974. 'Natural sequences in child second language acquisition', *Language Learning*, vol. 24, no. 1: 37–53.

Ellis, R. 1990. *Instructed Second Language Acquisition*, Blackwell, Oxford.

Ewer, J.R. and Latorre, G. 1969. *A Course in Basic Scientific English*, Longman, Harlow.

Frank, C. and Rinvolucri, M. 1987. *Grammar in Action: Awareness Activities for Language Learning*, Prentice Hall International, Hemel Hempstead.

Freeborn, D. 1987. *A Course Book in English Grammar*, Macmillan, London.

Greenbaum, S. 1991. *An Introduction to English Grammar*, Longman, Harlow.

Hall, N. and Shepheard, J. 1991. *The Anti-Grammar Grammar Book*, Longman, Harlow.

Harmer, J. 1987. *Teaching and Learning Grammar*, Longman, Harlow.

Hymes, D. 1972. 'On communicative competence', in Pride, J.B. and Holmes, J., *Sociolinguistics*, Penguin, Harmondsworth.

Jackson, H. 1982. *Analyzing English*, Pergamon, Oxford.

Krashen, S.D. 1985. *The Input Hypothesis: Issues and Implications*, Longman, Harlow.

Leech, G., Deuchar, M. and Hoogenraad, R. 1982. *English Grammar for Today*, Macmillan, London.

McLaughlin, B. 1987. *Theories of Second-Language Learning*, Edward Arnold, London.

Munby, J. 1978. *Communicative Syllabus Design*, CUP, Cambridge.

Murphy, R. 1985. *English Grammar in Use*, CUP, Cambridge.

Murphy, R. 1990. *Essential Grammar in Use*, CUP, Cambridge.

Owen, C. 1993. 'Corpus-based grammar and the Heineken effect: lexico-grammatical description for language learners', *Applied Linguistics*, vol. 14, no. 2: 167–87.

Palmer, H.E. 1940. *The Teaching of Oral English*, Longman, London.

Quirk, R., Greenbaum, S., Leech, G. and Svartvik, J. 1972. *A Grammar of Contemporary English*, Longman, Harlow.

Quirk, R., Greenbaum, S., Leech, G. and Svartvik, J. 1985. *A Comprehensive Grammar of the English Language*, Longman, Harlow.

Rutherford, W.E. 1987. *Second Language Grammar: Teaching and Learning*, Longman, Harlow.

Schmidt, R. 1990. 'The role of consciousness in language learning', *Applied Linguistics*, vol. 11, no. 21: 129–58.

Sinclair, J. (ed.) 1990. *Collins Cobuild English Grammar*, Collins, London.

Spolsky, B. 1989. *Conditions for Second Language Learning*, OUP, Oxford.

Swales, J. 1971. *Writing Scientific English*, Nelson, Sunbury-on-Thames.

Trudgill, P. 1974. *Sociolinguistics*, Penguin, Harmondsworth.

Ur, P. 1988. *Grammar Practice Activities*, CUP, Cambridge.

Wajnryb, R. 1990. *Grammar Dictation*, OUP, Oxford.

Wilkins, D.A. 1972. *Linguistics in Language Teaching*, Edward Arnold, London.

Wilkins, D.A. 1976. *Notional Syllabuses*, OUP, Oxford.

Willis, D. 1991. *Collins Cobuild Student's Grammar: Classroom Edition – Practice Material*, Collins, London.

Wilson, G. and Wilson, A. 1971. *Teaching English to Foreigners*, Batsford, London.

Woods, E. and McLeod, N. 1990. *Using English Grammar: Meaning and Form*, Prentice Hall International, Hemel Hempstead.

Young, D. 1984. *Introducing English Grammar*, Hutchinson, London.

Section 1

GRAMMAR AND GRAMMARS

Students' Grammar –
Teachers' Grammar –
Learners' Grammar

GEOFFREY LEECH

1. Introduction: three varieties of grammar

My purpose here is to share some thoughts on what kind of foreign language grammar should be presented to teachers. I hope my comments will be appropriate both for initial teacher education and for in-service courses for teachers. Although there are some grammatical books and materials written specifically for teachers (e.g. Edmondson *et al.*, 1977), all too often, I suggest, it is assumed that grammar for teachers is a variant either of academic grammar on the one hand or of pedagogical grammar (grammar for learners) on the other. Table 1 represents B (teachers' grammar) falling between the two stools of A (academic grammar) and C (learners' grammar).

Table 1: Types of grammar

A Academic grammar (for university students)	*B* Teachers' grammar	*C* Grammar for learners
Theoretical and descriptive	← − − − − ? − − − − →	Practical, selective, sequenced, task-oriented, etc.

I suppose it could be argued that teachers should ideally be well versed in both A and C: that they should have a sound, detailed academic knowledge of the language; and that they should also be thoroughly skilled in the methodologies of mediating grammar to learners at different stages. But perhaps, in the real world, this is too much to hope for; and in any case, it does not solve the problem of the necessarily indirect relation between academic knowledge and the way it can be put to use in the classroom. So we could usefully begin by seeing teachers' grammar as some kind of mediation between A and C.

In relation to grammar for learners, an issue which has been much discussed is: how far do learners need to become consciously aware of the grammar know-how they are acquiring? Opinions have ranged from those who favour traditional grammar instruction through *explicit* learning – through the presentation of rules, and so on – to those who advocate *implicit* learning of grammar through exposure to, and practice in, the language in use. Most of us will probably accept that in most institutional learning situations some kind of combination of explicit and implicit learning is necessary, and indeed unavoidable. Many will also take the view that the less the learners have to be bothered with grammatical terminology and grammatical explanation, the better.

On the other hand, when we come to teachers' grammar, it is difficult to deny the need for explicit knowledge – and for a higher degree of grammar consciousness than most direct learners are likely to need or to want. What kind of knowledge does the teacher need? I will call it a 'mature communicative knowledge' of grammar, and will use the rest of this article to suggest what it should be like and what requirements it should meet.

2. Grammar requirements for teachers

To begin exploring the knowledge that the teacher needs, let us begin with a list of what a teacher is ideally required to do with this knowledge.[1]

A 'model' teacher of languages should:

(a) be capable of putting across a sense of how grammar interacts with the lexicon as a communicative system (both 'communicativeness' and 'system' will need independent attention);

(b) be able to analyse the grammatical problems that learners encounter;

(c) have the ability and confidence to evaluate the use of grammar, especially by learners, against criteria of accuracy, appropriateness and expressiveness;

(d) be aware of the contrastive relations between native language and foreign language;

(e) understand and implement the processes of simplification by which overt knowledge of grammar can best be presented to learners at different stages of learning.

Let us look at each of these in turn.

(a) Grammar as a communicative system

The need for a communicative approach to grammar for teachers is perhaps obvious and does not need much argument here. It is true that Chomsky has argued that communication is by no means the only function of language (Chomsky, 1979: 87–8), suggesting that mental functions, such as the development of understanding, may be equally or perhaps even more important. But in the context of foreign language learning, communicative ability in the broadest sense – both productive and receptive – appears to be an overriding aim.

The systematic nature of grammar is also extremely important, although here we have to understand 'system' in an organic rather than a mechanistic sense. Both communicativeness and systematicness involve the interrelatedness of different things that need to be learned. I understand communicative grammar to mean an approach to grammar in which the goal is to explore and to formulate the relations (or 'relatednesses') between the formal events of grammar (words, phrases, sentences, and their categories and structures) and the conditions of their meaning and use. In linguistic terminology, this means relating syntax and morphology to semantics and pragmatics.

Seeing grammar as a system means being able to appreciate the relationships among units, rules, classes and structures within the grammar code itself, and between them and their functions, so that the whole adds up to more than the sum of its parts. Take, for example, the learning of verb categories in English. The different choices of tense, aspect, voice and modality operate conjunctively, and cannot be properly understood in abstraction from one another. We cannot understand or produce a sentence such as *It should be being published right now* unless we can put both the forms and their meanings together in the appropriate way.

Rutherford (1987) presents an organic view of grammar learning, and justly criticises the linear conception of grammar learning as an accumulation of discrete 'grammatical points', or separate parcels of learning – the building-block view of grammar learning that one often finds in textbooks. First one 'does' the present simple – or the present continuous – then one 'does' the past simple, then the present perfect, and so on. Now since syllabuses and textbooks are by their very nature linear, it may be a necessary evil that the learner has to proceed point by point in this linear way. But this should not be the viewpoint of the teacher. For grammar to be acquired progressively as a system, it is better to think, not so much linearly, as in terms of a cyclic progression: revisiting, developing and enriching what one has already learned, elaborating new and related knowledge as one goes, and building a sense of the interrelatedness of choices – for example, in the domain of the verb, between modality and tense. (The best syllabuses, of course, already give attention to this kind of need.) So grammatical knowledge evolves organically, rather than growing in discrete steps. The metaphor of the burgeoning plant is so much more appropriate than that of the wall which grows by the placing of one inert lump of stone on another.

(b) Analysing learners' grammatical difficulties

Two other reasons for emphasising the teacher's need for mature systematic knowledge have to do with the balance between productive and receptive learning. The productive side of grammar learning is inevitably more under the control of the grammatical coverage of the syllabus. The receptive side is more advanced but less controllable. In reading and listening to a foreign language, learners will encounter a wider range of grammatical phenomena than their explicit knowledge can deal with. Coming to terms with this knowledge gap is all part of the process of learning. But from the receptive angle, it is inevitable that learners need help with the problems they encounter. This shows up most clearly in those awkward and apparently unanswerable questions which teachers have to face from learners – particularly from the more alert and observant ones. In responding to the problems learners encounter, teachers need to draw on their own mature knowledge of grammar, and at the same time to mediate, or 'filter' that knowledge in a form which satisfies the learner's immediate need.

In connection with receptive grammar learning, I should also mention the value, in my own experience, of presenting teachers or trainee teachers with inductive tasks of grammar investigation – let us think of them as mini-research projects. This is the method of *discovery learning*, going from the data (or instances) to generalisations (or 'rules'), rather than following the traditional method of grammar instruction, going from the generalisations to the instances (cf. Higgins, 1986). Nowadays, many will be familiar with the method of using computer corpus data, in the form of concordances, focusing on particular grammatical or lexical items.[2] Each member of the group investigates a particular grammatical phenomenon by looking at a rather wide range of occurrences in actual texts, and almost invariably comes to a far richer understanding of how grammar works in practice, communicatively, than can be provided by the most detailed treatments in grammar books. The discovery that native speakers use the language in unforeseen ways and in ways which may even contradict the grammar 'experts' is itself a salutary experience, which teachers can hand on to their own learners. The grammar teacher needs to earn respect as an authority on the language, and yet there is nothing wrong with admitting occasionally to being fallible and ignorant! This is an indulgence which is difficult to grant in the traditional educational culture of the oracular teacher. But why should Teacher the Omniscient not occasionally give way to Teacher the Seeker, who (like the academic scientist or scholar) knows only some of the answers, and would like to know more – and can thereby aim to stimulate and challenge the class to be seekers too?

(c) Evaluating the use of grammar

Turning to the productive side, another function for which the teacher needs that mature grammatical communicative knowledge is to evaluate the learners' spoken and written productions, and to give appropriate guidance, especially for developing writing skills. What was said under (b) largely applies here, too. But some special abilities are needed to deal with productive problems. These include the ability to judge the likely source of errors, the best strategies for alerting the student to errors, and ways of restructuring the student's developing grammar system where necessary. Judgements will also have to be made about the gravity of errors (e.g. in terms of their impairment of communicative effect).

(d) Contrastive grammar

The value of contrastive knowledge – in particular, the explanation of the foreign language in terms of the native language – has been controversial in direct language teaching. But again, in teacher education surely it cannot be controversial that a teacher benefits greatly from having a knowledge of, and sensitivity to, the ways in which the two languages differ. This is beneficial both as an aid to identifying problem areas for the learner and as a vehicle for explanation, in giving learners feedback on their own speaking and writing.

(e) Processes of simplification

The problem of simplification is where the difference between teachers' grammar and learners' grammar becomes most apparent. Whereas ideally the teacher has a mature grammatical knowledge, the learner has only a developing proto-system, an immature competence necessarily incomplete and oversimplified. But if we accept that some elements of overt grammatical presentation and explanation are necessary for learners, we also have to accept the notorious stumbling-block for many learners of grammatical terminology, abstract rules, quasi-mathematical symbols and the like. To minimise this difficulty, whatever the level of learning, the degree of explicit explanation needs to be reduced to the simplest level consistent with its pedagogical purpose.

Simplification is necessarily in conflict with telling the whole truth about the language: by simplifying we indulge to some extent in fiction, by either overgeneralisation or undergeneralisation. (One convenient fiction often exploited at earlier stages of learning is that there is a one-to-one relation between form and meaning.) Hence, at a fairly elementary stage of learning English, it will be useful for the student to know a 'rule' that in questions, words like *any* are used rather than words like *some*: that the interrogative counterpart of *They lost some money* is *Did they lose any money?*. But at a more advanced stage it will be important to know that *Did they lose some money?* is also a possible question, implying a rather more specific context than the sentence with *any* (e.g. a context where *they* refers to inveterate gamblers, for whom losing money is a constant hazard). Similarly, at elementary and intermediate stages, it will be useful to know a rule that in *if* clauses we use the simple present tense, not *will*, in referring to the future. That is,

1. *If the party ends before midnight, we'll catch a bus home.*

is normal, not:

2. *If the party will end before midnight, we'll catch a bus home.*

But then at some later stage, learners have to be prepared to accept a sentence like this:

3. *If the party will end before midnight, it's time to start enjoying ourselves now.*

And at that stage the learners will need further and more sophisticated explanations (e.g. in the third sentence, the use of *will* implies the present predictability of the statement in the *if* clause).

One of the bugbears of the teaching tradition is the assumption that grammatical rules are immutable and without exception, and that teachers will make harsh judgements about learners who break them. But somehow, I believe, teachers have to convey the notion that grammar is not a tight, clear-cut system like mathematics. Grammar being an organic system, its rules and categories are frequently flexible, fuzzy, non-discrete, prototypical (see Karlsson, 1984; Lakoff, 1987; Legenhausen, 1989 – it is not important here what terminology one uses). The fascination of grammar, in fact, lies in the challenge of explaining where, how far and why rules break down. The familiar listing of exceptions, which one finds in traditional grammar presentation, is useful, but can so often be merely a mechanistic and superficial response to this challenge, which invites deeper explanations and deeper understandings.

To get this point over to learners requires a novel philosophy of language education: one that encourages teachers (and older and more advanced learners) to examine norms critically, rather than to accept them as prescribed by some higher authority. In the orthodox classroom, it may be difficult to say 'I am giving you this rule – see if you can find exceptions to it'. But I am convinced it is important to convey this attitude and, incidentally, by this means to encourage learners to be observant and engage intellectually with the language they encounter. Finally, it is important for teachers not to be deceived by their own unavoidable 'fictions'. Perhaps the best we can do in the earlier stages of grammar teaching is present to the learner a 'rule' which we might describe as 60 per cent or 85 per cent or 99 per cent true, a 'rule of thumb' (cf. Berman, 1979), like the rule about *any* in questions or the rule about *if* clauses. By making this clear, we may well prevent learners from sinking into cynicism or confusion when they discover (as they inevitably will) that what they accepted as 100 per cent rules do not always work.

3. A 'fuzzy' view of grammar: prototypes and scales

In the remainder of this paper I will try to explore further what is entailed in that 'mature communicative systematic knowledge' that the 'model teacher' ought to possess. I have already referred to the distinction between *inductive* and *deductive* learning, and would like to link this to another distinction I have alluded to – that between *receptive* and *productive* grammatical ability – as follows:

- Receptive skills (listening, reading) are more directly under the control of inductive learning.
- Productive skills (speaking, writing) are more likely to be aided by deductive learning.

The first of these two links is easier to make sense of than the second: if we are learning grammar from the receptive point of view, then we are doing so through exposure to, or confrontation with, given textual instances. For a reader or listener to achieve greater comprehension, precise formulation of 'rules of thumb' is probably unnecessary, since generalisations can be reached inductively. On the other hand, the second of the two statements proposes that to use language productively, in speaking and writing, we typically need a more 'top down' approach, making use of 'rules of thumb' as a short cut to an ability which could only be acquired more slowly and tentatively through the inductive method.

Although there is complementarity and some interchangeability between the strategies of deduction–production and induction–reception, there is also a mismatch in the level of attainment, as we have already noted. In receptive mode, learners will notice or acquire what they have not been taught. Whether consciously or not, they will gradually form new generalisations, which are often tentative and inexact, but which can be enhanced or strengthened as they are tested against new data. These generalisations will feed into productive learning, whereas the acquisition process by exposure to the language is often a slow, uncertain, hit-or-miss affair. On the other hand, while the short cut of explicit presentation of grammar by 'rules of thumb' can lead to an immediate sense of control over speaking and writing, this sense is to some extent built on false and simplified assumptions. How do we make sense of this mismatch between vague but wide-ranging receptive ability, and firmer but narrower productive ability?

The solution, I suggest, lies in the *prototype* approach to the teaching of grammar to teachers. Prototype theory, originating in cognitive psychology (Rosch, 1975; Rosch and Mervis, 1975) has had a major impact on linguistics (e.g. Lakoff, 1987; Taylor, 1989). It rejects the classical Aristotelean view that categories employed in human cognition are watertight categories based on necessary and sufficient conditions of membership: e.g. all women are (i) human, (ii) female and (iii) adult. Instead, it propounds the view that cognitive categories are often based on the recognition of prototypes, or typical members: e.g. the prototypical bird has feathers, flies, builds nests in trees, lays eggs, and so on. From this, it is seen that the criteria for judging whether something is or is not a bird are variably fulfilled, not all bird species being as 'birdy' as others. Typical species – 'good examples of birds' – such as robins or blackbirds, represent the prototype, whereas eagles, turkeys, ostriches and penguins are to different degrees and in different ways less prototypical (e.g. none of them builds nests in trees). In a similar way, the prototype concept – that categories are complex, with different degrees and variable criteria of membership – can also be applied to grammatical classes, such as adjective, subject, passive, etc., which are also cognitive categories, although of a different kind. Cognitive grammarians, such as Lakoff (1987) and Langacker (1991) have taken the view that grammatical categories are, in fact, no different in their basic composition from other conceptual categories. Unlike the Chomskyan model of grammar, which emphasises the difference between grammatical competence and other cognitive abilities, the cognitive grammar model claims a basic continuity between the two. The theoretical position of cognitive grammar therefore suggests that in childhood we acquire grammatical categories in much the same way as we acquire other categories, such as those of colour, space or time.

The prototype model is useful for our problem of teaching grammar, because it recognises both a hard core of clear and typical cases (the prototype), and also a periphery of less clear cases. The hard core can be thought of as that which is captured by an 80 or 90 per cent 'rule of thumb'. The periphery can be thought of as corresponding to the less typical cases which are, in some respect or other, exceptions to the rule. The fact that grammatical rules are difficult to fit into the 100 per cent classical mould is already face-value evidence in favour of the prototype model as applied to language. Besides, the prototype model invites us to take a more understanding view of all those exceptions to grammatical rules: let us think not so much of exceptions as of extensions to the rule.

Consider the apparently simple case of word-class categories, such as noun, adjective and verb. We all remember the schoolroom 'rule' that nouns are the names of things, persons and places; and we also remember the difficulty of explaining to children why this 'rule' breaks down with such words as *music*, *happiness* and *heat*. The truth is that this is not a 100 per cent rule, but a 'rule of thumb' – quite a useful one for young children at early stages of learning about grammar, since most of the nouns they encounter and use do indeed refer to persons, places and things (cf. Lyons, 1989). Such 'rules of thumb' are useful, for representing the stable core of a category; while the exploration of the penumbra, the unclear outer reaches of the category, is something that we can probably best leave to the process of induction from examples we encounter as listeners and readers.

Looking, now, at the formal aspects of nouns – their morphology – it can be proposed that the most typical, and recognisable, nouns are those which can be changed from singular to plural, by the addition of the *-(e)s* ending. By this standard, *bird* is more prototypical than (say) *goose* (which has an irregular plural), *chess* and *Paris* (which have no plural at all) and *amends* (which looks like a plural, but has no singular–plural alternation). Similarly, looking at the syntactic aspects of nouns, we recognise their typical ability to act as head of a noun phrase (e.g. following *the*) in the position of subject, object or prepositional complement in a sentence. But the word *stead* (as in *She sent her brother in her stead*) permits few of the possibilities which are available with other nouns, and so must be seen as a peripheral member of the noun category.

There is evidence (Anderson, 1975; Aitchison, 1987: 92) that both children and adults acquire meanings in a language by working from the prototypical to the less prototypical members of the category. Some reason exists, therefore, for thinking that this strategy will work best in the learning of the grammar of a second or foreign language. For the teacher, the guideline should be: 'Do not confront learners with the complexities of the whole category until they have grasped the prototype: work from the central to the peripheral cases'. So the 'rule of thumb', far from being merely a handy expedient for the teacher in a fix, may have a sound justification in terms of the psychology of language learning.

Prototype theory, and its use in cognitive grammar, is not the only useful theoretical background to the present approach to grammar teaching. Alongside Rosch's prototype, other more specifically linguistic accounts of the non-discrete nature of grammatical categories have been expressed in terms of scales, or continua. The terms used for such scales of difference vary, according to the author: *cline* (Halliday, 1961), *squish* (Ross, 1973), *gradient* (Bolinger, 1961; Quirk *et al.*, 1985: 90); but all emphasise the fact that grammar typically does not lend itself to clear-cut boundaries.

4. Some examples: gradience in English grammar

Almost *and* nearly

To begin with, let us examine an example. A few years ago (Leech, 1990) I discussed a rough corpus survey of the use of the pair of quasi-synonymous adverbs *nearly* and *almost*.[3] It was discovered that, far from being synonymous, these words have strikingly different, though overlapping, distributions. *Almost* tended to be the unmarked item, used for general approximation to some absolute quality, whereas *nearly* was characteristically related to a position on a scale (e.g. *nearly two days, nearly £100*) or to a path leading towards a goal or result (e.g. *I nearly fell over the cliff*). This more scalar, dynamic meaning of *nearly* seemed to be partly under the influence of a hidden metaphor: the etymological metaphor implicit in the use of the locative stem *near*. Thus, one could paraphrase the example above by the patent locative metaphor of *I came near to swearing at her*; *I came near to falling over the cliff*. In most examples, one felt that *almost* and *nearly* were broadly interchangeable; in other cases, only one of the two was acceptable. In yet other cases, one could perceive a slight difference of meaning: for example, *a nearly complete jug* is typically a jug not far from reaching completion (e.g. while the potter is still working on it), whereas *an almost complete jug* could be a jug permanently in a slightly incomplete state (e.g. an archaeological relic found with its handle missing).

Seem *and* appear

The same publication reported a similar corpus study of the quasi-synonymous copular verbs *seem* and *appear*.[4] Once again, it was evident that one of the two items, *seem*, is of more general application, whereas *appear* is more restricted and under the influence of an etymological metaphor. The metaphor is that of visual appearance, comparable to the literal meaning of *appear* as an intransitive verb, as in *A shadow appeared on the wall*. Consider, for example, *Mr Fell appeared to be in tears when he sat down*. Here *appeared* is more appropriate than *seem*, because the impression is clearly a visual one. A reasonable paraphrase would be: *Mr Fell looked as if he was in tears when he sat down*. But in the sentence *The night seemed loaded with thunder*, the choice of *seemed* evokes a general impression which might be due (say) to air pressure, humidity, temperature, even the behaviour of animals.

If the example had read *The night appeared loaded with thunder*, on the other hand, the dominant impression would have been visual.

5. The *'s* genitive and the *of* construction

In both of the above cases, the choice between one word and another is a scalar one: a matter of graduated preference due to the variant weightings of different factors. This is shown more clearly in a third example, that of the choice of the genitive *'s* as opposed to the quasi-synonymous *of* construction, which, with two colleagues, I have recently investigated with the help of corpus material (Leech, Francis and Xu, forthcoming). For clarity, the choice between these two constructions will be symbolised as the choice between *X's Y* and *the Y of X* (e.g. *God's will* and *the will of God*). In cases where they are grammatical alternatives, a number of factors of varying importance govern the preference of one form rather than the other. Of these, the most important include:

(a) The semantic category of X

What kind of noun phrase can occur in the position of *X* (the genitive expression)? One thinks of the prototypical genitive as referring to a person (e.g. *John's books*), but other types of noun phrase reference can be used, with diminishing acceptability, as in reference to an animal (e.g. *the dog's collar*), to a country (e.g. *Belgium's economic situation*) or to an organisation (e.g. *the company's recent successes*). Even inanimates occasionally occur in the *X* position (e.g. *the moon's surface*); but something like *gold's weight* is strongly disfavoured. There is a scale of decreasing 'personhood' leading from human *X*s, through organisational, animal and geographical *X*s (which all have some human associations) to inanimate and abstract *X*s. In general, the higher an *X* is on the 'animacy'[5] scale, the more likely it is to appear in the *X's Y* construction, and the less likely it is to occur in the *the Y of X* construction.

(b) The semantic relation between X and Y

What is the relation of meaning between *X* and *Y*? Again, we may assume there is a prototypical relation, often thought to be one of possession either in the narrow sense of 'ownership' (e.g. *Mary's book*), or in the wider sense of 'having' (e.g. *Mary's brother*). And, as in (a), there are degrees of acceptability for the genitive according to the type of relation it expresses. For example, the so-called subjective genitive, where *X* is in the position of 'doer' of the action represented by *Y*, is far more frequent than the opposite relation, called the objective genitive. Compare *the train's departure* (cf. *the train departed*) with *the railway's completion* (cf. *someone completed the railway*). Particularly in the second case, the alternative *of* construction is clearly more acceptable: *the completion of the railway*.

(c) The text type in which the construction occurs

The genitive is more frequent in certain types of text than in others. For example, it is more likely to occur in fictional texts or in journalistic texts than in more formal, academic writing.

There are many other factors which might influence the choice between *X's Y* and *the Y of X* (for example, one is the purely surface-structure one of the relative length, say, in words, of *X* and *Y*). But the important point is that this choice is not an all-or-nothing business, nor is it a random one. Rather, there are degrees of preference for one or the other, dependent on the weightings introduced by factors of form, meaning and context. These may be conceptualised and calculated in terms of bets taken out on two opponents in a two-horse race: the odds in favour of *X's Y* winning (i.e. the likelihood of *X's Y* winning as opposed to *the Y of X*) will vary from a probability of 0 to a probability of 1, according to the formula:

$$\frac{\text{Prob } (X's\ Y)}{\text{Prob } (the\ Y\ of\ X)}$$

By studying a large corpus of examples, one can arrive at strikingly precise predictions about the circumstances in which one or the other construction will be chosen. Regarding (a), predictably, the odds are found to be highest when *X* refers to a person, and to decrease progressively when *X* refers to a place, a human organisation or an animal, approaching zero when *X* refers to a thing or an abstraction. As for (b), the odds in favour of *X's Y* are highest when the relation is that of 'origin' (e.g. *Shakespeare's history plays*), and decrease progressively for the subjective, possessive, attributive, partitive and objective genitive, in that order. Although the subcategories themselves here are fuzzy-edged, the result points to a conception of the genitive as prototypically expressing a relation where *X* has a controlling or dominating role in respect to *Y*. It is at first glance surprising that the relational type which most favours the genitive is not the possessive genitive, but the genitive of origin. But the three genitive-favouring categories of (i) origin, (ii) subjective and (iii) possessive genitives all evoke a situation in which *X* has some control over *Y*. In (i) the originator of something exercises the ultimate degree of power in bringing it into being; in (ii) the subjective *X* is typically the agent, or doer of the action which causes the event or action *Y* to take place; and in (iii) the possessive *X* typically exercises control over something through the physical relation of 'having' the 'something' in one's sphere of influence, perhaps through right of ownership.

These scalar definitions of the difference between the two constructions are suggestive of a gradient linking two prototypes. But in one respect, the prototype theory is brought into question: the temporal genitive, although common, does not fit into the scale, but sticks out as an anomaly. This is because only one kind of semantic relation between *X* and *Y* accompanies a temporal *X* – namely a relation which is itself temporal (e.g. the temporal measurement relation found in *three weeks' holiday*, a holiday lasting for three weeks). Thus the temporal genitive stands aloof from the scales of personhood and control which seem to be influential in the choice of the genitive elsewhere. The conclusion here shows the limitations of the gradience view of grammar: sometimes there *are* discrete meanings and functions associated with a single word or grammatical form. One example is the split between the 'general' genitive and the temporal genitive – they divide straightforwardly enough into two categories. Grammar does not always have fuzzy boundaries.

6. Conclusion

In the preceding section, I illustrated the notions of gradience and prototype through practical examples of English grammar. This had a number of purposes, in relation to the preceding discussion of grammar teaching. My aims were:

- To exemplify how these notions of gradience and prototype apply, in practice, to areas of English grammar.
- To show, nevertheless, that the notion of *prototype* is not all-sufficient. In some areas at least, such as the genitive construction, there seems to be a fairly clear-cut distinction between two meanings of the same grammatical construction.
- To show, further, that the 'fuzzy' view of grammar which emerges from taking these notions seriously is not chaotic or haphazard: it has its own systematic nature which is subtle and organic rather than mechanistic.

My conclusions of a more speculative kind, applied to the teaching of grammar to teachers, are the following:

- The inductive method of arriving at generalisations on the basis of examples is the appropriate way of coming to terms with this fuzziness, whether we learn 'fuzzy grammar' implicitly or through explicit study of text data (research or discovery learning).
- Whereas in the less advanced stages of language learning inductive learning is simply implicit (by exposure), at a later stage it can profitably be made explicit. There is a natural continuity here between learners' grammar and teachers' grammar, but it is in teacher education, I would argue, that the method of explicit discovery learning will be particularly helpful. Hence the teacher can become critically aware of what, to the average learner, is an implicit learning process.
- The deductive method, on the other hand, is more fitted to the explicit presentation of grammar by 'rules of thumb' which are particularly useful when they identify the prototype – the central core of typifying cases. In the case of the genitive, the possessive use of *X's Y* is prototypical, as is also the genitive of origin and the subjective genitive, and all of these can be expected to co-occur with a prototypical human noun as *X*.
- The cognitive prototype which adults carry around with them may be the one they learned, as the most frequent variant, as children. Thus, returning to the

semantic relation between X and Y, while the genitive of origin is the one which most favoured the $X's$ Y construction in our corpus of adult English, it is quite plausible that the prototypical use for native speakers, learned in childhood, is the possessive genitive (e.g. *daddy's shoes*), which also happened to be the most frequently used semantic relation with the genitive in our data. If this is the case, then there is some reason for the same prototype use to be the most accessible to learners in earlier stages of learning a foreign language – particularly if the learners are children. By this argument, the initial focus on possessive meaning in teaching the genitive is a justifiable simplification.

I have argued in terms of the character of a 'model' grammar teacher – but such paragons are rather thin on the ground. Even so, I have said enough to explain why they are emphatically not to be equated with zealots who can parse a sentence in five seconds and recognise a split infinitive at a hundred yards. Being a good grammar teacher is far more (and less) than that.

There is also no model technique of teaching grammar, since selection and balance between methods will depend on many factors, such as the age and level of the learners, their degree of exposure to the target language, and so on. But perhaps I may venture one or two final general observations, thinking of grammar teaching as interacting with learning in evolving stages. Explicit learning of a new feature of grammar naturally starts with prototype, 'rule of thumb' cases. In later stages, there will be continuing interplay between the presentation of grammar and the acquiring of grammar through induction. At a later stage still, and particularly at the teacher education level, it is time to capitalise on the inductive processes of learning, which have remained largely implicit, and to make them explicit through the method of intelligently observing and studying textual data. Here the peripheral cases, as well as the prototype cases, will be noted, and a broader and deeper understanding of the language will result. There is no natural end to this grammar education process. A last recommendation for teachers, therefore, is that they continue this informal exploration of language – this self-education – by observation and critical engagement in the language that they encounter throughout their careers. The best language teacher is one who remains a student of language and languages.

Notes

1. This list derives indirectly from an earlier list given by Pauline Rea and Edward Woods in a lecture given at the British Council course 'Grammar and Language Learning' held at Lancaster in 1987.
2. This method has been widely advocated and demonstrated by Tim Johns (University of Birmingham). See also Tribble and Jones, 1990.
3. I owe to Kathleen Troy, then an M.A. student at Lancaster University, the benefit of an earlier corpus study of *nearly* and *almost*.
4. I owe a similar debt to an earlier corpus study of *seem* and *appear* by Sultaneh Bettaieb, then a Lancaster M.A. student.
5. This scale has been called the 'Silverstein hierarchy', after Michael Silverstein who used it to study phenomena unrelated to the genitive. See, however, Deane (1987) on the Silverstein hierarchy and genitives.

References

Aitchison, J. 1987. *Words in the Mind: An Introduction to the Mental Lexicon*, Blackwell, Oxford.

Anderson, E.S. 1975. 'Cups and glasses: Learning that boundaries are vague', *Journal of Child Language*, vol. 2, 79–103.

Berman, R. Aronson. 1979. 'Rule of grammar or rule of thumb?', *IRAL*, vol. 17, no. 4, 279–300.

Bolinger, D. 1961. *Generality, Gradience and the All-or-None*, Mouton, The Hague.

Chomsky, N. 1979. *Language and Responsibility* (based on conversations with Mitsou Ronat; translated from the French by John Viertel), The Harvester Press, Sussex.

Deane, P. 1987. 'English possessives, topicality, and the Silverstein hierarchy', in Aske, J. *et al.* (eds.), *Berkeley Linguistics Society: Proceedings of the 13th Annual Meeting, February 14–16, 1987: General Session and Parasession on Grammar and Cognition*, 65–76, Berkeley Linguistics Society, Berkeley.

Edmondson, W. *et al.* 1977. *A Pedagogic Grammar of the English Verb: A Handbook for the German Secondary Teacher of English*, Narr, Tübingen.

Halliday, M.A.K. 1961. 'Categories of the theory of grammar', *Word*, vol. 17, no. 3, 241–92.

Higgins, J. 1986. 'The computer and grammar teaching', in Leech, G. and Candlin, C.N. (eds.), *Computers in English Language Teaching and Research*, 31–45, Longman, Harlow.

Karlsson, F. 1984. 'Prototypes as models for linguistic structure', in *Papers from the Seventh Scandinavian Conference of Linguistics*, 583–600, Department of General Linguistics, Helsinki.

Lakoff, G. 1987. *Women, Fire, and Dangerous Things*, University Press, Chicago.

Langacker, R.W. 1991. *Concept, Image and Symbol: the Cognitive Basis of Grammar*, Mouton de Gruyter, Berlin.

Leech, G. 1990. 'The value of a corpus in English language research: a reappraisal', in *Linguistic Fiesta: Festschrift for Professor Hisao Kakehi's Sixtieth Birthday*, 115–26, Kuroshio, Tokyo.

Leech, G., Francis, B. and Xu, X. (forthcoming). 'The use of corpora in the textual demonstrability of gradience in linguistic categories', in *Proceedings of the International Round Table on the Continuum in Semantic Linguistics*, June 22–24, 1992, Caen.

Legenhausen, L. 1989. 'Grammatical fuzziness im Englischen', *Arbeiten aus Anglistik und Amerikanistik*, vol. 14, 73–88.

Lyons, J. 1989. 'Semantic ascent: a neglected aspect of syntactic typology', in Arnold, D. *et al.* (eds.), *Essays on Grammatical Theory and Universal Grammar*, 153–86, Clarendon Press, Oxford.

Quirk, R., Greenbaum, S., Leech, G. and Svartvik, J. 1985. *A Comprehensive Grammar of the English Language*, Longman, Harlow.

Rosch, E. 1975. 'Cognitive representations of semantic categories', *Journal of Experimental Psychology: General*, vol. 104, 192–233.

Rosch, E. and Mervis, C.B. 1975. 'Family resemblances: studies in the internal structure of categories', *Cognitive Psychology*, vol. 8, 382–439.

Ross, J.R. 1973. 'A Fake NP Squish', in Bailey, C.-J.N. and Shuy, R.W. (eds.), *New Ways of Analyzing Variation in English*, 96–140, Georgetown University Press, Washington, DC.

Rutherford, W.E. 1987. *Second Language Grammar: Learning and Teaching*, Longman, Harlow.

Taylor, J.L. 1989. *Linguistic Classification: Prototypes in Linguistic Theory*, Clarendon, Oxford.

Tribble, C. and Jones, G. 1990. *Concordances in the Classroom: A Resource Book for Teachers*, Longman, Harlow.

Pedagogical Grammar: Principles and Problems

SYLVIA CHALKER

1. Grammar and rules

If you ask classroom teachers to define grammar, various definitions emerge. But the word 'rules' crops up frequently. Grammar is rules.

If you then ask where the rules come from, this is something that many teachers have not considered. But since they are in awe of grammar, they usually incline to the 'God's truth' view – the rules are there in the language waiting to be discovered. This attitude – in essence similar to that of American structuralists from the 1930s on, who sought to discover rules objectively by scientific procedures, with little appeal to meaning – has various consequences.

Firstly, many teachers believe that there must be only one 'right' way of describing something. If two grammarians describe some language feature differently, one of them has strayed from the truth and got it wrong. Thus teachers ask questions like: 'This book says that in the phrase *to the lighthouse*, *lighthouse* is the object of the preposition, but another book says it's the complement. Which is right?' They find it difficult to see that more than one analysis is often possible – and that, anyway, in this case the label 'complement' could embrace 'object'.

Secondly, many teachers unquestioningly accept the rules as holy writ, even in the face of conflicting evidence. I once supervised a trainee who knew perfectly well that you could say '*Oh, it's good to sit down, I've been standing all the morning*', and yet solemnly taught his class that 'the present perfect continuous shows an action that is still continuing at the moment of speaking'. Usage contrary to a rule – if it is noticed at all – must be either wrong or an exception. Fortunately, with the emphasis in recent years on authenticity in language teaching, some teachers do collect examples of real English and refuse to accept patently misleading grammatical statements, but such teachers are probably in a minority.

A third consequence for teachers who take a rather structuralist approach is that they do not particularly expect grammatical rules to make sense. True, they know that tenses carry meaning, but even here a general feeling that the system is arbitrary is reinforced by the prevalence of superficial or misconceived rules. It is said, for example, that 'a future form becomes a present tense when we put it in a time clause'. But nobody turns future forms into present tenses in this way, except unlucky students who are made to do so.

Happily, there are signs that some of the more functional and meaning-based descriptions of grammar, as developed, for example, by Halliday, are eventually getting through to the classroom. But there is still a long way to go. Time and again new grammar books aimed at EFL/ESL learners make erroneous observations based on half-digested knowledge, like 'We use a passive verb and a by-agent when the object of the action is more important than the doer'. This simply would not be said by anyone who understood the relationship of word order to information structure, in terms of given and new or theme and rheme – or for that matter by anyone who understood the relevance of end-weight. (All of these factors are illustrated in the preceding sentence!)

A further problem with rules bedevils language teaching. Never mind where they come from – what are they for? Much confusion is caused by a failure to distinguish between rules as a full and accurate description of how the system works, which all teachers should understand, and simplified rules intended as useful do's and don'ts for learners. An example of the distinction needed is shown in the common treatment of *since*. The usual rule here states: 'With the word *since*, a perfect tense is used in the main clause', which sensibly discourages such deviant sentences as *I am living here since 1990*. The reason this rule usually works is that *since* covers the same 'then-to-now' (or 'then-to-a-later-then') span of time that a perfect tense does, so when the emphasis of the message is on this length of time, *since* and tense reinforce each other. But, although useful as a guideline, the rule is nevertheless superficial and mechanical. It suggests that other tenses with *since* are somehow deviant, e.g. *I am feeling better since I changed the treatment. We visit my mother more often since she moved south.* Yet such uses are entirely in accordance with English tense usage. A present tense is normal for a currently ongoing state or habit and, in a sentence with *since*, it is acceptable in a main clause if this state or habit may be traced back to an earlier cause.

2. What is pedagogical grammar?

If the words 'grammar' and 'rules' are confusing, we might hope for greater clarity by defining grammar as *pedagogical*. Alas, this term too is ambiguous.

Corder (1975) writes:

> Some people prefer to restrict the use of the term [pedagogical grammar] to those statements about, and exemplifications of, the language which are for the use of teachers rather than of learners, the object of which is then to guide the teacher in the way he is to present the language material to his pupils.

Pedagogical grammar, in other words, is grammar for pedagogues. Corder himself appears to take a wider view, but the word is often used in this way by linguists (who ought to know better) entirely without definition; which suggests that for some people this is the only meaning.

However, a different meaning is commonly understood. Greenbaum (1986) asserts:

> Pedagogical grammars [that is, grammar books] teach the language and not about the language. They are inherently prescriptive, since their purpose is to tell students what to say or write.

The following year, Greenbaum (1987) returns to the subject, and distinguishes basically four types of grammar book:

- reference
- pedagogical
- teach-yourself
- theoretical

However, he specifically excludes theoretical grammars from the discussion because their primary purpose 'is not to describe the grammar of English but to apply to English a specified model of how best to describe language'.

Greenbaum's main concern in this paper is to contrast reference grammars and pedagogical grammars. He recognises that they sometimes overlap, particularly in the way they are used, but basically he defines reference grammars as books intended for self-help and offering comprehensive coverage. A pedagogical grammar, to him, is a coursebook.

Greenbaum describes the five desirable characteristics of such a book:

1. It must be constrained by the length of class lessons.
2. It should be determined on psycholinguistic grounds (i.e. in accordance with the best methods for learning a foreign language).
3. Grammar topics and material should be graded.
4. Learners should be helped by having their attention drawn to general rules.
5. It should provide for practical applications (possibly with exercises in a separate book).

So here we have pedagogical grammar not merely as grammar for learners, but as a specific type of coursebook.

In this definition Greenbaum is not alone. Crystal (1987) lists six types of grammar:

- descriptive
- pedagogical
- prescriptive
- reference
- theoretical
- traditional

The six types are not strictly comparable, but this is a work for the general reader, and so the list may be read as a sort of glossary. Only three of Crystal's types of grammar seem to apply to actual books:

1. *Reference* grammars, which Crystal says must be as comprehensive as possible

(he instances Jespersen's seven-volume *Modern English Grammar* (1949) or *A Comprehensive Grammar of the English Language* (1985) by Quirk *et al*.

2. *Prescriptive* grammars, by which he means usage books for native speakers, such as Fowler's *Modern English Usage* (1926).
3. *Pedagogical* grammars, books 'specifically designed for teaching a foreign language, or for developing an awareness of the mother tongue'.

Crystal therefore agrees with Greenbaum that only a substantial book deserves the label 'reference', although in talking of pedagogical grammars as 'teaching grammars' he does not commit himself to say they have to be courses.

Some resolution of the conflicting definitions of pedagogical grammar – is it for teachers or for learners? – is offered by Dirven (1990). He defines pedagogical grammar as 'a cover term for any learner- or teacher-oriented description or presentation of foreign language rule complexes with the aim of promoting and guiding learning processes in the acquisition of that language.' This is a definition which would seem to accommodate both Corder and Greenbaum. Further, he says pedagogical grammar may be descriptive – or prescriptive – and may be a teaching grammar or a reference grammar, thus widening the definitions of Greenbaum and Crystal. So, except that it apparently excludes grammars for mother-tongue speakers, here we have a good all-embracing definition.

Taking a broad consensual view then we may say that pedagogical grammar:

• can be for reference or for course work (in either case it may be graded to meet a particular user level);
• could be comprehensive, but will probably be more modest in its aims;
• will draw attention to rules, thus probably combining prescription with description;
• will help foreigners to learn a language and/or help mother-tongue speakers to understand their own language;
• can be either for learners or for teachers.

3. Grammar books: a survey

In the classroom – rather than in academic circles – the distinction between grammar for teachers and grammar for learners may in any case be more theoretical than real. In practice, only a minority of teachers are likely to consult large reference grammars, and many EFL teachers learn their grammar from the same books as their students. Further, some of these learner-oriented books are definitely intended to be used for reference, even though (*pace* both Greenbaum and Crystal) they are not remotely comprehensive and do not pretend to be. Some in fact are aimed at quite elementary learners.

For the purpose of this study – to see how grammar is presented pedagogically – 25 books have been surveyed (see Appendix 1), mainly from British publishers, all claiming to be grammar books of some kind, and all but one (Swan, 1980) including the word 'grammar' in the title. They can be divided broadly into the following groups:

A: reference books, for consulting, not for working through;
B: alphabetically arranged grammars, forming a small subgroup of A;
C: grammar-cum-practice books, which give considerable amounts of grammatical information alongside the exercises.

In addition, two books for mother-tongue speakers at upper secondary or university level (D) were included for comparison; but, except for these, all the books are intended for EFL/ESL learners at secondary or adult level. Books for younger children were excluded from the survey, as overt grammar teaching is less usual here. Also excluded were books consisting mainly of exercises, or books narrowly concentrating on a particular area (e.g. tenses, comparatives).

The difference between the two main categories – the reference books and the grammar-plus-practice books – is not as great as may appear at first sight, as many books published purely as reference books in fact have back-up exercise books.

Several points emerge from the survey. Firstly, few of the authors use the magic word 'pedagogical'. One exception is Alexander (1988), who claims that his intermediate grammar (a book without exercises) is both a reference book and 'a true pedagogical grammar'. Secondly, only one of the exercise-less reference books claims that it could be used as a course. This is van Ek and Robat's *The Student's Grammar of English* (1984):

> What we have attempted to do in the present grammar is to apply the overall model of GCE [Quirk *et al.*, *A Grammar of Contemporary English*] to a pedagogical grammar with the comprehensiveness of Zandvoort's *Handbook* [1975]. The result is simultaneously a coursebook and a reference book.

Whilst this book undoubtedly can be used as a prescribed coursebook at university level, it would presumably fail the Greenbaum definition of 'pedagogical' by teaching *about* the language, and by not including 'practical applications'.

Almost all the other reference books examined specifically stress that they are not coursebooks: 'a simple grammar to refer to' (Bald *et al.*, 1986); 'can be used for easy reference by anyone with a knowledge of a few traditional labels' (Chalker, 1984); 'can be used as a general reference book or sourcebook on English grammar' (Leech and Svartvik, 1975).

Of the four alphabetically arranged grammars included in the survey (group B), none claimed to be anything other than a reference book. But interestingly, most of the practice books (group C), which might reasonably be expected to be courses, actually carry disclaimers, such as: 'Use the Index or contents list to find the unit(s) which deal with the particular point you want to study' (Beaumont and Granger, 1989); 'You are not expected to start at Unit 1' (Sinclair, ed., 1991).

One American practice book (Azar, 1985) did claim to be a course: 'The text is intended to be taught in the order in which it is presented'. This may possibly be more typical of American grammars. Among British authors, the only EFL book found that claimed to be a grammar course was *Using English Grammar* (Woods and McLeod, 1990). By contrast, both the grammars for native speakers are definitely coursebooks – Freeborn (1987), as is obvious from the title, and Leech *et al.* (1982), which claims in the preface: 'This is an introductory course in English grammar for use in English-medium schools, colleges and universities (especially in Britain)'. Like van Ek and Robat (1984), which is aimed at proficient non-native speakers, these two courses are primarily *about* language; unlike van Ek and Robat (1984), they contain exercises.

4. Who wants what?

Before looking in more detail at the way these reference and practice books are organised, three questions are worth considering:

1. What do learners want?
2. What do teachers (particularly EFL/ESL teachers) want?
3. What do grammarians/authors want?

Ideally these three aims should coincide. In practice they may diverge. Learners on the whole want language made easy – understandable rules that appear to work (e.g. 'Use a perfect tense with *since*'). They also want prescriptive guidance: they are uneasy if they are told that a sentence like *They convinced him to try* or *You know better than me* is in a grey area where native speakers disagree. Many teachers want much the same as their learners. If they are in the communicative tradition, they may want (or, more likely, profess to want) to understand how the grammar itself contributes to meaning. Both teachers and learners want grammar books to be simply arranged, and many are against 'too much terminology', even though in fact an understanding, say, of the way specific/generic meaning cuts across definite and indefinite would make much more sense of article usage than demonstrably false rules about using *the* 'for second mention' or 'with musical instruments'.

Writers of 'pedagogical' grammar books presumably want to meet these needs. But some may not like falsifying by oversimplifying – which conflicts with 'grammar made easy'. Some (an echo here of the belief that a reference book should be comprehensive) may aim at some sort of completeness, which again militates against simplicity. Some authors, too, are concerned about the grey areas, and this again conflicts with the desire of most learners and their teachers for guidance on right and wrong. Finally, some grammarians may be keenly interested in the underlying meaning of grammatical forms, while others are content – just as many teachers and learners are – with more superficial *ad hoc* rules.

A look at two best-selling EFL grammar books shows that consciously understanding the meaning of grammar ranks low for many people. A pioneer reference grammar for learners that first came out in the 1960s, Thomson and Martinet's *A Practical English Grammar* (1990), now in its fourth edition, presumably owes its enduring appeal to the fact that the examples are user-friendly and the grammar is presented in easily digestible chunks. Yet although there is some attention to

meaning, there are many questionable statements, including an 'illogical foreigners' rule: 'Note that in some European languages the definite article is used
before indefinite plural nouns, but that in English *the* is never used in this way.'
(This observation may serve as a guideline for some learners, but it is hardly
accurate to imply that some foreign languages confuse definite and indefinite reference simply because their article usage is not the same as the English system.)

A more recent favourite, a grammar-cum-practice book, *English Grammar in
Use* (1985), the first of several highly successful books by Raymond Murphy, also
presents grammar in manageable sections – an achievement not to be underesti-
mated – followed by manageable exercises. Users know where they are and get a
sense of achievement. However, some of the grammatical explanations do not
explain very much. Superficially it is true, as the book says, that *could* is the past of
can, that *could* often has present or future meaning, and (rather more dubiously)
that *could* (*do*) itself has a past tense – *could have* (*done*). But such observations
suggest that the tense system is arbitrary. In fact, although the modals are different
from other verbs, it is possible to draw people's attention to the fact that *could* and
would, like the past forms of other verbs, are also used for hypothesis and social
distancing. Once it is realised that the 'past' tenses are not always past in time, but
are marked as being in some way distant from the present, the tense system is
revealed as making consistent sense.

5. Specific issues in the writing of a grammar

Organisation

A major problem confronting anyone writing a grammar book is how to arrange in
a linear way an interlocking system, or set of systems. Wherever you start a
grammar book you presuppose other knowledge.

A fairly traditional arrangement is to take parts of speech as basic, though some
grammarians prefer to start with larger structural units, such as noun phrases or
adverbials, or even with simple sentences. Van Ek and Robat (1984) is perhaps a
good example of a middle way that manages to strike a balance between a form-
based and a meaning-based approach. There are two chapters on simple and
complex sentences, then some smaller units, but these are on noun phrases, verb
phrases, adverb phrases and so on, not parts of speech. Finally there are three
chapters on prominence (i.e. word order, fronting, cleft, etc.), word formation and
inter-sentence relations.

Woods and McLeod's course for intermediate students (1990) is also sophisticated in arrangement. They start, as many grammars do, with a brief overall view
on sentence organisation. Then they have an extensive section on verbs, another on
determiners (which rather incidentally includes nouns), a somewhat opaquely
labelled section on modification, and a final section on discourse, which includes
pronouns, connecters and conjunctions.

The other two coursebooks in the survey, Leech, Deuchar and Hoogenraad

(1982) and Freeborn (1987), are both for native speakers and are both sophisticated, Freeborn beginning with a section called 'Encoding experience in language',
and going on eventually to 'kernel clauses' and complex structures.

Among the reference grammars in the study, Leech and Svartvik (1975) is
notable for a functionally/meaning-based arrangement, under such headings as
'Concepts', 'Information, reality and belief', 'Mood, emotion and attitude' and
'Meanings in connected discourse'. The authors refer to 'the conventional method
of presenting English grammar in terms of structure', and claim that 'The student
who is primarily interested in making use of the language rather than in learning
about its structure (and this is true for the majority of foreign students) is not likely
to find such an arrangement particularly helpful.' While conventionally arranged
grammars admittedly do cause the user problems, it is not clear that a meaning-
based one is any easier. One can imagine a learner using a conventional grammar
and looking up *past* or *noun* in the index; would anyone look up *reality*, *belief* or
substance? The authors themselves felt the need to add a lengthy, alphabetically
arranged 'grammatical compendium'.

Concepts also feature in the main *Collins Cobuild English Grammar* (ed.
Sinclair, 1990), which makes a point of describing itself as a grammar of functions
and a grammar of meanings. It has a chart with such meaning-based headings as
'Concepts', 'Propositions', 'Circumstances' and 'Development'. However it still
loosely manages a more conventional grammatical arrangement because it
considers that each meaningful function is regularly expressed in English by one
particular type of structure. Thus 'concept' in this grammar largely equates with
noun group, and does not include, as it does in Leech and Svartvik (1975), time and
tense or degree. Similarly, the verb group and simple clauses are mainly dealt with
under 'circumstances', while 'development' covers compound sentences, reported
speech and conjunctions.[1]

Two university level grammars by Quirk and Greenbaum (1973) and Greenbaum
and Quirk (1990) have cyclical arrangements, with introductions on the general
framework, sections on basic constituents of simple sentences (i.e. parts of speech)
and then more complex structures (not only complex sentences, but noun phrases
recycled in more detail, and so on).

Of the simpler books in the survey, aimed at beginner or elementary level, Bald
et al. (1986) is unique in favouring a sophisticated arrangement of three main
sections – 'Sentences', 'Verb Phrases' and 'Noun Phrases', with a final section
called 'Communicative Situations'. The rest mostly have a straightforward 'parts of
speech' arrangement, as do most of the practice books, though some of them single
out items like conditionals or reported speech for special treatment.

It is noticeable that almost all the books, some after an opening overview, start
with either nouns or verbs, and usually leave conjunctions (and hence more compli-
cated sentences) for later. This applies both to the straight reference books and to
the reference-cum-practice books. No explanations are offered for this ordering,
but possibly it is because nouns and verbs are felt to be basic. Starting with nouns
fits in with studies of early child language that show a heavy preponderance of

nouns, reflecting our primary need to name things. On the other hand, grammarians who start with verbs perhaps recognise that (as we all learnt at school) no proper sentence should be without one.

So most of these reference books and practice books give the impression that they make most sense if worked through from the beginning, with the most difficult or longer structures left to the end. This is particularly so where there are opening sections offering some sort of overview on simple sentences and basic word order. Yet almost all the authors specifically state that this is *not* how to use these books.

The alphabetical grammars, being in dictionary format, are clearly not intended to be worked through from *A* to *Z*, and might seem an extreme example of authorial opt-out. But it is obvious from this survey – and from general observation – that grammarians cannot agree on how to arrange their material, and that those who do take some trouble to produce a simple-to-complex sequence then usually deny that such organisation has any purpose.

From the point of view of learners and teachers, a dictionary-style grammar may be good sense. In a survey carried out by Leitner (1990) among students at the Free University of Berlin a few years ago, a majority of the learners said that, when confronted with a problem (assuming they had time to check on it), they would go first to a dictionary; if that failed 70 per cent would try another strategy (i.e. 30 per cent would not pursue the problem) and that second strategy might be a grammar book. In other words, a big majority of the learners in Leitner's survey found a dictionary easier to use than a grammar book. This must particularly be so if the problem is related to a particular word.

Location and indexing of items

With larger grammatical problems, the user of any type of grammar has the primary problem of finding out where to look, and this will depend on the writer's decision of where-to-put-what. This can be a real problem for the user, since grammarians vary considerably as to where they locate even central concerns to EFL teachers, such as:

- comparative clauses (*Anna is as clever as Dick is* or *These things are more expensive than they were*);
- relative clauses;
- reported/indirect speech;
- conditionals.

An examination of just a few of the 25 books surveyed reveals considerable variation. Comparatives are dealt with under subordination by Greenbaum and Quirk (1990), under the noun group in Sinclair (ed., 1991), and under adjectives by Beaumont and Granger (1989) and Thomson and Martinet (1990). All these solutions can be justified, though the adjective classification has the disadvantage of excluding the same structure used with adverbs (*Anna runs as fast as . . . faster than . . .*).

Relative clauses, an important teaching concern, may be in one of several places. Surprisingly to traditionalists, who regard them simply as a type of subordinate clause (along with noun clauses and adverb clauses), they are to be tracked down in Greenbaum and Quirk (1990) under the noun phrase, since these authors persuasively analyse them as a type of postmodification (i.e. as part of the noun phrase and not directly subordinate to the main clause at all), though this leads to the somewhat difficult concept of a simple sentence possibly having more than one finite verb. Other grammarians, who do consider relative clauses to be directly subordinate, may include them under some heading like 'Sentence structure' or may deal with them under pronouns (despite the awkward fact of contact clauses). Some authors give them a separate section.

Reported speech, a third serious concern for EFL, may be dealt with as complex sentences (Greenbaum and Quirk, 1990), under subordinate clauses or even under verbs (Sinclair, ed., 1991); or, again, there may be a separate section. Conditional sentences may be grouped with other adverbial clauses, or treated under sentence structure or allotted their own section.

Giving these items their own sections at least makes them easy to locate. The disadvantage is that it makes such structures as reported speech or conditionals seem to have their own unique rules. In the case of reported speech, this often means misleading rules for the mechanical backshift of tenses; with conditionals there is often too great an emphasis on form and the implication that only three or four types are normal. In both cases, the underlying consistency of English tense usage is concealed.

But even dividing the grammar up into small sections does not overcome the problem of terminology, which can also affect an alphabetical grammar.[2] There could for example be a real difficulty for anyone who did not realise that their problem was called 'comparatives'. Some grammar books are good at indexing alternative terms. So anyone looking up *deletion* or *omission* in Greenbaum and Quirk (1990) is referred to *ellipsis*, and at *continuous* and *progressive* there is a cross-reference to *aspect*. Similarly, a user searching the Cobuild reference grammar (Sinclair, 1990) for *agreement* is referred to *concord*. But neither *agreement* nor *concord* is indexed in *Cobuild Student's Grammar* (1991), where the item is to be discovered only with difficulty. It is not at *singular* or *plural nouns*, nor at *verbs*. Eventually by looking up *count nouns*, the diligent searcher will find a couple of exercises. One has to have some idea of terminology or sometimes a knowledge of alternative terms to use even an apparently well-indexed grammar.

Contextualisation

Another problem for grammar book writers is contextualisation. Grammar as a matter of acceptable structure, can be illustrated – and usually is illustrated – by isolated sentences. But interest in language as communication and developments in discourse analysis and text linguistics make us aware that what is grammatically correct out of context may be virtually unacceptable in context. Use of a passive rather than an active verb may not depend, as is often said, on formality or a 'scientific' text, but on what has gone before, and therefore on the given–new information structure of the sentence. A word that can apparently take two different patterns interchangeably (e.g. *He seems (to be) a nice person*) does not do so in all contexts (e.g. *He seems to be a director of the firm*, but not **He seems a director*).[3] There are also questions of register and general appropriacy. Some grammar books do address some of these, but grammar above sentence level, the grammar of cohesive devices in long texts, is missing from many grammar books.

6. Coursebooks

In older and more traditional approaches to language teaching, where teaching a language was largely equated with teaching the grammar, a coursebook was primarily a grammar book. Today's coursebooks seem a world away, with their wealth of illustrations, their large casts of characters, and their emphasis on language in use and learning as fun. Chapters may be labelled by themes or topics (advertising, crime, health, etc.); there may be units on functions and situations (warning, persuading, taking notes, etc.); space is probably given to pronunciation practice; sections may be devoted to pair work or projects, to games or problem solving. In addition, the course may include specific sections on consolidating the 'four skills' or even some designed to promote 'learner training'.

Nevertheless these new-style coursebooks do tackle grammar. It may therefore be of interest to take three older coursebooks from the 1950s and 1960s, when structuralism was still the dominant EFL orthodoxy, and compare them with four new ones – all seven intended for beginners, from young teenagers to adults (see Appendix 2). There are some obvious differences. The new courses have bigger pages, come as packages with cassettes and, except for Willis's *First Lessons* (1990), are full of glossy full-colour photographs and cartoons. Secondly, the 1990s courses try much harder to be lively. *WOW!* (1990) has a framework described as a fictitious television programme; *Streets Ahead* (1990) has a soap opera story. All try to involve the learners more – beginning the very first lesson with greetings (*Hi. I'm Jim*) rather than *This is a chair*.

However, the newer coursebooks, like their forerunners, are structure-based. This seems to apply even to *First Lessons*, with its ostensibly task-based approach. Nor is there any great difference in the ordering of the grammar between the older and newer courses, which all introduce early on, in a controlled way, *be*, *have*, personal pronouns, possessives, demonstratives, selected modals and some tenses of lexical verbs. Interestingly, though, the three earlier books all introduce the present continuous several units before the present simple (presumably *do*-support was considered difficult). All four 1990s books take the reverse line, with the present simple coming first: perhaps it is felt to be more useful. The 1990s books are not afraid of grammar summaries. *Streets Ahead* even has simple tree diagrams, incorporating the assertion that every English sentence has an auxiliary which in simple tenses is omitted. Allegedly, this makes word order easier to understand.

7. Coursebooks versus grammar books

From a grammatical point of view, a major difference between the coursebooks and the grammars in the survey is that coursebooks build up from structures judged to be useful or frequent (or perhaps easiest to teach), and continually recycle, thus meeting Greenbaum's criterion of grading. The grammars to some extent progress from simple to more difficult, but the primary arrangement is by grammatical categories.

To some extent modern coursebooks also meet some of Greenbaum's other criteria: units of lesson length, a supply of practice material, and (presumably) what the authors consider to be the right conditions for learning. But with so much else going on in these books, they hardly seem to qualify as pedagogical grammars.

The overall picture is that most classes today are expected to use a coursebook which contains some grammar; and then to reinforce the grammar with reference and practice books. As noted, only a very few of the grammar books claim to be courses – 'pedagogical grammars' in a strict sense.

8. Conclusion

All the books in the survey are concerned with 'surface' structure – what is said or written – and not with any abstract theoretical models of grammar. The grammar included is in the mainstream tradition, though that tradition has itself been influenced by transformational grammar, case grammar, modern semantics and so on. However, these books vary in the extent to which they have incorporated the ideas of modern linguistics. Even some of the elementary books take the line, for example, that English has no future tense as such. Other authors (Alexander, 1988; Thomson and Martinet, 1990) prefer a more traditional approach here. Some are generally reliable; others still repeat inaccurate rules.

The major influence on the more linguistically aware grammars is the work of Quirk and his colleagues. Halliday is a noticeable influence on the Cobuild grammar, but there is no great conflict here: Leech and Svartvik (1975), for example, acknowledge their particular debt to Halliday's functional approach.

One problem that can arise from the separation of coursebooks from grammar books is that learners may find early on that their coursebooks and their grammars explain things differently, using different terminology and even offering different rules. This can be turned to advantage. Teachers can use this opportunity to raise learners' awareness that language may be analysed in different ways. They should also help learners to get a 'feel' for the grammatical system, and learn to judge for themselves which explanations are satisfactory. Learners certainly need to realise that most guideline rules are simplifications which will have to be revised as their knowledge and confidence grow.

Notes

1. About half the books in this survey use parts of speech labels, and about half go either for verb group, noun group, etc. (the Hallidayan labels) or for verb phrase, noun phrase, etc. (the terms favoured by Quirk *et al.*).
2. The alphabetical grammars are not in fact as similar as this cover term suggests. Broughton's entries are almost entirely under grammatical labels (from 'Active and passive voice' to 'Zero forms'). Both Swan's usage book and Leech's grammar have mixed entries, with grammatical headings ('Conjunctions', 'Indirect speech', etc.) interspersed with individual words. Chalker (1990) is closest to a dictionary, with headwords consisting solely of high-frequency words (*a/an* to *yourself/yourselves*) and with a glossary defining the grammatical terms used in the entries.
3. The difference may be that *seems* + noun phrase is acceptable for a more internal subjective evaluation, but an intervening *to be* is preferred when the judgement is based on more objective external fact.

References

Corder, S.Pit. 1975, in Allen, J.P.B. and Corder, S.Pit (eds.), *The Edinburgh Course in Applied Linguistics*, vol. 2, 1–15, OUP, Oxford.

Crystal, D. 1987, *The Cambridge Encyclopaedia of Language*, CUP, Cambridge.

Dirven, R. 1990, 'Pedagogical grammar', *Language Teaching*, vol. 23, no. 1, 1–18.

Fowler, H.W. 1926, *A Dictionary of Modern English Usage*, OUP, Oxford.

Greenbaum, S. 1986, 'English and a grammarian's responsibility: the present and the future', *World Englishes*, vol. 5, no. 2/3, 189–95.

Greenbaum, S. 1987, 'Reference grammars and pedagogical grammars', *World Englishes*, vol. 6, no. 3, 191–7.

Jespersen, O. 1949, *A Modern English Grammar on Historical Principles*, Munksgaard, Copenhagen.

Leitner, G. 1990, 'Students' uses of grammars of English: can we avoid teaching?', *International Review of Applied Linguistics in Language Teaching*, vol. xxvii, no. 2, 153–67.

Quirk, R., Greenbaum, S., Leech, G. and Svartvik, J. 1972, *A Grammar of Contemporary English*, Longman, Harlow.

Quirk, R., Greenbaum, S., Leech, G. and Svartvik, J. 1985, *A Comprehensive Grammar of the English Language*, Longman, Harlow.

Zandvoort, R.W. 1975, *A Handbook of English Grammar*, Longman, Harlow. Seventh edition.

Appendix 1: Grammar books surveyed

A *General reference grammars*

Alexander, L.G. 1988, *Longman English Grammar*, Longman, Harlow.

Allsop, J. 1989, *Making Sense of English Grammar*, Cassell, London.

Bald, W-D., Cobb, D., Schwarz, A. 1986, *Active Grammar*, Longman, Harlow.

Bing, J.M. 1989, *Grammar Guide*, Prentice Hall Regents, Englewood Cliffs, NJ.

Bolton, D., Oscarson, M., Peterson, L. 1986, *Basic Working Grammar*, Nelson, Walton-on-Thames.

Chalker, S. 1984, *Current English Grammar*, Macmillan, London.

Greenbaum, S. and Quirk, R. 1990, *A Student's Grammar of the English Language*, Longman, Harlow.

Leech, G. and Svartvik, J. 1975, *A Communicative Grammar of English*, Longman, Harlow.

Quirk, R. and Greenbaum, S. 1973, *A University Grammar of English*, Longman, Harlow.

Sinclair, J. (ed.) 1990, *Collins Cobuild English Grammar*, Collins, London.
van Ek, J.A. and Robat, N.J. 1984, *The Student's Grammar of English*, Blackwell, Oxford.

B Alphabetical grammars

Broughton, G. 1990, *Penguin English Grammar A–Z*, Penguin, Harmondsworth.
Chalker, S. 1990, *English Grammar Word by Word*, Nelson, Walton-on-Thames.
Leech, G. 1989, *An A–Z of English Grammar and Usage*, Arnold, London.
Swan, M. 1980, *Practical English Usage*, OUP, Oxford.

C Grammar practice books

Alexander, L.G. 1990, *Longman English Grammar Practice*, Longman, Harlow.
Azar, B.S. 1985, *Fundamentals of English Grammar*, Prentice Hall Regents, Englewood Cliffs, NJ.
Beaumont, D. and Granger, C. 1989, *The Heinemann English Grammar*, Heinemann, London.
Hill, J. with Hurst, R. 1989, *Grammar and Practice*, Language Teaching Publications, Hove.
Murphy, R. 1985, *English Grammar in Use*, CUP, Cambridge.
Murphy, R. 1990, *Essential Grammar in Use*, CUP, Cambridge.
Sinclair, J. (ed.) 1991, *Collins Cobuild Student's Grammar*, Collins, London.
Thomson, A.J. and Martinet, A.V. 1990, *Oxford Pocket English Grammar*, OUP, Oxford.
Woods, E. and McLeod, N. 1990, *Using English Grammar*, Prentice Hall, Hemel Hempstead.

D Native speaker grammars

Freeborn, D. 1987, *A Course Book in English Grammar*, Macmillan, London.
Leech, G., Deuchar, M. and Hoogenraad, R. 1982, *English Grammar for Today*, Macmillan, London.

Appendix 2: Coursebooks surveyed

Abbs, R. and Freebairn, I. 1990, *Blueprint One*, Longman, Harlow.
Alexander, L.G. 1967, *First Things First*, Longman, London.
Aston, P. and Edmondson, E. 1990, *Streets Ahead*, OUP, Oxford.
Candlin, E.F. 1962, *Present Day English for Foreign Students*, University of London Press, London.
Hornby, A.S. 1954, *Oxford Progressive English for Adult Learners*, OUP, Oxford.
Nolasco, R. 1990, *WOW! Window on the World*, OUP, Oxford.
Willis, J. 1990, *First Lessons*, Collins, London.

Design Criteria for Pedagogic Language Rules

MICHAEL SWAN

1. Introduction: pedagogic[1] and non-pedagogic rules

In this article, I shall discuss the characteristics which distinguish pedagogic language rules from other kinds of language rule. By 'pedagogic rules' I mean rules which are designed to help foreign-language learners understand particular aspects of the languages they are studying (whether these rules are addressed directly to the learners, or to teachers and materials writers who are expected to pass on the rules to the learners in one form or another, is immaterial). I shall refer to a collection of such rules, unoriginally, as a 'pedagogic grammar'. This term can also reasonably be applied to a collection of rules designed for students who are learning about the structure of their own language, and much of what I shall have to say is relevant to mother-tongue language instruction.

'Pedagogic' rules can be more or less pedagogic. At one extreme, we can conceive (with some idealisation) of a rule designed for one specific learner, whose background, stage of development and preferred learning styles are all known. (This is the kind of rule that a good teacher might aim to give to an individual student.) Such a rule would probably be very different from a standard reference grammar's description of the same linguistic facts. At the other extreme is the type of broad-spectrum rule which one might find in a pedagogic grammar designed for teachers and advanced students from a variety of backgrounds; rules of this kind do not always differ in many respects from the equivalent non-pedagogic descriptions.

Implicit in this discussion is the belief that pedagogic rules can be useful to language learners. The question is notoriously a controversial one: it is of course possible that teaching language rules contributes nothing to learners' development. This issue is, however, outside the scope of my paper.

2. Six criteria

Assuming, then, for the sake of argument, that language rules are useful to learners, good rules must be more useful than bad rules. But what makes a 'good' rule? I believe that one can identify at least six 'design criteria' for pedagogic language rules: *truth, demarcation, clarity, simplicity, conceptual parsimony* and *relevance*. (Not all of these terms are transparent, but I hope that the following

45

discussion will make it clear what I mean by them.) The first three criteria are relevant to any kind of rule, while the others are especially important to the design of pedagogic rules. Some of them overlap; nonetheless, I feel that they are sufficiently distinct to merit separate consideration. Not all of them are compatible; indeed, I shall argue that some of the criteria necessarily conflict.

(a) Truth

Rules should be true.

It is obviously desirable to tell learners the truth. However, as Oscar Wilde said, the truth is rarely pure and never simple: it can be difficult to be sure exactly what the facts are, and to decide how much of the truth to tell. This criterion, therefore, is likely to conflict with others, and one will often need to compromise with truth for the sake of clarity, simplicity, conceptual parsimony or relevance. All other things being equal, though, it is best if language rules correspond reasonably well to the linguistic facts; since grammarians are fallible human beings like everybody else, this does not always happen. Readers may like to decide what is wrong with the following rules, taken from well-known pedagogic and general-purpose reference works. (For comments, see the end of the article.[2])

1. The past tense refers to a DEFINITE time in the past. (Leech and Svartvik, 1975)
2. *In case* is a subordinator referring to possible future conditions: *Do this in case a fire breaks out* means 'Do this in the event of a fire breaking out'. However, in British English *in case* in this sentence could also have the meaning of negative purpose: 'Do this to prevent fire breaking out'. (Quirk *et al.*, 1985)
3. Unlike the simple genitive, the double genitive usually implies non-unique meaning. Compare:
   He is my brother. (suggests I have one, or more than one brother)
   He is a brother of mine. (suggests I have more than one brother) (Leech and Svartvik, 1975)
4. When the main verb of a sentence is in a past tense, verbs in subordinate clauses must be in a past tense also. (Thomson and Martinet, 1980)
5. The plain infinitive is used with *had better*, *had rather*, *had sooner*. (Zandvoort, 1957)
6. Spelling: *-ise* and *-ize* . . . It is safer to write *-ize*: with a very few exceptions, this is always correct. (Swan, 1984)

In the interests of telling the truth, a pedagogic grammarian must of course try to suppress his or her own prescriptive prejudices and resistance to language change. One may, for instance, personally disapprove of the use of *like* as a conjunction (as in *It looks like the tickets are sold out*), or one may feel that many people use *hopefully*, *refute* or *disinterested* in undesirable ways, but one is doing no service to learners by telling them, as some writers do, that such things are incorrect (though one may well want to point out that some people believe them to be so). If educated native-speaker usage is divided, the grammarian's job is to describe and account for the division, not to attempt to adjudicate.

(b) Demarcation

A pedagogic rule should show clearly what are the limits on the use of a given form.

Telling the truth involves not only saying what things are, but also saying what they are not. If you ask me what a pika is, and I tell you that it is small and furry, has four legs and is found in the United States, you have grounds for complaint. My answer is descriptive, in that it gives you some accurate information about pikas, but it has no defining or predictive value, because it does not enable you to distinguish between pikas and other creatures such as squirrels, martens, weasels, prairie dogs, chipmunks, moles, rats or cats. If I want to do better than this, I must, so to speak, demarcate the territory occupied by the concept of 'pika' from that occupied by similar concepts, by telling you what makes pikas unique.

In the same way, a pedagogic rule, however true and well expressed, is useless unless it demarcates clearly the area within which a given form is appropriate, so that a learner will know when to use the form and when not to. Here is an example of a rule that does not meet this criterion.

> The PERFECT OF EXPERIENCE expresses what has happened, once or more than once, within the speaker's or writer's experience. (Zandvoort, 1957)

One can see what Zandvoort has in mind, but his description does not distinguish between different ways of talking about 'experience', and so fails to provide a basis for predicting whether or not the present perfect will be appropriate in a given case. As formulated, in fact, Zandvoort's rule could be interpreted as meaning that one uses the present perfect to refer to everything that has happened in one's lifetime!

Here is another rule which fails to demarcate.

> The present perfect continuous tense . . . is used for an action which began in the past and is still continuing, or has only just finished. (Thomson and Martinet, 1980)

What is said here is perfectly true, as well as being admirably clear and simple. The problem is that the present perfect continuous is not the only tense that is used to talk about actions which began in the past and are still continuing. The present continuous is also used for this purpose – much more often, in fact, than the present perfect continuous. The rule does not list the features (e.g. specification of duration) which demarcate the use of the present perfect continuous from that of the present continuous, and so provides no basis for predicting which of the two tenses will be appropriate in a given case.

The demarcation criterion is particularly important, and notoriously difficult to satisfy, in pedagogic lexical definition. Learners of English often have enormous difficulty in distinguishing close synonyms such as *evil* and *wicked*, *box* and *tin*, *shut* and *close* or *begin* and *start*. Dictionary definitions do not usually help – indeed, ordinary dictionaries are not designed to settle demarcation disputes between synonyms. (One of the learner's dictionaries on my shelf defines *evil* as 'causing harm and morally bad', and *wicked* as 'immoral and harmful'; the others do no better.) Perhaps as computerised corpus studies make more usage data available, it will at last become possible to give really helpful rules about the distinctions between words.

(c) Clarity

Rules should be clear.

Teachers tend to be good at making things clear. Their professional training and experience make them skilled at presenting information in an orderly fashion, using examples constructively, putting proper emphasis on what is most important, eliminating ambiguity, and so on. Modern pedagogic grammars, which are often written by people with teaching experience, do generally put things clearly, and it is much easier to find rules that are clear but untrue than rules which are true but unclear.

Where rules are unclear, it is often because of the use of unsatisfactory terminology, and this may conceal the fact that the writer does not himself or herself really understand the point at issue. Vague terms like *emphasis*, *definite*, *habitual*, *pronoun*, *condition*, *modality* or *style* can give the illusion of explanation without really conveying very much. When formulating pedagogic explanations, it is always worth asking oneself if one really understands exactly what is meant by the terms one is using; and assuming one does, whether one's audience is likely to understand the same things by them as one does oneself.

Here are two examples of rules where writers have perhaps failed to put a premium on clarity.

> The perfect tense usually denotes an action that falls within the time-sphere of the present. (Zandvoort, 1957)

> La modalité est le filtre coloré de notre subjectivité, au travers duquel nous voyons le réel. (Charlot, Hocmard and Morgan, 1977)

Zandvoort's time-sphere and the French authors' filter are both striking images, but neither of them successfully conveys the relevant information to someone who does not already possess it. After studying these rules, the learner is no better able than before to make valid choices of tense or modality. (How can we decide, after all, whether a given past action is 'within the time-sphere of the present' or whether facts that we wish to refer to are or are not seen through the 'coloured filter of our subjectivity'?) The concepts are evocative, but they simply do not have enough precision to give them predictive value. Perhaps metaphors are better avoided in pedagogic grammar.

(d) Simplicity

A pedagogic rule should be simple. There is inevitably some trade-off with truth and/ or clarity. How much does this matter?

Simplicity is not quite the same thing as clarity (though it may contribute to it). Clarity, as I have used the term, relates above all to the way an explanation is worded; simplicity to the way it is constructed. Clarity is the opposite of obscurity, and means the avoidance of ill-defined concepts and vague or misleading terminology. Simplicity is the opposite of complexity – simplifying a description involves trimming it to make it more manageable, for example by reducing the number of categories or subdivisions or by leaving out inessential details.

One of the things that distinguish pedagogic rules sharply from general-purpose descriptive rules is the requirement that they be simple. The truth is of no value if it cannot be understood, and since ordinary language learners tend to have limited prior knowledge and are not usually natural grammarians, some degree of simplification is nearly always necessary. In addition, clear and simple rules are psychologically valuable: they make students feel that they can understand and control the very complex material that they are faced with. How much one can reduce complexity without excessive distortion is a matter for individual judgement: one person's skilful simplification is another person's irresponsible travesty, and teachers' journals are consequently full of articles in which pedagogic grammarians take each other to task for giving over-simple rules of thumb. In some cases, of course, a point of grammar may be so complex that a successful simplification is actually impossible: there are aspects of language which cannot be taught (though they can be acquired).

The following rule, on article usage, seems to me an excellent example of a carefully thought-out trade-off between truth, clarity and simplicity.

> The best simplification is that the form of the article is determined by the interplay of the features 'definite' and 'known to the listener', thus giving four possible realisations:
>
> 1. Both definite and known to the listener » *the*
>   *Look at the sun!*
> 2. Definite but not known to the listener » *a/an*
>   *I passed through a village.*
> 3. Indefinite but known to the listener » *the/a/0+s*
>   *The lion is dangerous.*
>   *A lion is dangerous.*
>   *Lions are dangerous.*
> 4. Neither definite nor known to the listener » *a/an*
>   *If a person wants something* . . .
>
> (Todd and Hancock, 1986)

Some clarity has been lost in the simplification – *definite* is not explained, and *known to the listener* is used as something of a catch-all term. The authors have also cut one or two corners – in particular, they have decided not to deal with the use of articles to make *general/specific* distinctions. But what is left gives a good deal of the truth about the use of articles, and gives it in a form that makes this very complex point accessible to the average advanced student or teacher.

Here is another impressive simplification, from an article on teaching the present perfect.

We often think that there are endless rules for this tense. In fact these can be boiled down to just two simple precepts:

1. To describe actions beginning in the past and continuing up to the present moment (and possibly into the future): *I've planted fourteen rose bushes so far this morning.*
2. To refer to actions occurring or not occurring at an unspecified time in the past with some kind of connection to the present: *Have you passed your driving test?*

Every use of the present perfect (for example with *since*, *for* and so on) will fit into one of these rules. Proliferating rules without end makes this tense sound more difficult than it actually is.
(Alexander, 1988b)

Whether or not a particular simplification is valid depends ultimately on who it is addressed to, how much they already know, how much they are capable of taking in, and what value they and their teachers place on complete accuracy. Nonetheless, one can reasonably ask whether Alexander, excellent pedagogic grammarian though he is, has not on this occasion paid too high a price for simplicity. It is easy to share his impatience with the jungle of rules that are often supplied in a desperate attempt to pin down the use of the present perfect. On the other hand, the point *is* a difficult one; that is why grammarians make such heavy weather of it. (Defining the use of the present perfect is rather like trying to fit a balloon into your pocket – as soon as you manage to get one bit in, another bit bulges out again.) It is interesting that, in his *Longman English Grammar* (1988a), Alexander actually devotes quite a lot of space – over 140 lines – to the point. In comparison, *Cobuild* (Sinclair, ed., 1990) has 58 lines and Greenbaum and Quirk's *Student's Grammar* (1990) has 80. Thomson and Martinet (1980), locked in a fight to the death with this most elusive of tenses, have over 380.

(e) Conceptual parsimony

An explanation must make use of the conceptual framework available to the learner. It may be necessary to add to this. If so, one should aim for minimum intervention.

Simplicity and clarity may not be enough. One can drastically reduce the complexity of an explanation, use terminology that is perfectly precise in its reference, and still be left with something that is difficult for the non-specialist to grasp. When new information is communicated, there is often a conceptual gap between writer/speaker and reader/listener. Not only does the former know more than the latter; he or she may also analyse the material using concepts and categories which, though clearly defined, are unfamiliar to the recipient. In order to communicate effectively, it can be important to take into account the conceptual framework available to one's reader or listener, and to try to work within this as far as is reasonable. If the way in which one analyses a topic is too far removed from the analysis which one's audience initially brings to it, communication is likely to break down.

A professional grammarian writing for colleagues or well-informed amateurs does not of course need to make too many concessions to this principle of conceptual parsimony. He or she can assume that most readers will be familiar with the concepts and terminology used; if they are not, they can be expected to do the work necessary to grasp precisely what is meant by, say, 'theme and rheme', 'ergative', 'raising' or 'NP-trace'. On the other hand, a pedagogic grammarian or a teacher giving learners a rule can usually assume very little conceptual sophistication on the part of his/her readers or listeners. He or she must try to get things across using the simplest possible grammatical notions. Terminology will be chosen for its familiarity rather than for its precision. It will sometimes be necessary to provide students with new concepts in order to get a point across, but one must aim for minimum intervention. This will often mean compromising – perhaps quite seriously – with the truth.

Which of the following rules is more likely to be understood by the average learner?

1. We use *much* with uncountable nouns and *many* with plural countables.
2. We use *much* with singular nouns and *many* with plurals.

It seems to me that, in this instance, the added precision gained by referring to countability is not worth paying for, unless the student to whom the rule is addressed is already totally familiar with the concept. (Students who can distinguish between singular and plural are unlikely to try to use *much* with countable singulars anyway, because phrases like *much horse* do not make sense, so 'singular nouns' will effectively direct them to uncountable nouns in this case.) Similarly, one might (possibly gritting one's teeth) decide that it was more cost-effective with a particular student or class to talk about 'possessive adjectives' rather than 'possessive determiners', 'infinitive' rather than 'base form', 'tense' rather than 'tense plus aspect', or 'conditional' rather than '*would* + infinitive', however unsatisfactory these labels might be from a strictly descriptive point of view. (If one's students speak a language in which the equivalent of *would go* is an inflected verb form with a name such as *conditionnel* or *condizionale*, it is surely perverse not to use the cognate term when talking about the English structure.)

(f) Relevance

A rule should answer the question (and only the question) that the student's English is 'asking'.

Pedagogic grammar is not just about language; it is about the interaction between language and language learners. A good pedagogic rule does not present a neutral analysis of a set of linguistic data; it answers a question, real or potential, that is asked by a learner, or that is generated by his or her interlanguage. Consider the following concocted examples.

1. *My sister Ksenija lives in Belgrade. She is hairdresser.*
2. *My sister Marie-France lives in Lyon. She is hairdresser.*

Despite the surface equivalence, the two instances of *She is hairdresser* can be seen as reflecting totally different interlanguage rules. In the first case (given the fact that Slav languages have no article systems), the learner's interlanguage rule – if this sentence is typical of his/her usage – might be paraphrased as 'There are no indefinite articles in English' or 'English articles are too hard to understand, so don't use them'. The second learner's interlanguage rule is more likely to be something on the lines of 'Articles are not used in English before classifying complements such as the names of professions'. In a teaching situation, one could regard each of the sentences as generating a question, or a request for a rule: respectively 'How are (indefinite) articles used in English?' and 'How does English article usage differ from French in the case of classifying complements?'. Clearly the pedagogic rules that will be appropriate in each case will be totally different one from the other. While the Serbo-Croat speaker will need a good deal of information about the meaning and use of the English articles, there is no point in giving a French-speaking learner a similarly complete account, since he/she already knows in general how article systems work.

The following rather fanciful examples show how failure to produce an English plural inflection might reflect four different interlanguage rules (so that four different pedagogic rules would be potentially relevant to the correction of the mistakes).

1. *I run an import–export business in Taipei with my two brother.*
   (Chinese does not inflect for number.)

2. *I run a carpet factory in Teheran with my two brother.*
   (Farsi nouns inflect for number, but singular forms are used with numerical determiners.)

3. *I run a call-girl network in Dijon with my two brother.*
   (Although written French commonly adds -*s* for plural, like English, the -*s* is not pronounced. This carries over into the spoken English of French-speaking learners, and – because of subvocalisation – quite often into their written English.)

4. *I run a brewery in Heidelberg with my two brother.*
   (Many German nouns form their plural by adding -*er*; many others have both singular and plural in -*er*. German speakers quite often drop -*s* off the plurals of English words ending in -*er*: presumably this is because the ending already 'feels plural' to them.)

Because it is important to focus closely on a learner's point of difficulty and to exclude information that is irrelevant to this, it can sometimes be useful to present what is, objectively speaking, a thoroughly bad rule. Conditional structures are a case in point. The standard pedagogic analysis of sentences with *if* into 'first', 'second' and 'third' conditionals is, from a strictly descriptive point of view, total nonsense. (All sorts of possible combinations of verb forms are possible with *if*; in so far as it makes sense to categorise them, they can more usefully be divided into two main groups – those with 'ordinary' tenses, and those in which 'special' tenses are used to express a hypothetical kind of meaning.) However, given that students do tend to have trouble with the three structures that are presented in the standard pedagogic analysis, and that they can generally manage the others without difficulty, one could argue that – whatever its theoretical defects – this analysis gives students what they need.

Similar considerations apply to the teaching of indirect speech. This is very nearly a pseudo-category in English. Despite the monstrous apparatus of rules about backshift, deictic changes and so on that appear in many pedagogic grammars and coursebooks, nearly all English indirect speech utterances are constructed in accordance with the general rules that determine the form of most other English sentences. A few kinds of indirect speech sentence do involve tense usage that is specific to this grammatical category (e.g. *Are you deaf? I asked you how old you were*), but these are the exception. On the other hand, indirect speech is very definitely a live category for many learners of English, either because in their languages it does follow special syntactic rules, or because their mother tongues have no equivalent of the structure at all. This being so, it may after all be appropriate for a pedagogic grammar to provide a full-scale account of indirect speech as a separate topic, even if this would arguably be out of place in a purely descriptive grammar.

Failure to focus on the learner's linguistic state as well as on the language itself is responsible for a good deal of bad grammar teaching. In old-style mother-tongue English lessons in secondary schools, a great deal of emphasis was put on parsing: identifying parts of speech and their syntactic roles, labelling clause types and so on. This effectively amounted to saying 'Their grammar is defective; therefore we must teach them grammar', without consideration of whether the grammar they were allegedly getting wrong and the grammar they were being taught bore any relation to each other. But there is not much value, for instance, in teaching people to identify noun clauses, if the ways in which their language is unsatisfactory do not include failure to operate the category of noun clauses. This is like saying 'Jake got lost on the way back from the pub last night; he needs geography lessons' or 'Annie put salt in her tea this morning instead of sugar; she needs chemistry lessons' or (in the immortal words of *Yes, Minister*) 'Something must be done; this is something; therefore let us do it'.

Effective grammar teaching, then, focuses on the specific problems (real and potential) of specific learners. This will necessarily mean giving a somewhat fragmentary and partial account of the grammar of the target language, rather than working through a 'complete' grammar syllabus giving 'complete' rules. There is nothing at all wrong with this, though the approach may look messy and unsystematic: the grammar classroom is no place for people with completion neuroses. To quote a very apposite old American saying: 'If it ain't broke, don't fix it'.

3. Crossing linguistic categories: grammar, lexis or pragmatics?

When we formulate fine-tuned pedagogic rules, the need to focus on the learner as well as the language not only affects the shape of the rules; it may even determine whether a particular language element is seen as involving grammar, lexis or pragmatics. Consider the various possible ways of handling *because* clauses. In a general-purpose reference book, these will be unambiguously classified under grammar. Whether a pedagogic rule treats them as grammar, however, will depend on who the rule is for. A learner whose language does not have clause subordi-nation – or does not express cause through subordination – will certainly approach *because* clauses as an aspect of grammar. But a speaker of a European language is likely to have few problems with simple subordination; for such a student, the relevant information about *because* will be that it is the equivalent of *weil*, *parce que*, *porque*, *fordi*, *potamou sto* or whatever. He or she will learn *because* as a vocabulary item, and may well need no grammatical information at all in order to begin using it correctly.

Or consider ways of asking for help. For some learners, the English use of a negative declarative question structure to make requests (as in *You couldn't give me a hand for a minute?*) will correspond closely to what happens in their own languages, and their task will be the relatively simple one of mastering the English version of the form. For speakers of other languages, in contrast, the very fact of asking for help by means of a direct question may be quite alien, so that they will not only have to learn a new point of grammar – how to construct this kind of interrogative – but also an aspect of pragmatics – how to associate questions with a new kind of speech act. In pedagogic grammar work, therefore, the very way in which items are assigned to linguistic categories may depend as much on what the learner knows as on the structure of the target language.

4. Conclusion: in defence of rules of thumb

'School grammars' is a term that is often given a pejorative edge (sometimes with good reason). But it is easy to forget what it is like to know little about a subject and to have little aptitude for it. People who are inclined to be dismissive of popular pedagogic grammars might usefully consider in what form they themselves would like to be given information about quantum mechanics, laser technology, plant genetics, crystallography or the physics of black holes. A little truth goes a long way when one is off one's own ground.

Teachers often give students explanations of a kind that they would not dream of producing if an inspector was in the room. And yet the teacher's corner-cutting rules of thumb, half-truths and unscientific terminology might on occasion work better than anything that the inspector would be capable of. Good teaching involves a most mysterious feat – sitting, so to speak, on one's listener's shoulder, monitoring what one is saying with the listener's ears, and using this feedback to shape and adapt one's words from moment to moment so that the thread of communication never breaks. This is art, not science, and there is a great deal of such art in the production of successful pedagogic language rules. These rules may on occasion be very different from those found in a standard reference grammar; but it may be this very difference – the fact that they satisfy specifically pedagogic criteria such as simplicity, conceptual parsimony and relevance – that makes them succeed where more descriptively 'respectable' rules would fail.

Notes

1. I make no distinction between the terms *pedagogic* and *pedagogical*, but prefer the shorter word.
2. Notes on the quotations under 'Truth':
    1. What is a 'definite' time? How definite is *once upon a time*? How about *an indefinite time ago*? How about *Nobody knows when . . .*?
    2. Suppose you insure a house in case fire breaks out. This doesn't mean either 'in the event of fire breaking out' or 'to prevent fire breaking out', but 'to guard against the consequences of fire breaking out'.
    3. What about *How's that brother of yours*? The 'non-unique' meaning in Leech and Svartvik's example comes from the indefinite article, not from the 'double genitive', whose function is simply to circumvent the English constraint on the co-occurrence of possessives with articles and demonstratives.
    4. This is only true of certain kinds of subordinate clause in certain kinds of structure.
    5. *Had rather* lives on in grammars, but is virtually obsolete in normal usage.
    6. The opposite is closer to the truth.

References

Alexander, L.G. 1988a, *Longman English Grammar*, Longman, Harlow.

Alexander, L.G. 1988b, 'The three best kept secrets about grammar', *Practical English Teaching*, vol. 9, no. 2, 59–60.

Charlot, M., Hocmard, G. and Morgan, J. 1977, *Let's Go On! Classe de Seconde*, Armand Colin/Longman, Paris.

Greenbaum, S. and Quirk, R. 1990, *A Student's Grammar of the English Language*, Longman, Harlow.

Leech, G. and Svartvik, J. 1975, *A Communicative Grammar of English*, Longman, Harlow.

Quirk, R., Greenbaum, S., Leech, G. and Svartvik, J. 1985, *A Comprehensive Grammar of the English Language*, Longman, Harlow.

Sinclair, J. (ed.) 1990, *Collins Cobuild English Grammar*, Collins, London.

Swan, M. 1984, *Basic English Usage*, OUP, Oxford.

Thomson, A.J. and Martinet, A.V. 1980, *A Practical English Grammar* (3rd edition), OUP, Oxford.

Todd, L. and Hancock, I. 1986, *International English Usage*, Croom Helm, Andover.

Zandvoort, R.W. 1957, *A Handbook of English Grammar* (1st edition), Longmans, Green & Co., London.

A Lexical Approach

DAVE WILLIS

1. Introduction

The purpose of a pedagogic grammar is to provide the learner with useful insights into the language under study. To be useful, any insight should obviously be accessible to the learner. It should be accessible in two ways. First, it should be comprehensible. Material should be offered to learners in such a way that they can not only repeat its surface form but also process it for meaning to discover what lies beneath the surface form. Material should also be generalisable in two ways: it should enable learners to generate language for themselves, and it should be informative when applied to other samples of the language encountered by the learners.

In helping learners manage their insights into the target language we should be conscious that our starting point is the *learner's* grammar of the language. It is the learner who has to make sense of the insights derived from input, and learners can only do this by considering new evidence about the language in the light of their current model of the language. This argues against presenting them with pre-packaged structures and implies that they should be encouraged to process text for themselves so as to reach conclusions which make sense in terms of their own systems.

Before proposing a way of tackling this problem, I would like to look at alternative ways of approaching three items which take up a good deal of time in most intermediate courses. I will begin by looking at the passive, and then go on to discuss the 'second conditional' and 'reported speech'. The consensus view seems to be that these items are of central importance and that they cause learners particular difficulties, therefore justifying the expenditure of a good deal of time in the classroom and a good deal of space in coursebooks, not to mention supplementary materials devised by teachers.

2. Three areas of grammar: alternative views

(a) The passive

The uses of the past participle are illustrated in these five examples:

1. *I would be **interested** to hear an account of your experience.*

2. *Thank you very much for your **detailed** letter.*
3. *I think they must have got **mixed up**.*
4. *A van **equipped** with a loudspeaker toured the reservoir.*
5. *He was **rescued** by one of his companions.*

Four of the patterns in which the past participle appears are closely paralleled by patterns with adjectives in the following:

6. *I would be **happy** to hear an account of your experience.*
7. *Thank you very much for your **cheerful** letter.*
8. *She must have got very **angry**.*
9. *One man, **happy** with the results of his efforts, was able to take home a large sum of money.*

Sentences 1 and 6 are examples of an adjective as complement after the verb *be*; 2 and 7 show an adjective qualifying a noun; 3 and 8 have an adjective after *get* (several other verbs, like *look*, *grow* and *become* display this pattern); sentences 4 and 9 show an adjective followed by a prepositional phrase (all adjective phrases of this kind come after the noun). There seems, therefore, to be a good *prima facie* case for regarding the past participle as an adjective. If we do this, it need no longer be seen as presenting any special difficulty beyond those that learners already have to tackle in learning how adjectives work in English.

Some teachers, however, may baulk at regarding 5 as adjectival. In 1, the past participle *interested* is descriptive: it tells us how the recipient of the letter felt; whereas in 5, *rescued* tells us what happened to the subject. Semantically the past participle *interested* is stative and the past participle *rescued* is dynamic.

There is a large class of past participles which are stative in meaning (*delighted*, *tired*, *worried*, *broken*, etc.) and which are therefore better regarded as adjectives. But the distinction is not entirely clear-cut. In a sentence such as *The windows were broken*, the past participle *broken* could be regarded as either stative (cf. 10) or dynamic (cf. 11).

10. *The house was a mess. The paintwork was peeling and the windows were **broken**.*
11. *The windows were **broken** by the force of the explosion.*

The case is similar with *frightened* in the next two sentences:

12. *Little Miss Muffet was **frightened** of spiders.*
13. *Little Miss Muffet was **frightened** by a spider.*

In 12, the past participle is descriptive or stative, but in 13 it is dynamic.

But it is not only past participles that can be either stative or dynamic. The same is true of adjectives.

Stative and dynamic adjectives differ in a number of ways. For example stative adjectives such as *tall* cannot be used with the progressive aspect or with the imperative: **He's being* *tall*; **Be tall*. On the other hand we can use *careful* as a dynamic adjective: *He's being careful . . . Be careful . . .* (Quirk *et al.*, 1972)

A Grammar of Contemporary English goes on to list well over 50 adjectives – some of them extremely common, such as *nice* and *kind* – which can be used dynamically.

It seems, therefore, that the only real distinguishing feature of the passive is the use of *by* with a noun phrase to mark an agent. Rather than picking out the passive as a feature of the verb group for special treatment, an economical teaching strategy will allow the past participle to be treated adjectivally. One of the consequences of this is that the collocation of *be* with *-ed* forms is noted, but not given undue prominence. This is simply to say that *-ed* adjectives are commonly predicative; that is, they are commonly found as complement after a link verb. This can be put together with the use of *by* as a marker of agency, as in the following examples:

14. *Wally was awakened by the telephone ringing.*
15. *Handicrafts made by the people in the third world . . .*
16. *Is that magazine published by Macmillan?*

and then the learner has all that is needed to produce the passive with agent.

The main difficulties with the passive, as exemplified in sentence 5, are not structural, but textual and semantic. In terms of textuality, we need to look at the use of the passive. In this respect the strategy suggested here is likely to be more effective than an approach which derives the passive voice transformationally from the active form. If the participle is treated adjectivally, it will quite naturally be used when the subject of the clause is given and it is the information contained in the past participle that is new.

In effect this is the approach that is often taken. Chalker (1993) suggests the following sequence as a way of introducing the passive:

Lots of objects have labels on them showing the country of origin, so you could start by looking at some. *Can you read the label on my bag? My bag was made in China. And my shoes? My shoes were made in Brazil. What about my camera? Can you guess where it was made? Yes, it was made in Japan . . .* Agents are for another lesson, where the by-agent is important new information we want to keep to the end.

This seems to be a useful strategy in providing insights into the use of the passive – it helps to meet the textual difficulties. But it highlights one of the semantic problems. The shoes, bag, camera and so on are here and now. The natural comment would seem to be: *My bag is made in China, my shoes are made in Brazil.* The use of the past tense marks the past participle in these examples as dynamic. This needs to be brought out clearly.

Another way of introducing the passive would be to assemble a set of sentences taken from texts that are already familiar to learners and ask them to identify adjectives, including past participles, in a predicative position. On the following questions, for example,

My father's called John.
Are you tired?

Bridget is English.
Those are very nice.
They're married.
The house was built in 1890.
Her jeans are blue.
Wally was awakened by the phone ringing.

the teacher might ask: 'What words follow the verb *be*? Which of these words are related to verbs? What about *married* – does it describe someone or does it tell you what happened? What about *awakened*? What about *built*?'

This tackles the textual problems by relating past participles and adjectives, and also highlights the dynamic meaning of some past participles.

(b) The 'second conditional'

Many ELT grammars and coursebooks talk about the 'three conditionals':

1. *If it rains we'll get wet.*
2. *If it rained we would get wet.*
3. *If it had rained we would have got wet.*

These patterns are highlighted for the learner and offered as paradigms. This is done, presumably, in the belief that the learner will be able to generalise from these patterns. Of course other modals can be used in conditionals; for example:

4. *If it rains, we could/may/might get wet.*
5. *If it rained, we could/might get wet.*
6. *If it had rained, we could/might have got wet.*

There are 'mixed' conditionals:

7. *If United had won they'd be top of the table.*
8. *If they caught the train they'd be here any minute.*

There are many sentences in which *if* marks a condition but in which the subordinate clause is not conditional:

9. *Even if I had the time, I feel too tired.*
10. *If you want a beer there's one in the fridge.*

Conditionals are simply the sum of their parts. The second conditional contains a main clause with the modal *would*. The Cobuild 7.6 million corpus, which was used for the early research which went into the production of the *Collins Cobuild English Dictionary* (1987) contains just under 15,000 occurrences of the word *would*. It is the forty-fourth most frequent word in the corpus and the most frequent modal, much more frequent than *will*, for example, which has 8,800 occurrences. In around half of its 15,000 occurrences, *would* is used to talk of events which are of a hypothetical nature at the time of being mentioned, either because they are in the future, or because they depend on events which may or may not occur. Examples include:

> *A picnic wouldn't be any fun without you.*
> *Wouldn't it be quicker to chop it down?*
> The Tempest *would make a wonderful film.*
> *I suspect that the West Germans would still be a bit cautious.*

In these examples a condition has been established earlier in the text, or is implicit in the word *would*. This accounts for around 7,500 of the occurrences in the corpus. A subcategory of this, accounting for a further 1,200 occurrences, is *would* used in explicitly conditional sentences; for example:

> *I would be surprised if sterling strengthened.*
> *It would be funny if it wasn't so sad.*

In these sentences *would* is combined with the past tense. Hypothesis is also one of the meanings carried by the past tense; for example:

> *I wish I lived in a caravan.*
> *Suppose you got lost.*

The second conditional does not create these meanings, it simply brings them together.

It is clear that all the modals, not only *will* and *would*, are commonly found in conditionals, and that *would* used to talk of hypothetical events and situations is much more commonly found without *if* than with *if*. Most modals are taught lexically. Students learn that *might* and *could*, for example, are used for possibility. It is not thought necessary to teach as standard patterns conditionals like 4, 5 and 6 above. Provided that learners know what *if* means, and they know what *might* and *could* mean, and they know that the past tense is used for hypothesis, it is assumed that they can create for themselves sentences like 4, 5 and 6. In exactly the same way, if *would* is taught lexically with its main meaning of hypothesis, learners will be able to generate for themselves sentences like 2.

The strategy of highlighting word meaning is a much more productive one than the strategy of teaching structural patterns. If the second conditional is taught as a means of introducing learners to the meaning of the word *would* and the hypothetical meaning of the past tense, this seems to me to be an economical teaching strategy. Learners may then be led to the generalisation that *would* also occurs in all sorts of environments without *if*. But this is not generally what happens. The second conditional is normally taught as if it had some life of its own, as if there were something unique about this combination of the past tense and the modal *would*. But both these elements carry the meaning of hypothesis quite independently of the second conditional. In fact, *would* in conditionals is no more difficult than *might* or *could* in conditionals. It is simply more common.

(c) *Reported statements*

It is a fact of the English language that the tense we select is liable to change if we take a different standpoint in time. If George says 'I'm tired' and I report this as 'George said he was tired' I choose the past tense because George's being tired occurred in the past, rather than because the verb *said* is past tense. Even if George is still tired, I may nevertheless choose to say 'George said he was tired'. But if George is still tired and I want to make this clear I can choose to report what he said by saying 'George said he's tired' or even 'George says he's tired'. So the choice between past and present does not simply indicate when something happened. It may also indicate whether or not I think the happening is still relevant.

The fact that we sometimes have a choice between past and present tenses is not simply a feature of reported speech. I might talk about something which happened in the past by saying 'We stayed in the Grand Hotel. It was an awful place.' If the hotel still exists and is still awful, I can nevertheless choose to use the past tense if I do not think my statement has any relevance to the present. On the other hand, I can choose to give my assessment some present relevance by selecting the present tense: 'We stayed in the Grand Hotel. It's an awful place. You certainly shouldn't stay there.'

While preparing the *Collins Cobuild English* course materials we asked someone to rewrite a story as a radio script. The story included this passage:

> 'What part of London are you headed for?' I asked him.
> 'I'm going through London and out the other side,' he said, 'I'm going to Epsom, for the races. It's Derby Day today.'
> 'So it is,' I said. 'I wish I were going with you. I love betting on horses.'
> 'I never bet on horses,' he said, 'I don't even watch them run. That's a stupid silly business.'
> 'Then why do you go?' I asked.
> He didn't seem to like that question. His ratty face went absolutely blank and he sat there staring straight ahead at the road saying nothing.
> 'I expect you help to work the betting machines or something like that,' I said.
> 'That's even sillier,' he answered.
> (Roald Dahl, *The Hitch-hiker*)

This summary was produced:

> The other day I picked up a hitch-hiker who was heading for London and then going on to Epsom for the Derby. I got very curious about him because it transpired that although he was going to the Derby he didn't like horses or racing, he didn't bet on horses and he didn't seem to have any kind of job at the race-track.

The interesting thing about this is that although the second version reports what was said, there are no verbs of saying. There is no past tense verb like *said* to trigger a tense change. The report is in the past tense because the reported events happened in the past.

There is nothing difficult about tense in reported speech in English. The logic it follows is the same as for the rest of the language. In spite of this, many coursebooks insist on regarding reported statement as a structure of some kind which has a system of rules to itself. Instead of looking for broad generalisations about the language, there is an attempt to cordon off sections and treat them as if they were in some sense unique. Reported speech, particularly the use of tense, is treated in this way and is seen as creating great difficulties for learners, even at quite an advanced level.

One practice book for the Cambridge First Certificate, for example, solemnly lists the rules for reported speech. It explains that changes have to be made to certain items with the result that *this* becomes *the* or *that*, *today* becomes *that day* and *I* becomes *he* or *she*. To complicate the issue further, it is explained that if the reporting verb is in the past tense, then all the tenses 'go one step backward in time'. These backward steps are then listed. Present simple becomes past simple, present perfect and past simple become past perfect and so on.

This is all totally unnecessary. These differences in person and in phrases of time and place occur because we are taking a different standpoint from the original writer or speaker. It would be stupid to refer to something as happening today if I am well aware that it happened several days ago. Similarly, if someone asked me the question 'Do you think I'll be late?', it would be silly to reply by saying: 'Yes, I probably will'. We are constantly changing reference to person, time and place to accommodate the standpoint of a different speaker at a different time. This is a feature of language as a whole, not simply a feature of reported speech. It is a confusing and uneconomical teaching strategy to single out reported statements and treat them as if they were unique in some way.

It is in fact difficult to sustain the argument that reported statement is a grammatical category at all. An analysis of noun clause phrases introduced by *that* in the texts for the *Collins Cobuild English Course* level 3, produced examples like these:

1. *Cecil Sharpe felt that the old songs of England might disappear for ever.*
2. *If it's a job interview try to show that you're interested in the job.*
3. *The government brought in a rule that children under thirteen weren't allowed to work.*
4. *The unsuccessful artist decided that his prayer had been answered.*
5. *The monkey said that there was no such thing as food, only fruit.*
6. *A long time ago there was this theory that women always passed first time.*

Altogether in the texts which make up the CCEC level 3, there were 212 occurrences of *that* used to introduce a noun clause. Of these 212 occurrences,

- 87 are introduced by verbs of thinking (*think, feel, assume, decide, realise, understand, conclude, believe, know, wish, recall, remember*).
- 40 are introduced by verbs of saying (*say, tell, demand, report, explain, suggest, point out, assure, argue*).
- 38 are introduced by nouns (*rule, fact, idea, theory, problem, situation, thing, information, implication, promise, belief, impression, assurance, grounds, speculation, claim, announcement, signs, concern, conclusion, feeling, case, background*).

- 13 are introduced by adjectives (*glad, clear, sure, likely, incredulous, satisfied, convinced*).
- 34 are introduced by miscellaneous other words (*show, see, it, except, mean, imply, turn out, hear, notice, pretend, reveal*).

This tells us a number of things. First of all, comparatively few of the 212 occurrences could accurately be described as reported speech. Reported thought is much more common than reported speech. But reported thought does not figure in pedagogic grammars with anything like the same inevitability as reported speech. Secondly, a large number of occurrences (such as 2, 3 and 6 above) could not be described as reports at all. Thirdly, noun clauses are by no means always dependent upon a verb.

What, then, does the learner need to know about clauses of this kind? As I have pointed out, many pedagogic grammars imply that the difficulty lies particularly with tense, and with changes in time and place reference. But I have argued that there is nothing unique about tense or about time and place in these noun clauses. I would suggest that, as with the passive, the most important thing about noun clauses is not how they are formed, but how they are used. They are used, for example, in the way that I have used them earlier in this paragraph with words like *argue* and *suggest* to help develop an argument. They are used with nouns like *thing*, *problem*, *situation* and *theory* to help define and develop ideas. In particular, they have an important function in identifying and highlighting a notion that is going to be developed in the text:

> *thing*
> *problem*
> *The situation is (that)* . . .
> *theory*
> *difficulty*

Of the 1,000 commonest words in English approximately 350 function as nouns. Of these, some 35, about one in ten, are found with a report clause.

3. Lexis as a starting point

I have suggested that three of the items traditionally regarded as difficult for the learner are not in fact generally difficult in the way they are believed to be. They are generally regarded as being difficult structures. I have argued that the passive and the conditionals do not need to be presented as structures, since they can readily be created by learners for themselves, provided that they have an understanding of word meaning.

A lexically based approach is likely to be more powerful than a structural approach in three ways. In the first place, it offers more powerful generalisations.

Once learners are aware of hypothetical use of the past tense and *would* to encode hypothesis, they are in principle capable of producing sentences like:

> *I think* The Tempest *would make a wonderful film.*
> *I wish I lived in a caravan.*

They are also in a much better position to make sense of further input. They will be more likely to identify the general hypothetical use of the past tense and *would* if they are able to abstract them from the 'second conditional' pattern. Similarly, once they identify the passive as adjectival, a range of uses is open to them. It may be some time before they take advantage of this, but they are more likely to do so if this is the starting point rather than if the passive is treated transformationally and if the past participle is linked entirely to the verb *be*.

Secondly, and as a corollary, the fact that a lexical description depends on a more powerful generalisation means that the learner will have more evidence on which to base useful generalisations about the language. I have shown, for example, that *would* expressing hypothesis occurs six times without *if* for every time it occurs with *if*. You may search for some time before you come across a full-blown conditional clause, particularly if you are looking for one of the kind usually presented to learners, stripped down to its essentials. You will not go very far, however, without coming across *would* in its hypothetical meaning. The evidence suggests that it will occur on average around once every thousand words.

A similar lesson can be drawn from our look at the noun clauses which realise, among other things, reported statements. There are four examples in this paragraph so far, none of them a reported statement. This noun clause, therefore, is likely to be a much more useful concept than reported statement. It is not linguistically complex, since it follows the general rules governing the use of tenses and adverbials of time and place in English. Once learners become aware of this, they can begin to work on the variety of uses of such clauses and, in particular, the words that introduce them. If we assume that learners have an understanding of clause and group structure, what we should go on to look at is the meaning and use of the elements within the clause, the meaning of *would* and of past participles, and the use of words that introduce noun clauses with *that*.

This is a task which learners are able to accomplish for themselves with a little guidance from the teacher. We have already suggested an exercise which focuses on the meaning of past participles and their use as predicative adjectives. In the same way learners might be asked to look at sentences such as:

> *Cecil Sharpe felt that the old songs of England might disappear for ever.*
> *He was sure that he was right.*
> *There was this theory that women always passed the first time.*

and identify and attempt to classify words followed by *that*. They may later be asked to identify cases where the word *that* has been omitted, and to find out when it is obligatory. They could be asked to identify the past tense forms in a short text like this:

A: What would you cook if someone dropped in unexpectedly and stayed for a meal in the evening? What would you do, David?
B: I'd cook whatever vegetables happened to be there.
C: I'd take them to a restaurant.
A: Supposing they arrived after the restaurants had shut?

The teacher might ask: 'Do these forms refer to past time? What about the word *would*?' It is not asking too much of the learners to recognise that this is a hypothetical situation.

What I am proposing here is that words are more amenable to learner analysis and discovery than 'structures'. This is partly because words are more immediately recognisable and partly because they are more frequent than any 'structure' that might incorporate them. Instead of receiving a decontextualised and teacher-controlled presentation, learners can be asked to analyse texts which they have already processed for meaning. This may involve an analysis of a specific text, as in the case of the dialogue above. On the other hand, it may involve treating the texts learners have already processed as a 'pedagogic' corpus. Items from this corpus can then be reprocessed for analysis, as was proposed for the exercises on past participles and noun clauses. Just as lexicographers and grammarians analyse a corpus of texts to produce their linguistic descriptions, so learners can analyse a corpus for insights into the language which will help develop their own grammar.

All this does not mean that clause structure is not important. But there is nothing unusual about the clause structure in conditionals and noun clauses. They follow the same SVO/C order as other clauses of English. Learners need to discover the structure of the clause and of the elements within it, but this is not a learning difficulty associated specifically with any particular structure, such as first or second conditional.

A concern with the transmission of abstract sentence patterns teaches nothing about the meanings and use of particular words. Indeed it can obscure the function of words like *would* by implying that the meaning is given by a particular structural configuration rather than residing in the word itself. There is a danger that we concern ourselves too much with manipulating reported speech and ignore the much wider use of noun clauses, such as their signalling function in discourse in association with words like *thing*, *problem* and *situation*. Too much time has been given to presenting learners with target structures which are simply the sum of their parts. Too little time has been given to looking at the items which make up those structures.

As a starting point I have looked at three patterns which, I have argued, conceal more about the language than they reveal. A closer look at the frequent words in the language may well provide information of value to the language teacher. A look at 1,200 occurrences of the word *can*, for example, reveals that in one case out of seven it is followed by the word *be*. This suggests that there are powerful collocational patternings in the language which owe nothing to any grammatical description. Clause structure may cause initial problems for the language learner but it is not long before a close look at the meanings and uses of words and their common patternings begins to pay much greater dividends.

References

Chalker, S. 1993, 'Teaching grammar', *past present future*, p. 6.
Quirk, R., Greenbaum, S., Leech, G. and Svartvik, J. 1972, *A Grammar of Contemporary English*, Longman, Harlow.
Sinclair, J. (ed.) 1987, *Collins Cobuild English Dictionary*, Collins, London.
Willis, J. and Willis, D. 1988, *Collins Cobuild English Course*, Collins, London.

Section 2

TEACHERS' KNOWLEDGE OF GRAMMAR

The Grammatical Knowledge/Awareness of Native-Speaker EFL Teachers: What the Trainers Say

STEPHEN ANDREWS

1. Introduction

The teaching of EFL by non-native speakers has a long and distinguished history. Before 1600, for example, such teaching was already established in the Netherlands and France (Howatt, 1984). Nowadays, the great majority of learners of EFL worldwide study with non-native-speaker teachers, usually as part of a system of compulsory education.

The involvement of native speakers in the teaching of EFL is, by contrast, a more recent phenomenon. Berlitz schools may have been offering EFL taught by native speakers at the turn of the century (Howatt, *op. cit.*), but it is only in the last 40 years or so that such teachers have become relatively commonplace around the world, very often working in private language schools set up to support, complement or compensate for the tuition provided by the state.

In the early years of native-speaker EFL teaching, the approach was distinctly amateur. As Haycraft describes it:

> At that time, the EFL profession hardly existed, and private language schools were regarded generally as rackets, in which untrained undergraduates figured prominently in part-time jobs on summer courses. Those who taught EFL frequently had the attitude: 'I'm English, aren't I? So I can teach my own language, can't I?' (Haycraft, 1988)

During this period, the mere fact that such teachers were native speakers of English was often seen as a distinct commercial advantage by many language schools. As time passed, however, the limitations of such teachers became increasingly apparent. As a result, various training courses, starting with the RSA Certificate (later Diploma) in the Teaching of English as a Foreign Language in 1967, were developed in an attempt to remedy these deficiencies and enhance the professionalism of native-speaker teachers of EFL, with the initial focus being on those who already had substantial experience of teaching EFL.

In spite of such developments, there are still a number of ways in which, it might be argued, native-speaker teachers of EFL are less well prepared than many of

69

their non-native-speaker counterparts. For instance, the majority of native-speaker teachers of EFL have not studied Education and have not studied the subject they teach (i.e. English language) since school – indeed, when such teachers are below a certain age, it is doubtful whether they will have studied the English language at all, even at school. These are disturbing reflections, particularly at a time when native-speaker practitioners in our field are striving to establish TEFL as a credible profession: how many 'real' professions would tolerate a situation where the primary activity of that profession is being conducted by so many inadequately trained people?

In the development of training schemes for native-speaker EFL teachers, the nature of the pedagogical content – whether it should be rooted in the broader study of education or whether it can legitimately be limited to EFL concerns – has long been the subject of lively debate. Rather less attention, in contrast, seems to have been given over the years to the adequacy of the subject knowledge of such teachers, presumably because it has been assumed (as by Haycraft's 'typical teacher' above) that native speakers by definition 'know' their own language.

The experience of many people involved in TEFL, however, especially those who encounter native speakers at the start of their careers, casts serious doubts as to the validity of such an assumption (for example, see Davis, 1990). A survey of the experience of one such group of people is described in this paper in an attempt to throw a little more light on the subject knowledge of native-speaker EFL teachers.

2. The survey

The focus

Two fundamental questions emerge in any initial thinking about the native-speaker teacher's subject knowledge:

1. If one takes the view that a prime aim of teaching EFL is to help learners develop an understanding of how the English language works as a system, to what extent are native-speaker teachers adequately equipped, by their own knowledge/understanding of that system, to do so?
2. What do we consider to be 'adequate' knowledge/awareness for the teacher of EFL?

The survey described in this paper represents an attempt to begin to address these issues, with specific regard to grammar, and to find out a little more about the grammatical knowledge/awareness of native-speaker EFL teachers, by investigating the views of those who encounter such teachers at the start of their careers: the trainers who work on pre-service courses. The specific aims of the survey were as follows:

1. to find out a little more about the native speakers who follow courses of initial

training in TEFL, in particular their age, previous experience, language background and educational background;

2. to find out the trainers' views and experience of such people's grammatical knowledge/awareness: its relative strength and weakness and how it might be characterised;

3. to find out whether, in the trainers' experience, variations in grammatical knowledge/awareness seem to relate in any way to the factors mentioned in 1 above;

4. to gain some idea of the extent to which grammatical knowledge/awareness changes as careers in TEFL develop, and of the factors which appear to cause such changes.

The methodology

In order to gain a broad picture of how trainers perceived their trainees' grammatical knowledge/awareness, a questionnaire format was adopted. This methodology had its obvious limitations. It ruled out the possibility of clarifying face-to-face the wording of the questions and the precise meaning of the responses. It also provided no opportunity for following up interesting replies. It did, however, offer a means of gathering insights from a wide range of people involved in initial training, insights which can be followed up in subsequent 'harder' research.

The trainers

The trainers whose views were sought are all involved in work on courses leading to the RSA/Cambridge CTEFLA (Certificate in the Teaching of English as a Foreign Language to Adults). Most of those whose views were solicited are also CTEFLA 'assessors' as well as being course tutors. This means that they have been appointed by a committee of their peers to moderate the standards of courses offered by other institutions participating in the scheme.

The CTEFLA

The CTEFLA is a scheme of initial TEFL training for which there are courses both in the UK and overseas. It was set up in the late 1970s as the Preparatory Certificate, and was aimed at 'those without previous experience in teaching adult foreigners and for practising teachers with no previous training in EFL' (RSA, 1980). It is by a long way the largest scheme of its kind in the world. There are currently more than 4,000 candidate entries for the scheme each year and consequently a large number of trainers actively involved.

The decision to focus attention on the CTEFLA was a way of ensuring that it would be possible to ask the opinions of a wide range of trainers working in a variety of institutions and locations, all of whom had a common frame of reference. It also provided an opportunity to follow up on one of the findings reported by

Davis in his initial evaluation of the four-week CTEFLA course, where nine out of ten employers (all Directors of Studies in UK language schools) stated that the aspect of performance of CTEFLA holders with which they were least satisfied was their ability to analyse and teach grammatical structures.

It is probably useful at this stage to provide one or two items of information about CTEFLA which may help to contextualise the views of the trainers for those readers without first-hand experience of the scheme. The CTEFLA is a 'starter' course: it gives people an introduction to TEFL, nothing more. It lasts for a minimum of 100 hours and may be taught over four weeks full-time, over a year part-time or anything between the two. It aims to develop on the one hand a practical awareness of learners, language and materials and on the other hand practical ability in classroom management and lesson planning, in the presentation and practice of new language and in developing the skills of reading, listening, speaking and writing. With so many topics to be covered in such a short time, grammatical knowledge/awareness inevitably receives limited attention. It is also worth mentioning that CTEFLA courses are internally assessed and externally moderated (by staff of other institutions participating in the scheme) and that the CTEFLA scheme has a 95 per cent success rate.

The respondents

Two hundred questionnaires were sent out (the questionnaire is reproduced in appendix 1 at the end of this article). A total of 82 trainers returned fully completed questionnaires (a response rate of roughly 40 per cent). Of those who responded 35 per cent were based in UK institutions which might be regarded as belonging to the private sector (including those which are charitable trusts). A further 16 per cent belonged to UK public-sector institutions. The remainder all had some overseas experience of the CTEFLA: they had spent their entire careers as trainers over-seas, were currently based overseas, having previously worked in the UK, or were at present working in the UK, having been involved with overseas courses in the past. Almost all had experience of visiting other types of centre as course assessors.

The results

Section B: Questions 1 and 4

The first question was an attempt to elicit a profile of those entering the profession as encountered by the respondents. It should be emphasised that these figures represent the impressions of those surveyed. The information is not culled from centre records and therefore should in no way be treated as hard data.

Respondents were asked about the age, educational background, previous experience and language background of the trainees they had encountered. A summary of their responses is given in Table 1:

Table 1: The age and background of the trainees

Age				
Under 25	25–30	31–40	41–50	Over 50
28%	31.6%	23.5%	11.5%	5.4%
Educational background				
Arts graduate	Graduate (non-Arts)	Non-grad. T. Cert.	Other HE quals.	No post-sch. quals.
48%	22.5%	12.7%	10.4%	6.4%
Full-time TEFL experience				
None	Up to 1 yr	1–3 yrs	4–5 yrs	Over 5 yrs
63.5%	20.1%	10.4%	3.7%	2.3%
Language background				
British native sp.	Nth. Am. native sp.	Austr./NZ native sp.	Other native sp.	Non-native sp.
76.5%	8.2%	10.2%	2.6%	2.5%

Interestingly, given that the requirements of the scheme are merely that candidates should be at least 20 years old and educated to university matriculation standard (i.e. two 'A' levels), more than 70 per cent of CTEFLA candidates encountered were thought to be 25 years old or over, and a similar percentage were thought to be graduates.

Question 4 asked respondents whether they felt that markedly weak or markedly good grammatical knowledge/awareness seemed to be linked to a significant extent with any of the categories mentioned in question 1. The majority of respondents reported that in their experience there was no such link, though a number of potential links were referred to by others. The points in Tables 2 and 3 were mentioned by several respondents.

Table 2: Factors said to link positively with grammatical knowledge/awareness

1) Experience of foreign language learning
   Proficiency in a foreign language
   Study of foreign languages to 'A' level or degree level
2) Age
3) Educational background ('at school before 1970')
4) EFL teaching experience
5) Background in linguistics
6) Degrees in Science/Law

The appearance of 'age' in both lists calls for comment. Those citing it as a factor linking positively with grammatical knowledge/awareness qualified this with remarks suggesting that there was not a simple correlation. Age was seen by some as a plus factor if it was accompanied by a good grounding in formal grammar or if

Table 3: Factors said to link negatively with grammatical knowledge/awareness

1) Age (over 50 and under 25)
2) Non-foreign language Arts degrees (especially English)
3) North American/Australian/NZ language and educational background

it was linked to confidence in approaching grammatical topics. However, some trainers reported that in their experience advantages of this sort were often counterbalanced by such problems as an over-prescriptive attitude or a tendency to lecture rather than facilitate. Those who mentioned age as a factor linking negatively with grammatical knowledge/awareness identified two specific age groups: the under-25s and those referred to by one respondent as the 'change of lifers': men and women over 50.

Section B: Questions 2 and 3

These questions were aimed at finding out a little more about the concept of grammatical knowledge/awareness, how it might be characterised in relation to teachers of EFL and the extent to which trainers perceived initial trainees as being weak or good in this area.

Question 2 asked for a global rating of the grammatical knowledge/awareness of trainees at the start of a CTEFLA course. The suggested spread of trainees was as follows:

Table 4: Grammatical knowledge/awareness of trainees at the start of a CTEFLA course

Very weak	Weak	Adequate	Good	Very good
22%	31.5%	31.3%	11.1%	4.1%

Although these responses (and others in the survey) were made without an explicitly defined and agreed standard of 'adequate' grammatical knowledge/awareness, one might suggest that the common frame of reference of the respondents and their familiarity with the standards of the CTEFLA scheme provide a reasonable basis for equating one person's view of *adequate* with another's. It certainly seems worthy of note that, even after centres have screened prospective course participants, filtering out up to 5 per cent (many because of poor language awareness), more than 50 per cent of those embarking on CTEFLA courses are still perceived by trainers as having inadequate grammatical knowledge/awareness.

In question 3, respondents were asked to characterise grammatical knowledge/awareness. The list in Table 5 presents a selection of the points mentioned. The selection was made in order to reflect the range of points rather than the frequency with which an individual point was mentioned. A number of the points overlap. Some of them seem to relate more to knowledge, others more to awareness. Still others seem to involve aspects of technique as well. Together they illustrate something of the complex multiplicity of factors which seem to constitute the grammatical knowledge/awareness required of EFL teachers.

Table 5: What characterises grammatical knowledge/awareness?

1) Knowledge of grammatical terminology
2) Understanding of the concepts associated with terms
3) Awareness of meaning/language in communication
4) Ability to reflect on language and analyse language forms
5) Ability to select/grade language and break down grammar points for teaching purposes
6) Ability to analyse grammar from learners' perspective
7) Ability to anticipate learners' grammatical difficulties
8) Ability to deal confidently with spontaneous grammar questions
9) Ability to think on one's feet in dealing with grammar problems
10) Ability to explain grammar to students without complex metalanguage
11) Awareness of 'correctness' and ability to justify an opinion about what is acceptable usage and what is not
12) Sensitivity to language/awareness of how language works

Section B: Questions 5, 6 and 7

Respondents were given the seven areas listed in Table 6 and were asked to rate the adequacy of the trainees they had encountered in relation to each area.

Table 6: The adequacy of the trainees: areas for rating

1) Explaining grammatical points
2) Using grammatical terms correctly
3) Demonstrating an understanding of major elements of English grammar
4) Identifying correctly students' grammatical errors
5) Controlling the grammatical complexity of one's own speech when talking to low-level students
6) Speaking grammatically correct English
7) Writing grammatically correct English

Respondents were also invited to suggest other areas connected with grammatical knowledge/awareness which they considered important enough to warrant a separate rating. A number of the areas suggested reflected points mentioned in Table 5 above. Others included the area listed in Table 7.

Table 7: The adequacy of the trainees: additional areas for rating suggested by respondents

1) Confidence with regard to learning about English grammar
2) Contextualising language to facilitate understanding/practice
3) Using reference grammars effectively
4) Planning the grammatical aim(s) of a lesson
5) Identifying the main grammar point in a text/task

The confidence factor is one which was referred to by a number of respondents at this point, and one which was a recurrent theme in many replies. Clearly a large number of native speakers begin their careers as EFL teachers with a marked lack of confidence in their own knowledge/awareness of grammar, experiencing feelings variously described as insecurity, inadequacy, fear and panic.

Respondents were asked to rate trainees at the start of a CTEFLA course, and again at the end of the course. It should once more be emphasised that the figures in Table 8 are in no way 'hard' data about trainees: they are a summary of the impressions and memories of the trainers.

Table 8: Ratings of trainees' teaching performance at the beginning and end of the CTEFLA course

	Very weak (%)	Weak (%)	Adequate (%)	Good (%)	Very good (%)
Explaining grammatical points					
Start of CTEFLA	25.8	38.4	25.4	7.8	2.6
End of CTEFLA	3.1	14.0	50.1	24.1	8.7
Using grammatical terms correctly					
Start of CTEFLA	18.4	36.5	29.1	12.0	4.0
End of CTEFLA	2.6	10.4	47.1	28.8	11.1
Demonstrating understanding of major elements of English grammar					
Start of CTEFLA	15.1	38.4	29.7	11.5	5.3
End of CTEFLA	3.2	12.0	44.6	30.3	9.9
Identifying correctly students' grammatical errors					
Start of CTEFLA	24.0	35.0	27.9	9.5	3.6
End of CTEFLA	3.4	15.5	44.3	26.4	10.4
Controlling grammatical complexity of own speech when talking to low-level students					
Start of CTEFLA	20.9	31.4	34.5	10.3	2.9
End of CTEFLA	4.1	11.8	40.2	32.3	11.6

Of the first five areas of grammatical knowledge/awareness, those in which the greatest percentage of trainees were considered to be weak at the start of a CTEFLA course were explaining grammatical points (64.2 per cent of trainees weak or very weak) and identifying correctly students' grammatical errors (59 per cent weak or very weak). At the end of a CTEFLA course, explaining grammatical points would appear to be the area with which trainees still have the greatest difficulty, with only 32.8 per cent being adjudged good or very good (compared, for instance, with 43.9 per cent for controlling grammatical complexity of own speech when talking to low-level students). The relative similarity of pattern across these first five areas calls for comment. It may well be partly a result of the survey format (see appendix 1). However, it may also reflect the way in which a number of the points overlap and interrelate.

The last two areas of trainees' grammatical knowledge/awareness considered by the respondents were different in nature from the first five, as they were concerned solely with the quality of the trainees' own English. As expected, a different pattern presented itself in the responses for these two areas, with many fewer trainees being placed in the weak/very weak categories (4.1 per cent for speaking grammatically correct English and 9.8 per cent for writing grammatically correct English) and almost no discernible change occurring during a CTEFLA course.

Table 9: Ratings of trainees' English language skills

	Speaking grammatically correct English				
	Very weak (%)	*Weak (%)*	*Adequate (%)*	*Good (%)*	*Very good (%)*
Start of CTEFLA	0.9	3.2	19.1	35.9	40.9
End of CTEFLA	0.5	2.1	17.9	38.0	41.5
	Writing grammatically correct English				
	Very weak (%)	*Weak (%)*	*Adequate (%)*	*Good (%)*	*Very good (%)*
Start of CTEFLA	1.5	8.3	26.8	31.6	31.8
End of CTEFLA	1.0	6.5	26.9	30.9	34.7

In attempting to explain this difference in pattern, one might reasonably assume that it simply reflects the fact that the trainees being described are native speakers and in the main well educated, and that therefore one would expect them to be proficient users of their own language. This explanation might well apply to those who are actually admitted on to CTEFLA courses. It would not, however, give a wholly accurate reflection of the proficiency of all native speakers who *want* to follow CTEFLA courses. As mentioned above, most centres have pre-course interviews and other screening procedures on the basis of which they exclude potential trainees about whom they have doubts. The widespread use of such procedures is frequently cited by those involved in the CTEFLA scheme to justify the high pass-rate referred to earlier. The procedures used, the criteria applied by centres in this pre-course selection and indeed the firmness of such criteria in times of economic recession have not been investigated. However, one reason for applicants being rejected which was mentioned by a number of respondents was the quality of their English. It can therefore be assumed that the quality of the spoken and written English of native speakers *wishing* to take pre-service courses is somewhat lower than that indicated in Table 9.

Section C

The last part of the survey invited respondents to reflect upon their own grammatical knowledge/awareness, to rate it at various stages of their careers and to indicate to what they attributed any improvement. The ratings are shown in Table 10.

Table 10: Trainers' ratings of own grammatical knowledge/awareness

	Very weak (%)	Weak (%)	Adequate (%)	Good (%)	Very good (%)
At start of TEFL career (before training)	13.9	36.7	24.1	21.5	3.8
After initial training (if any)	3.1	9.4	40.6	37.5	9.4
Now	0.0	1.3	2.6	34.6	61.5

The trainers' self-ratings were much as expected, with 50.6 per cent recalling their grammatical knowledge/awareness as being weak or very weak at the start of their careers (compared with their corresponding rating of 53.5 per cent for trainees beginning CTEFLA courses). A handful of respondents were modest about their improvement, continuing to classify their grammatical knowledge/awareness as weak or only adequate. Others emphasised that there was a process of developing grammatical knowledge/awareness which was a voyage of continuing self-discovery: 'The more I know, the more I know I don't know' was the statement of one respondent. The vast majority (more than 96 per cent), however, felt that they would now rate their grammatical knowledge/awareness as good or very good.

The factors influential in causing an improvement fell into the following broad categories:

1. response to teaching environment (including colleagues)
2. informal self-study
3. participation in courses of formal study
4. experience of general class preparation and teaching
5. reaction to new professional challenges.

Examples given in relation to each category are mentioned below in Table 11.

Table 11: Factors contributing to improvement in trainers' grammatical knowledge/awareness

---

1) Working in good teaching environment
   Discussion with stimulating colleagues
2) Study (informal)
   Research
   Intrinsic interest
3) In-service training
   Doing a DTEFLA course
   Completing PGCE/MA
4) Classroom experience
   Using coursebooks with good teachers' manuals
   Students' questions/students' errors
5) Teaching exam classes (FCE/CPE)
   Becoming a trainer/a trainer trainer
   Teaching language awareness courses
   Writing EFL coursebooks/teachers' resource books

The most frequently mentioned points were those in category 5). Involvement in teaching exam classes, in training and in writing for publication – a sequence of professional challenges talked of by several respondents – all seem to be stages of career development at which trainers have been particularly conscious of short-comings in their own grammatical knowledge/awareness and inspired to take remedial action. The fear factor seems to be instrumental in motivating such action. In relation to teacher training, for instance, respondents referred to the need to be on top of what one teaches and fear of a loss of credibility if caught out, while those involved in textbook writing mentioned having to get everything right or, as one put it, 'having to tell the truth'.

3. Conclusions

Clearly, much more work needs to be done in order to go beyond the collation of impressions contained in this initial survey and to obtain rather more precise information from a variety of sources. However, it seems worthwhile to make the following observations and comments at this point:

1. There is an apparent contradiction between trainer perceptions as summar-ised in this paper and the experience of employers reported in Davis (1990): while trainers seemed to consider 80–85 per cent of trainees at the end of CTEFLA to be adequate or better in the categories mentioned in the survey, nine out of ten employers considered CTEFLA holders unsatisfactory in their ability to analyse and teach grammatical structures. This contradiction may be the result of a mismatch of perceptions about what is adequate or satisfactory.

It may in part reflect a tendency for the trainers to look favourably on the results of their own endeavours. It may also, however, be related to employers' false expectations about CTEFLA holders. As one respondent put it: 'CTEFLA is a glorified selection process [for entry to the TEFL profession] with a few hints/tips thrown in'. It needs to be regarded as such by employers. CTEFLA holders are *not* the finished product: their knowledge will be at best very patchy. They will have shown improvement in those areas covered on the course, they will know what they need to prepare and where to refer for help, but their knowledge will be in no way comprehensive.

2. Following on from the suggestion that employers perhaps have false expectations of CTEFLA holders is the related question of the guidance (if any) which employers give to their new appointees who have just obtained the CTEFLA. The descriptions of CTEFLA pass grades – A, B, Pass (see appendix 1) – and the levels they reflect clearly underline the need for successful candidates to continue to receive guidance from employers to help them to develop their potential and broaden their range of skills as teachers. My suspicion (based on intuition rather than data) is that if such support is given in any systematic or structured way – a very big if – its main focus is likely to be on methods and techniques rather than grammatical knowledge/awareness.

3. It would appear from the responses of the trainers that the process of developing grammatical knowledge and heightening grammatical awareness is one which potentially continues throughout one's career. Rather than this being a smooth, steady process of improvement, however, it seems that significant leaps in progress are triggered off by certain specific sorts of career change which offer new challenges and an increase in pressure because of the accompanying risk of exposed ignorance. At the same time, for some people improvements occur in response to the intellectual stimulus of further study, together with the support and encouragement provided by a good working environment and committed colleagues.

4. It should not be assumed from 3, however, that the process of developing grammatical knowledge and heightening grammatical awareness is, for the mass of people working in TEFL, similar to that described by the trainers: one must keep in mind that the latter are from that minority of people who have 'succeeded' in the profession. If one were to look instead at the majority of native-speaker teachers of EFL, the picture might be rather bleaker. One might well wonder, for example, what happens to the grammatical knowledge/awareness of the following groups of people:

   • those who are not accepted on to CTEFLA courses but who nevertheless go into EFL teaching
   • the 60 per cent or so of CTEFLA candidates (i.e. up to 2,500 per year) who secure a bare Pass and who may therefore be assumed to straddle the survey's *weak/adequate* categories for grammatical knowledge/awareness

- those who do not go on to DTEFLA or further study, but who stay in the profession
- those who do not teach examination classes, become involved in teacher training or write textbooks
- those who do not work with professionally stimulating colleagues or in an environment conducive to continuing professional development.

My worry is that there must be many native speakers working in TEFL who belong to one or more of these groups of people. If so, the likelihood is that the majority of those EFL students worldwide who are studying with native speakers are being taught by people whose subject knowledge is very shaky.

5. One very interesting area for future research would be a longitudinal study of entrants to the profession. Such research would, unfortunately, be difficult to conduct because of the geographical spread of people working in TEFL and the peripatetic nature of the profession. It would also be difficult because of the number of CTEFLA holders who either do not immediately go into teaching or who leave the profession within one to five years. According to Phillips (1989):

> There is general agreement that a particularly large number leave after three to five years of teaching. A good number probably leave after one or two years, having entered the profession in the first place simply to finance a year or two of foreign travel.

It must be a source of yet more concern about the level of grammatical knowledge/awareness of native-speaker EFL teachers that there is such a high turnover for, during the short career spans of those who leave TEFL after one to five years, there is little likelihood of any development of the sort reported by the trainers.

If there is any cause for optimism, it lies in the fact that there seems to be an increasingly strong feeling among those involved in EFL teacher education that language development needs to be a specific component of training schemes for native speakers. This would seem to be clearly indicated, for example, by the responses to the questionnaire sent out by UCLES as part of a recent review of their TEFL schemes, including CTEFLA (UCLES, 1992). Should this feeling be translated into action, then in the long term we may perhaps begin to see a certain degree of improvement within the profession, or at the very least employers might be able to have somewhat greater confidence in the level of grammatical knowledge/awareness of future generations of CTEFLA holders.

References

Davis, H.T. 1990, *The four-week CTEFLA Course: A First Step Towards Evaluation*, Cambridge TEFL Research Report No. 1, University of Cambridge Local Examinations Syndicate, Cambridge.

Haycraft, J. 1988, 'The First International House Preparatory Course: an historical overview', in Duff, T. (ed.), *Explorations in Teacher Training*, Longman, Harlow.

Howatt, A.P.R. 1984, *A History of English Language Teaching*, OUP, Oxford.

Phillips, D. 1989, *Pilot Study of the Career Paths of EFL Teachers*, Centre for British Teachers, London.

RSA 1980, *Certificates In The Teaching Of English As A Second Or Foreign Language*, Royal Society of Arts Examinations Board, Orpington.
UCLES 1992, *Cambridge Integrated TEFL Scheme – Brief Report on the Analysis of the Data Collected in the First Phase of the Review*, University of Cambridge Local Examinations Syndicate, Cambridge.

Appendix 1

QUESTIONNAIRE

SECTION A

1. Please identify:

   a) the type(s) of institution in which you are working/have worked on CTEFLA courses:

      ☐ Private-sector U.K.
      ☐ Public-sector U.K.
      ☐ Overseas private-sector
      ☐ British Council
      ☐ Other (please specify) _____

   b) the type(s) of CTEFLA course with which you are/have been involved

      ☐ 4/5 week intensive
      ☐ Up to 3 months part-time
      ☐ 1 academic year part-time
      ☐ Other (please specify) _____

   [Please show clearly if you have experience of different types of course/institution. If, as you complete the questionnaire, you find your response would vary depending on the type of course/institution, please indicate in relation to specific questions or in a general comment at the end. Also, please indicate any other variable which, from your experience, would significantly affect your response to any question(s), e.g. daytime cf. evening courses, summer courses cf. courses at other times, etc.]

2. Please indicate:

   a) the number of CTEFLA courses you have been involved with:

      i. as course tutor _____
      ii. as support tutor _____
      iii. in some other capacity involving direct contact with trainees _____
      (Please specify: _____)

   b) the number of years you have been involved with CTEFLA courses in one of the ways mentioned above _____

   c) the estimated total number of trainees with whom you have had direct contact in one of the ways mentioned above _____

3. a) Are you also a CTEFLA assessor? _____

   b) If you are not a current assessor, have you been an assessor in the past? _____

   c) If your response to a) or b) was YES, approximately how many courses have you assessed? _____

SECTION B

1. In your experience and to the best of your knowledge, the CTEFLA trainees you have encountered:

   a) are aged:

Under 25	25–30	31–40	41–50	Over 50
☐	☐	☐	☐	☐

   (PLEASE GIVE APPROXIMATE % OF TRAINEES IN EACH CATEGORY)

   b) have the following educational background:

Arts graduate	Graduate (non-arts)	Non-graduate Teacher's Cert.	Other Higher Ed. quals.	No post-school quals.
☐	☐	☐	☐	☐

   (PLEASE GIVE APROXIMATE % OF TRAINEES IN EACH CATEGORY)

   c) have the following amount of previous full-time (or equivalent) TEFL experience:

None	Up to 1 year	1–3 years	3–5 years	Over 5 years
☐	☐	☐	☐	☐

   (PLEASE GIVE APPROXIMATE % OF TRAINEES IN EACH CATEGORY)

   d) have the following language background:

British native speaker	Nth. American native speaker	Australian/NZ native speaker	Other native speaker	Non-native speaker
☐	☐	☐	☐	☐

   (PLEASE GIVE APPROXIMATE % OF TRAINEES IN EACH CATEGORY)

2. How would you rate the grammatical awareness/knowledge of trainees at the start of a CTEFLA course?

Very weak	Weak	Adequate	Good	Very good
☐	☐	☐	☐	☐

   (PLEASE GIVE APPROXIMATE % OF TRAINEES IN EACH CATEGORY)

3. How would you characterise this grammatical awareness/knowledge? (PLEASE GIVE EXAMPLES, IF POSSIBLE)

   _____
   _____
   _____
   _____
   _____

4. a) In your experience and to the best of your knowledge, are those trainees with markedly weak or markedly good grammatical awareness/knowledge linked to a significant extent with any of the categories mentioned in SECTION B question 1?

   _____

   b) If yes, please specify: _____
   _____
   _____
   _____

5. How would you rate trainees' proficiency *at the start of a CTEFLA course* in the following areas?

(PLEASE GIVE APPROXIMATE % OF TRAINEES IN EACH CATEGORY)

a) explaining grammatical points

Very weak	Weak	Adequate	Good	Very good
☐	☐	☐	☐	☐

b) using grammatical terms correctly

Very weak	Weak	Adequate	Good	Very good
☐	☐	☐	☐	☐

c) demonstrating an understanding of major elements of English grammar

Very weak	Weak	Adequate	Good	Very good
☐	☐	☐	☐	☐

d) identifying correctly students' grammatical errors

Very weak	Weak	Adequate	Good	Very good
☐	☐	☐	☐	☐

e) controlling the grammatical complexity of own speech when talking to low-level students

Very weak	Weak	Adequate	Good	Very good
☐	☐	☐	☐	☐

f) speaking grammatically correct English

Very weak	Weak	Adequate	Good	Very good
☐	☐	☐	☐	☐

g) writing grammatically correct English

Very weak	Weak	Adequate	Good	Very good
☐	☐	☐	☐	☐

h) _____

Very weak	Weak	Adequate	Good	Very good
☐	☐	☐	☐	☐

i) _____

Very weak	Weak	Adequate	Good	Very good
☐	☐	☐	☐	☐

(USE h) AND i) IF THERE ARE OTHER AREAS CONNECTED WITH GRAMMATICAL AWARENESS/KNOWLEDGE WHICH YOU CONSIDER IMPORTANT)

Comments: _____
_____ (additional space allowed)

6. How would you rate trainees' proficiency in the same areas *at the end of a CTEFLA course*?

(PLEASE GIVE APPROXIMATE % OF TRAINEES IN EACH CATEGORY)

a) explaining grammatical points

Very weak	Weak	Adequate	Good	Very good
☐	☐	☐	☐	☐

b) using grammatical terms correctly

Very weak	Weak	Adequate	Good	Very good
☐	☐	☐	☐	☐

c) demonstrating an understanding of major elements of English grammar

Very weak	Weak	Adequate	Good	Very good
☐	☐	☐	☐	☐

d) identifying correctly students' grammatical errors

Very weak	Weak	Adequate	Good	Very good
☐	☐	☐	☐	☐

e) controlling the grammatical complexity of own speech when talking to low-level students

Very weak	Weak	Adequate	Good	Very good
☐	☐	☐	☐	☐

f) speaking grammatically correct English

Very weak	Weak	Adequate	Good	Very good
☐	☐	☐	☐	☐

g) writing grammatically correct English

Very weak	Weak	Adequate	Good	Very good
☐	☐	☐	☐	☐

h) _____

Very weak	Weak	Adequate	Good	Very good
☐	☐	☐	☐	☐

i) _____

Very weak	Weak	Adequate	Good	Very good
☐	☐	☐	☐	☐

Comments: _____
_____ (additional space allowed)

7. If you are involved in DTEFLA courses, how would you rate the proficiency of DTEFLA course participants in the same areas?
   (PLEASE GIVE APPROXIMATE % OF COURSE PARTICIPANTS IN EACH CATEGORY)

a) explaining grammatical points

Very weak	Weak	Adequate	Good	Very good
☐	☐	☐	☐	☐

b) using grammatical terms correctly

Very weak	Weak	Adequate	Good	Very good
☐	☐	☐	☐	☐

c) demonstrating an understanding of major elements of English grammar

Very weak	Weak	Adequate	Good	Very good
☐	☐	☐	☐	☐

d) identifying correctly students' grammatical errors

Very weak	Weak	Adequate	Good	Very good
☐	☐	☐	☐	☐

e) controlling the grammatical complexity of own speech when talking to low-level students

Very weak	Weak	Adequate	Good	Very good
☐	☐	☐	☐	☐

f) speaking grammatically correct English

Very weak	Weak	Adequate	Good	Very good
☐	☐	☐	☐	☐

g) writing grammatically correct English

Very weak	Weak	Adequate	Good	Very good
☐	☐	☐	☐	☐

h) _____

Very weak	Weak	Adequate	Good	Very good
☐	☐	☐	☐	☐

i) _____

Very weak	Weak	Adequate	Good	Very good
☐	☐	☐	☐	☐

Comments: (Please specify (i) any area in which there is a marked change in proficiency during a DTEFLA course and (ii) any additional area of grammatical knowledge/awareness which becomes significant at the DTEFLA level)

_____
_____ (additional space allowed)

SECTION C

1. Please indicate your own qualifications:

a) First degree

English	Mod. Langs.	Other Arts subject(s)	Other non-Arts subject(s)	None
☐	☐	☐	☐	☐

b) Non-graduate Teacher's Cert.

☐ If yes, please specify subject(s) _____

c) PGCE ☐

d) CTEFLA

Pass	Pass 'B'	Pass 'A'
☐	☐	☐

e) DTEFLA

Pass	Distinction (written)	Distinction (practical)	Distinction (written and practical)
☐	☐	☐	☐

f) Other qualifications (please specify):

_____
_____
_____
_____

2. How many years' full-time TEFL experience do you have?

3. How would you rate your own grammatical awareness/knowledge:
   a) at the start of your TEFL career (i.e. before any training)?
Very weak	Weak	Adequate	Good	Very good
☐	☐	☐	☐	☐

   b) after your initial TEFL training (if any)?
Very weak	Weak	Adequate	Good	Very good
☐	☐	☐	☐	☐

   c) now?
Very weak	Weak	Adequate	Good	Very good
☐	☐	☐	☐	☐

Comments: _____
_____ (additional space allowed)

4. At the start of your career, was your grammatical awareness/knowledge markedly weak or markedly good in any particular areas? If yes, please specify:
_____
_____
_____

5. At what stage of your career did you reach your present level of grammatical awareness/knowledge
_____
_____
_____

6. To what do you attribute any improvement in the ratings you have given yourself in 3?
_____
_____
_____

Comments: _____
_____

Thank you very much for taking the trouble to complete and return the questionnaire. If you have any general comments, please write them below.

Stephen Andrews

Appendix 2

Syllabus areas

The aim of this initial scheme is to develop:

(i) Practical awareness of:
   Learners. Cultural and individual needs, approaches to learning difficulties, and the motivation of adult learners.

Language. Linguistic form, function and meaning including, e.g. a knowledge of grammar and its terminology, appreciation of structure and function; an understanding of the principles of selection and grading and an introduction to how subject matter and context affects language, and the importance of phonology.

Materials. Coursebooks and supplementary materials and their teachers' books; provision of special interest texts; authentic and non-authentic materials; commercially produced and teacher-made materials and reference works for both teachers and learners.

(ii) Practical ability in:

Classroom management and lesson planning. The ability to arrange the physical environment appropriately for different learning situations and to establish an appropriate atmosphere for learning. The ability to plan both individual lessons and a series of lessons appropriate to student needs.

General procedure: setting up group work
Possible techniques: deciding on size and composition of groups
- giving instructions on group tasks
- giving instructions on getting into groups
- ensuring that all groups are working appropriately

Presentation and practice of new language. The ability to select language items appropriate to students' needs and level, to divide the items into learnable units, to present the language clearly and efficiently to students, to devise and operate appropriate activities for the controlled and free practice of the language presented and to check learning and understanding at all stages of the process.

General procedure: checking of learning and understanding
Possible techniques: devising context-checking questions
- using questions to check understanding of forms, concept and function of language
- devising non-verbal checks of understanding and learning
- using simple tests of achievement

Developing the skills of reading, listening, speaking and writing. The ability to develop the four skills using techniques which require not only their individual development but also their integration; to select appropriate materials and to have the ability to use a wide range of techniques to this end.

General procedure: improving global listening ability
Possible techniques: deciding on the aims of a lesson within a series of lessons
- selecting listening texts of the right length and level of difficulty
- devising tasks or questions which check general understanding

Mode of assessment

Assessment is carried out on a continuous basis. Trainees are assessed in all the syllabus areas. Particular emphasis is given to the trainees' ability to foster learning in their students and the training and use of the English language is an integral part of the assessment.

During the course trainees are required to produce two pieces of written work of a practical nature of between 500–1,500 words or one piece of written work of no fewer than 1,000 and not more than 3,000 words. Written work will be moderated by the visiting assessor.

Certificates are awarded with or without endorsement at the following levels:

(i) The Certificate for the Teaching of English as a Foreign Language to Adults is awarded to candidates who have satisfactorily fulfilled all the requirements of the scheme. They will have shown potential for further development after the course, an awareness of language learning problems and of classroom techniques. In terms of a performance profile:

   (a) The candidate has demonstrated an awareness and understanding of adult learners, of language, and of basic principles of language learning.
   (b) The candidate has demonstrated a practical working knowledge of English and of materials for learning/teaching English.
   (c) The candidate has demonstrated an ability to plan appropriately for parts of and for complete lessons within a sequence of lessons.
   (d) The candidate has demonstrated an ability to manage classes effectively and to provide appropriate presentation, practice, and production activities.
   (e) The candidate has demonstrated a willingness and an ability to benefit from teaching practice feedback and to work effectively with colleagues.
   (f) The candidate has demonstrated the capacity to develop as a teacher.

   Successful candidates at this level will continue to need guidance from their employers to help them to develop their potential and broaden their range of skills as teachers.

(ii) Certificates at 'Pass B' level are awarded to trainees who have demonstrated a level of achievement significantly higher than that required to pass in both language awareness and classroom approaches.

   It may be expected that they will continue to need a degree of guidance, once employed.

(iii) Candidates awarded certificates at 'Pass A' level will have demonstrated an overall excellence and a degree of independence that will allow them to work with much less guidance than is generally required by teachers at this level of qualification.

Grammar, Syllabuses and Teachers

ROSAMOND MITCHELL

1. Introduction

The place of grammar in the language classroom is an ancient question, debated over the years in methodological advice given to teachers of first, second and foreign languages. Under the influence of styles of teaching developed earlier for the classical languages, the teaching of both first and foreign languages in academic institutions in the late nineteenth century was strongly centred on the explicit teaching of grammar (Howatt, 1984). In the twentieth century, for a wide variety of reasons, methodological advice has moved strongly away from such a focus, first for the teaching of mother tongues (especially English) and, somewhat later, for second/foreign languages. The 'natural' image of the young child successfully learning its first language apparently without conscious, systematic attention to language form has powerfully influenced L2/FL pedagogy in the 1970s and early 1980s. For example: 'We prefer to avoid oral grammar explanations in the classroom simply because they take time away from acquisition activities' (Krashen and Terrell, 1983: 144). From the mid-1980s, some reaction set in. Faerch commented soon afterwards on this particular generalisation of Krashen and Terrell:

> When we discuss FL teaching in relation to countries that have a long tradition in teaching FLs, and often with very successful results, such generalizations are considered extremely arrogant by practising teachers . . . Before we have proceeded much further [with a variety of research questions], it seems completely uncalled for to bring into question the pedagogic validity of meta talk in FL teaching. (Faerch, 1985: 197–8)

More generally, many of Krashen's numerous critics argued the proposition that 'learning *can* become acquisition', and writers such as Rutherford (1987) have argued for a productive role for grammatical 'consciousness-raising' with respect to critical features of the target language system. Recent research activity in the areas of so-called 'instructed second language acquisition' (e.g. Ellis, 1990) and 'learner strategies' (e.g. O'Malley and Chamot, 1990) necessitate further reconsideration of the question of the contribution of grammar study to language learning.

However, while debates among theoreticians and researchers run their course, the translation of methodological advice into the actual classroom experience of language learners remains the responsibility of teachers, not 'expert' methodologists. There is now a substantial educational research tradition (reviewed from a language teaching perspective by White, 1988) which reminds us that teachers are by no means 'implementation machines', as far as innovatory methodological advice is concerned. Teachers' classroom practices at any one time have a variety of origins, to do with craft tradition, personal preferences and specific cultural features of the local educational context, as well as current methodological orthodoxy, as has been shown in numerous studies (e.g. Mitchell, 1988, on innovation in the British foreign language classroom). As far as grammar is concerned, therefore, we need to know not only what is being said to teachers, but also what teachers are making of this advice at any particular time, if we are to understand better the role of grammar in classroom language teaching and learning. Relevant published empirical studies, both of teacher thinking about grammar and of classroom practice in this area, are still few in number, though Faerch's observational study of FL teachers' classroom explanations (Faerch, 1986; see a fuller discussion in 'Grammar and Teaching', Section 4 of this volume) and Chandler's questionnaire-based exploration of English L1 teachers' views on the teaching of grammar (Chandler, 1988) are useful, if isolated, examples. The issue is also touched on briefly in a number of wider studies (e.g. Mitchell, 1988; Peck, 1988; Breen, 1991).

In order to exemplify contemporary expectations of teachers in this area, this chapter will critically review some of the advice currently on offer both to teachers of English as a mother tongue and to teachers of second/foreign languages, in one specific context, that of the curriculum initiatives of the late 1980s in British schools. (While this volume is mainly concerned with grammar in the second language classroom, debates on the issue in the British context have recently been much more prominent with respect to English mother-tongue teaching, and these discussions form an instructive contrast with British second/foreign language teaching initiatives.)

2. The reforms of the 1980s and 1990s

The school curriculum in England and Wales saw two curriculum reforms in very rapid succession in the late 1980s. The long-debated unification of national examinations at 16+ into the new General Certificate of Secondary Education (GCSE) culminated in 1988, when pupils took the new examination for the first time (Gipps *et al.*, 1986; Grant, 1989). But this development was rapidly overshadowed by the introduction of proposals for a new ten-subject National Curriculum for ages 5–16, and legislation enacting it in 1988 (DES/WO, 1987; Education Reform Act, 1988). (The intention is that National Curriculum assessment will ultimately absorb or supersede GCSE assessment at 16+, but at the time of writing the precise means by which the two assessment schemes will ultimately be merged remain very unclear. Various interim proposals for modification of GCSE assessment on the road towards the eventual merger have already been made; here, however, we will review versions of the GCSE syllabuses produced just prior to the merger proposals.)

In following subsections we will examine the assumptions, expressed in a selection of documents arising from both these reforms, regarding grammar, what teachers can be expected to know about it, and how they are expected to exploit grammatical knowledge in the classroom.

GCSE in foreign languages

In England, the General Certificate of Secondary Education is administered by four national examining consortia (London and East Anglia Group, Midlands Examining Group, Northern Examining Association, Southern Examining Group). These bodies are semi-mergers between a larger number of bodies which ran the previous General Certificate of Education and Certificate of Secondary Education, and offer alternative syllabuses across the whole curriculum spectrum. The four bodies are regional in origin, but have been encouraged to compete nationally for the 'custom' of secondary schools. Schools increasingly make a cafeteria-style choice from the range of syllabuses offered by different examining groups.

The syllabuses produced by the various GCSE groups for a range of foreign languages are very similar in a number of important respects, reflecting the influence of the so-called 'national criteria' on which they are based. They mark a substantial departure from tradition in foreign language teaching in Britain, in that the specification of content is much more detailed than was previously the case, right down to the provision of specified vocabulary lists.

The influence of the Council of Europe language teaching projects of the 1970s and 1980s (e.g. van Ek, 1976) has been very apparent in the phraseology and organisation of these specified syllabuses. Thus, for example, the Northern Examining Association (NEA) divided its 1990 French syllabus content into the following sections:

1. Settings and Topics
2. Language Tasks
3. Language Functions
4. General Notions
5. Structures and Grammar
6. Communication Strategies
7. Vocabulary – Lists by Topics
            – Alphabetical list (NEA, n.d.).

The Southern Examining Group (SEG) divided its German syllabus similarly:

1. General Contexts
2. Relationships
3. Topics and Settings
4. Functions
5. General Concepts
6. Language Tasks
7. Structures and Grammar.

A vocabulary list is available separately (SEG, n.d.).

A closer examination of the 'Structures and Grammar' sections of these syllabuses reveals something about the notion of grammar which teachers are assumed to possess; however, it also reveals the absence of any clear model of language as a foundation for the syllabus design. As an example, the complete 'Structures and Grammar' section for the SEG German syllabus is reproduced here as Table 1.

Essentially, this consists in a listing of the traditional 'parts of speech', with a central focus on morphology. (It is evidently assumed that teachers will be familiar with the relevant terminology.) Sentence grammar, however, is hardly referred to, except as 'word order' in the brief final section, where mentions of 'appropriate word order' are brief, generalised and selective. How the morphosyntactic elements listed in the syllabus can be exploited to promote intersentential cohesion is even more effectively ignored, apart from a passing, imprecise mention of 'word order changes according to emphasis intended'.

The limitations of such a treatment of grammar become much clearer when the handling of virtually any major topic in sentence grammar is considered in more detail. For the purposes of this paper, we shall limit ourselves to two such topics: interrogation and negation. Under 'Structures and Grammar' (pp. 24–27), the SEG syllabus does list a range of interrogative forms (pronouns and adverbs), and mentions the negative form *nicht* (though no others). However, the sentence patterns in which such forms may be used are not represented there. Instead, for a fuller treatment of interrogation and negation, it is necessary to turn to the 'Functions' section of the syllabus (pp. 10–18). Interrogative sentences or part-sentences are scattered through the example exponents for a number of functions, and cluster under the heading of 'Giving and Seeking Information'; negative forms are found here also, under a lengthy subheading, for which it is difficult to claim any functional coherence: 'Denying or correcting a simple proposition, answering questions negatively, and making negative statements' (SEG, n.d.: 11).

The syllabuses of the Northern Examining Association (NEA) cut the cake somewhat differently. In the 1990 NEA French syllabus, for example (NEA, n.d.), the 'Structures and Grammar' section is similarly focused on the morphology of French, and makes similar assumptions about teachers' technical knowledge of it. However, it includes nothing at all on word order or sentence structure, interpreting 'structure' exclusively as a matter of morphology.

Negation and interrogation are also handled strikingly differently in the NEA syllabus. In this case, the subsection on verb forms within 'Structures and Grammar' does include a list of 'negatives' (*ne . . . pas, ne . . . jamais*, etc.), though there are no explicit models of sentence patterns using them. However, interrogative forms do not appear in this grammatical section, nor do the actual target language interrogative forms appear in the 'Language Functions' section (as they did in the SEG syllabus). Instead, these forms are listed under 'General Notions' (in a special subsection, with the simple heading 'Question words'!). Again, no sentence patterns are given.

Teachers studying these documents could thus be forgiven for forming the impression that 'grammar' has to do essentially with the minutiae of word morphology,

Table 1: Grammar in a GCSE syllabus (SEG German)

General level	*Extended level*

Articles

1 Definite: nominative singular and plural
accusative singular and plural
dative singular
* genitive singular and plural
* dative plural

2 Indefinite: nominative, accusative and
dative
* genitive singular

3 *kein*:   nominative singular and plural
accusative singular and plural
dative singular
* genitive singular and plural
* dative plural

Nouns

1 Gender
2 Cases as for articles
3 Singular
4 Plural of nouns as appropriate
5 Simple noun formation (e.g. *-in*, *-er*: *der
Lehrer, die Lehrerin*; *spielen, der Spieler*)

Pronouns

1 Personal pronouns in nominative,
accusative and dative:
ich, du, er, sie, es, wir, ihr, sie, Sie

2 *man*
* *jemand, niemand*

3 Reflexive pronouns – accusative only	Also dative forms
4 Interrogatives *wer? was? was für . . .*?	Also *wen? wem? wo?* + preposition
	5 Relative pronouns

Verbs

1 Tenses: Present
         Present tense for future time
         Perfect tense
         Imperfect tense of *haben, sein*,
         plus verbs of saying and asking
         * Imperfect tense
         * Future tense	

	Pluperfect Conditional (*würde* plus infinitive) Imperfect subjunctive of *sein* and *haben* in conditional sentences
2 Forms: all persons, singular and plural	

Table 1: Grammar in a GCSE syllabus (SEG German) (*cont.*)

General level	Extended level
3 Modal verbs: *können, müssen, wollen* (present and imperfect tenses only) *dürfen, mögen* (present tense only) *möchtelmöchtest könntest dulkönnten Sie* (requests) * *sollen* * *dürfen, mögen* (imperfect) * *dürfen, mögen* (imperfect)	
4 * Infinitive with *zu*, including *um . . . zu* construction	
	5 * Passive
	6 * *lassen* + infinitive

Adjectives

1 Possessives (cases as for articles)

2 * *dieser*, jeder

3 *welcher?*

4 Adjectives used predicatively

5 * Adjectives used attributively

6 Common comparatives used predicatively   Also attributively

7 * Common superlative forms

Adverbs

1 Adjectives used adverbially: common adverbs of manner

2 Interrogatives *wie? wie lange? wieviel(e)? wo(hin)/(her)? warum?*

3 Common comparative forms

4 * Common superlative forms

5 * Adverbs with the prefixes/suffixes *hin* and *her*

Prepositions

1 With accusative:
durch, für, entlang
bis, gegen, ohne, um (in set phrases, e.g.   *bis, gegen, ohne, um*
bis morgen)

2 With dative:
aus, bei, gegenüber, mit, nach, von, zu

Table 1: Grammar in a GCSE syllabus (SEG German) *(cont.)*

General level	*Extended level*
3 With accusative or dative: *an, auf, hinter, in, neben, über, unter, vor, zwischen*	
	4 With genitive: *statt, trotz, während, wegen*
5 Common contractions: e.g. *am, ans, beim, im, ins, vom, zum, zur*	
	6 * Other prepositions (any case)
Conjunctions	
1 Co-ordinating: *aber, oder, und* * *denn, sondern*	
2 Subordinating: *als, daß, weil, wenn* * *bevor, bis, nachdem, obwohl, während*	Also *damit, ob* * Also *als ob, falls*
Word order	
1 Appropriate word order in main clause: position of main verb, adverbs, *nicht*, infinitive, past participle	Also accusative/dative (direct/indirect object)
2 Appropriate word order after *als, daß, wenn, weil*	Remaining conjunctions
3 Inversion after adverb (e.g. *gestern*)	Inversion after subordinate clause
	4 * Word order changes according to emphasis intended

while other formal aspects of the language system belong somewhere else. But where else? The treatment of sentence structure in these syllabus specifications is highly unsystematic and incomplete; grammar itself has been disarticulated. The SEG German syllabus provides long lists of sample German sentences as exponents for its set of 'functions', as we have seen. But these are structurally very disparate, and unaccompanied by any guidance whatever on how to analyse them in formal terms. (The set of 'functions' which they exemplify of course also embodies some familiar problems of poor definition, fuzzy boundaries, etc., characteristic of such models.) The NEA French syllabus does not even provide this basic kind of exemplification. And above the level of the sentence, the role of grammar in the construction of coherent texts (e.g. the use of formal devices to signal thematisation, or information structure) is an issue which is effectively ignored in both these sample syllabuses.

Apart from implicit messages, which teachers may infer from the organisation of the syllabuses, regarding those aspects of language form which merit any kind of systematic attention in the teaching/learning process, these syllabus documents do convey some more explicit views on the role of grammar. To quote the SEG document once more:

> Communication and understanding of a language *are aided* by the ability to use effectively

the common structures of the language. Some structures may be more useful for under-standing, others for the productive use of language. (SEG, n.d.: 24; emphasis added)

This remarkable statement would seem to imply that 'communication and under-standing' are frequently possible *without* any ability to use effectively the 'common structures of the language'. The suggestion that (at an elementary level!) the grammar of a language can usefully be divided into mutually exclusive receptive and productive sections is also very odd. Adding further to the confusion, the document goes on to refer to 'structures which have been learned communicatively' (p. 24), in a context which makes it clear that the authors are referring to rote-learned, unanalysed holophrases.

More than ten years ago, Canale and Swain (1980) drew our attention to a minimalist interpretation of 'communicative competence', which consisted in the rote learning of a cluster of holophrases useful for everyday survival. Of course, these authors argued that true communicative competence must in principle go beyond this stage and involve the internalisation of a generative language system. GCSE has, however, been criticised increasingly as an examination which rewards 'phrasebook learning' (e.g. Clark, 1989). The present analysis certainly suggests that the organisation of these syllabuses is likely to predispose teachers to concep-tualise early FL learning in holophrastic terms, and lends them little help in think-ing systematically about their pupils' evolving mastery of syntax.

Modern foreign languages in the National Curriculum

The proposals for modern foreign languages in the National Curriculum were first produced in draft form in 1990 (DES/WO, 1990a). The final, statutory curriculum provisions were published in 1991 (DES/WO, 1991). As the legal prescriptions in both documents are similar, but the draft document contained rather more exten-sive discussion of the 'grammar' issue, both draft and final versions will be con-sidered here.

The working party which produced the draft curriculum document was handi-capped by the requirement that they produce a syllabus specification which would be appropriate for all languages legally recognised as eligible for the Modern Foreign Languages (MFLs) slot in the National Curriculum. As this list includes the heritage languages of a variety of minority speech communities in England (e.g. a number of South Asian languages) as well as genuinely 'foreign' languages, the document had to be written in extremely general terms, and all exemplification was in English only. A 'four skills' model was adopted, with broad descriptors of attainment at each of ten levels for each individual skill. (The ten-level model had been prescribed for all subject areas, and was not negotiable.) In addition, seven 'areas of experience' were identified, which were intended to provide a broad content focus for FL learning activities. These are:

A. Everyday activities
B. Personal and social life

C. The world around us
D. The world of work
E. The world of communications and technology
F. The international world
G. The world of imagination and creativity.
(DES/WO, 1990a: 39–40)

It was assumed that there would be 'defined syllabuses' of some kind for specific languages (p. 37), and functions, notions, grammar and lexis were all mentioned as possible components (p. 38); indeed, 'the syllabus for any course of study must . . . set out clearly how learners will progress through the content which is specific for that language' (p. 37). However, no detailed guidance was given on how these language-specific syllabuses would be developed.

On the learning of grammar, the draft report began optimistically with a quotation (from Widdowson, 1989), to the effect that communicative competence develops through holophrastic learning and subsequent analysis of the language 'chunks' thus internalised (p. 54, 9.2). The report writers displayed strong hostility to the systematic exposition of grammar in the classroom, and said so several times (e.g. p. 35, 6.11; p. 56, 9.14). Yet, they also argued *in favour* of promoting learners' 'awareness of underlying structures and verbal relationships' (p. 35, 6.11), presumably through inductive procedures. The following quotation illustrates what seems to be a fundamental internal contradiction in the draft report's argument on this point:

> Much confusion arises from the use of the word grammar to refer to two quite different things: first, the framework of structures which forms the skeleton of any language; secondly, the attempt to describe these structures in more or less formal terms, rarely using the target language. The latter is at best of very limited value to most pupils, but an increasing awareness of the former can be an important ingredient in learners' progress towards a truly independent use of language. (p. 56)

How is it that 'awareness' of the 'framework of structures' can be developed, if these are never to be described? A later paragraph (9.17) tried to illustrate this process, suggesting as an example the visual demonstration of gender categories (using pictures, objects, etc.), without any perceived need for the teacher to supply an explicit conceptual key. Instead, it was suggested that *pupils* might be asked from time to time 'to summarise their understanding of a structure and give examples of its use' (9.19): surely an extremely optimistic application of discovery learning principles! Indeed, in developing this argument, the authors referred explicitly to 'good primary practice' as a model of active learning; they were apparently unaware of the persistent current of sympathetic criticism of 'good primary practice' in contemporary educational discussions (e.g. Alexander *et al.*, 1991) and arguments from a Vygotskyan perspective in favour of teachers sharing their conceptual frameworks explicitly with their pupils, rather than conducting experiential guessing games (e.g. Edwards and Mercer, 1987).

The draft National Curriculum MFLs document implicitly accepted some of the criticisms levelled at the GCSE model of communicative competence, and does argue more clearly for the development of a generative target language system, capable of dealing with a wider world than that of immediate tourist survival. However, it represents no advance on the GCSE documentation in its treatment of the grammar question. In so far as grammatical models appropriate for syllabus design and/or for teaching frameworks are mentioned at all in the document, Council of Europe style terminology is used, but the scope and relationship of functions, notions, syntax and so on are left quite undefined. On grammar as a structuring element in texts longer than a single sentence, the report is silent. On the pedagogy of grammar, which is considered at some length, the report reflects deep confusion, and no clear set of principles. The foreign language teacher seeking guidance on the grammar question here would surely experience only frustration.

The final, statutory version of the document (DES/WO, 1991) presents the ten-level 'four skills' model in similar terms to the draft, and adopts the proposed 'areas of experience', but with far less in the way of accompanying argument. The sole references to grammar study occur in a subsection of 'Programmes of Study', entitled 'Developing language learning skills and awareness of language'. Here we are told that pupils should have regular opportunities to:

> use knowledge about language (linguistic patterns, structures, grammatical features and relationships, and compound words and phrases) to infer meaning and develop their own use of language. (DES/WO, 1991: 25)

It is difficult to make very much sense of such a condensed statement. Presumably the intention is to refer to explicit, conscious 'knowledge about language', including some sort of explicit grammatical knowledge, but even this is not altogether clear. No further guidance is given on the kind of grammatical knowledge which might be pedagogically useful, nor on how and when this knowledge is to be developed. It seemed that teachers would have to await the production of language-specific syllabuses (plus their accompanying testing schemes) to clear up continuing confusion deriving from the draft report.

English as a mother tongue: from GCSE to LINC

While in foreign language curriculum development there is a movement away from traditional concerns with grammar, and a decline even from the mid-1980s level of interest in 'language awareness' (as expressed, for example, in Donmall, 1985), the reverse has been happening in the teaching of English as a first language. In curriculum documents for English, there is a steady rise of interest in so-called 'knowledge about language' (a term we have already seen in marginal use in the MFLs documentation), and an increase in sophistication of the linguistic models appealed to as an underpinning for this interest.

In the GCSE documentation for English, little explicit attention has been paid to grammar, even though awards in 'English' as distinct from 'English Literature' are available. A syllabus document of the Midlands Examining Group (MEG) may be taken as fairly typical. Here grammar is explicitly referred to only with respect to writing, for example in Assessment Objective 7 (out of eight such objectives): 'Exercise control of appropriate grammatical structures, conventions of paragraphing, sentence structure, punctuation and spelling in their writings' (MEG, n.d.: 3). (It is further mentioned that in order to be awarded the higher grades, control of 'complex' sentences is required!)

The reference to 'paragraphing' here is worthy of note, as it is the first expression of concern with the *discourse* level so far encountered; such a concern was entirely absent in the foreign language documentation. However, the reference to paragraphing is itself both brief and non-technical. And apart from these summary statements in Objective 7, all references to language (for both speech and writing) have to do with issues of style, register, appropriacy and audience, rather than with grammar itself. This balance is in line with trends in the teaching of English over recent decades, where a profession with a mainly literature-oriented academic training has proved willing to take on board a range of ideas rooted in contemporary sociolinguistics, but highly resistant to the notion that 'core' linguistics could be useful (Stephens, 1989).

Simultaneously with the introduction of GCSE English, however, politicians' concerns with educational standards, and with a perceived decline in standards of literacy in particular (itself not a new 'problem': see Milroy and Milroy, 1985), have led to external pressure on the English teaching profession to take grammar more seriously. This pressure manifested itself first of all in the commissioning of the Kingman report (DES, 1988), and found expression in terms largely acceptable to the profession in the Cox proposals for English in the National Curriculum (DES/WO, 1989).

Subsequent developments have made it clear that the location of grammar study in a broader framework of 'knowledge about language', which characterises both these documents, is very unlike the normative sentence-level grammar teaching centred on Standard English which ministers probably had in mind. (Brian Cox himself has documented the conflicts surrounding production of the 1989 proposals: Cox, 1991.) However, the broad 'knowledge about language' idea was adopted (though not as a fully fledged independent dimension) by the first statutory version of the English National Curriculum documentation.

As a result, 'English in the National Curriculum' (DES/WO, 1990b) shows a substantially increased concern with issues to do with language form, compared with previous GCSE syllabuses, and also makes somewhat more ambitious assumptions about the linguistic sophistication of its readership. As an example, we may take the following extract from the programme of study for Key Stage 3:

> In order to achieve *level 6* [of the ten possible Levels of Attainment], pupils should come to understand the functions of the impersonal style of writing ... and to recognise the linguistic features, *e.g. the passive, subordination*, which characterise it. This should be done by reading and discussing examples.
>   Teaching should bring out the fact that as speech typically takes place in a situation where both speaker and listener are present, it can be accompanied by gestures and words like 'this', 'that', 'here', 'now', 'you', etc., whereas writing generally requires greater

verbal explicitness. Pupils should be helped to recognise that because writers are not able to use the voice to emphasise key points in a sentence, they have to use a wide range of grammatical structures (such as the passive, or other alterations of word order) to bring about the desired emphasis. They should also recognise that writing is often more formal and more impersonal than speech: lexical and grammatical features of language both reflect and create these contrasts. (DES/WO, 1990b: 40)

This quotation deals with supposed *syntactic* features of 'impersonal style', and also with syntactic differences between speech and writing, in much more specific detail than the GCSE documentation. It has also shifted the level of concern somewhat towards discourse (note the pedagogic recommendation to 'read and discuss examples' of impersonal texts). It is noteworthy, however, that the authors are willing to assume readers' familiarity with only very limited grammatical terminology. The term 'deixis' is avoided by clumsy circumlocution, and a whole host of possibilities are covered by the phrase 'other alterations of word order'.

The accompanying 'statements of attainment' for Level 6 (supposedly, criterion-referenced statements of pupils' knowledge and skills) also refer to syntax, in distinguishing spoken Standard English from non-Standard, and speech from writing.

In the case of English, however, the 1990 National Curriculum documentation has not been the last word on the topic of grammar. Firstly, as a follow-up to the Kingman Report, the Department of Education and Science launched in 1989 a two-year in-service training programme for teachers, intended to start to remedy English teachers' well-known lack of linguistic expertise. Though originally independently conceived, this programme became merged with National Curriculum developments, and is now known as the Language in the National Curriculum (LINC) project.

The LINC programme was directed by an academic linguist (Professor R.A. Carter of Nottingham University) and employed a large network of trainers across the country. To support its work, a substantial pack of materials was also produced, with the intention that these would subsequently be published by the government publishing agency (HMSO) and remain permanently available to the profession. Publication of the materials was aborted in 1991, on ministers' instructions, it seems because, once more, the academic product was perceived as insufficiently focused on instruction in Standard English. However, the materials have circulated widely in desk-top-published form, and provide a useful record of the evolution of the Kingman/Cox perspective on grammar in the English classroom.

Among ten sets of materials produced by LINC, one is entitled *Grammar in Action*. This unit conveys a number of new messages, as the following quotation shows:

Language is used to make, exchange, convey and record meanings and information. It is able to do these jobs because it works according to systems that are understood by the people who 'speak the same language'. Of these systems grammar is the major one.

There are, however, other complementary systems, sometimes less fixed and usually less well defined, that are also important in constructing and conveying meaning. Most notably there are systems that operate at the level of a whole text. These interact with grammar at sentence level and choices at word level to create the significance of text.

Thus, although this part of the LINC material is called 'Grammar in Action', grammar is not viewed in a narrow and sentence bound way.

In what follows the way that English grammar operates is illustrated through analyses of some written and spoken texts. It is not the intention to present a comprehensive description of English grammar but to show how the grammatical choices made every time language is used create distinctive meanings and distinctive types of texts. (LINC, n.d.: 1)

First of all, these paragraphs show that LINC has clearly expanded the scope of 'grammatical' analysis beyond the phrase or sentence, to the discourse level. Secondly, the materials offer a new motivation for teachers' study of grammar, compared with the previous documents discussed above. Here, grammar is offered as a diagnostic tool, and as an aid to planning:

Grammar is usually taken to mean the analysis of how units of language such as sentences are constructed. In this sense grammatical analysis can be likened to an act of linguistic dissection. As with dissection, this provides an understanding of the structures and systems. However, just as doctors use their knowledge of physiology to diagnose and remediate, so it is possible to use a working knowledge of grammar to make an *informed* appreciation of pupils' uses of language. The knowledge gained from grammatical analysis can also be used in supporting the creation of ever more sophisticated and successful texts. (*ibid*)

A series of texts (predominantly ones produced by children, in line with the intended 'diagnostic' purpose, but also including literary and scientific texts, and conversational transcripts) is then presented. The accompanying analyses focus on a range of dimensions, including sentence structure, but also exploiting such diverse concepts as schema theory, transitivity, cohesion, thematic structure, turn taking, and exchange structure. As a teaching text, the 'Grammar in Action' unit is fairly sketchy; it seems doubtful whether teachers unfamiliar with the concept of 'modality', for example, will master it fully via a commentary on a single Thomas Hardy poem (LINC, n.d.: 25). But this broad interpretation represents a clear development beyond previous formulations of 'grammar', even in English mother-tongue documentation.

National Curriculum English: second thoughts

Following the refusal of DES to permit publication of the LINC materials, however, subsequent developments in official policy have further disrupted these evolving interpretations of 'grammar'. Only two years after publication, and before it was fully introduced in schools, the first, 1990 version of the National Curriculum for English was revised by the National Curriculum Council. Among the main criticisms advanced of the programme were the breadth and perceived vagueness of the 'knowledge about language' (KAL) strand, and the handling of it in particular:

While KAL is receiving greater attention than previously, pupils still need to develop a better understanding of grammatical terms. Part of the problem is that the Order, as it is currently drafted, takes a broad view of what children should know about the way in which language works. Teachers can give equal weight, for example, to studies of accent and dialect, on the one hand, and to the teaching of grammatical terms and syntax, on the other. . . .

The emphasis throughout the programmes of study is on the development of grammatical understanding 'in the context of discussion' about the pupils' 'own writing'. Nowhere is this essential understanding defined with any precision. (NCC, 1992: 7–8)

The subsequent consultative document produced by the Secretary of State incorporating the proposed revisions (DFE/WO, 1993) has an increased emphasis on explicit sentence-level grammatical analysis, in the service of the normative teaching of Standard English, and a corresponding reduction in the broader 'knowledge about language' framework. Adoption of these proposed revisions is, however, uncertain at the time of writing.

3. Advice to teachers: conclusion

L1 and L2 teachers in the British context are thus receiving changing and conflicting messages in official documentation, on what grammar *is*, and why it should be studied. In the foreign language literature, it is interpreted in a narrowly traditional way, as consisting in parts of speech plus (perhaps) sentence patterns; it may have some place in the ingredients of a defined syllabus, but certainly is not seen to provide an explicit conceptual framework to be shared between teacher and learners. In the L1 documentation, grammar has increasingly been presented as if it operates on rather more levels, up to that of the complete (written?) text; it is a diagnostic tool for teachers, and ultimately may even provide a metalanguage for analysing/reflecting on texts *with* pupils. However, in so far as the teaching of grammar has become involved with the 'Standard English' question, it too has become an area of conflict between traditionalist and progressivist camps.

These changing messages addressed to teachers working in different parts of the same school system are striking in their variety. They have in common, however, a general failure to make fully explicit the theoretical foundations on which they are based, either in terms of a model of language or a language learning theory. Recommendations about content and pedagogy thus appear, cloaked in the authority of Government/Examinations Board policy, which may not bear even limited analytic scrutiny. If such policies are to be turned into an effective sequence of learning experiences for our pupils, with a degree of coherence across language boundaries, it will be necessary for teachers themselves to adopt a critical, independent stance with respect to such advice, as far as the grammar question is concerned. The article 'Grammar and Teaching' in Section 4 of this volume explores the question of how well prepared British L1 and L2 teachers are to make sense of government policies for grammar.

References

Alexander, R. *et al.* 1991, *University of Leeds Primary Needs Independent Evaluation Project: Interim Evaluation Reports 10 and 11*, School of Education, University of Leeds.

Breen, M. 1991, 'Understanding the language teacher', in Phillipson, R. *et al.*, *Foreign/Second Language Pedagogy Research*, Multilingual Matters, Clevedon.

Canale, M. and Swain, M. 1980, 'Theoretical bases of communicative approaches to second language teaching and testing', *Applied Linguistics*, vol. 1, no. 1, 1–47.

Chandler, R. 1988, 'Unproductive busywork', *English in Education*, vol. 22, no. 3, 20–8.

Clark, R. 1989, *Problems in Testing Oral Communicative Competence: the NEA German Speaking Test at GCSE*, MA (Ed) dissertation, University of Southampton.

Cox, B. 1991, *Cox on Cox*, Hodder & Stoughton, London.

DES 1988, *Report of the Committee of Inquiry into the Teaching of English Language* (Kingman Report), HMSO, London.

DES/WO 1987, *National Curriculum Task Group on Assessment and Testing: A Report*, HMSO, London.

DES/WO 1989, *English for Ages 5 to 16* (Cox Report), Department of Education and Science.

DES/WO 1990a, *Modern Foreign Languages for Ages 11 to 16*, Department of Education and Science and Welsh Office.

DES/WO 1990b, *English in the National Curriculum (No. 2)*, HMSO, London.

DES/WO 1991, *Modern Foreign Languages in the National Curriculum*, Department of Education and Science and Welsh Office.

DFE/WO 1993, *English for Ages 5 to 16 (1993)*, Department for Education and Welsh Office.

Donmall, B.G. (ed.) 1985, *Language Awareness*, NCLE Reports and Papers 6, CILT, London.

Edwards, D. and Mercer, N. 1987, *Common Knowledge*, Methuen, London.

Ellis, R. 1990, *Instructed Second Language Acquisition*, Blackwell, Oxford.

Faerch, C. 1985 'Meta talk in FL classroom discourse', *Studies in Second Language Acquisition*, vol. 7, no. 2, 184–99.

Faerch, C. 1986, 'Rules of thumb and other teacher-formulated rules in the foreign language classroom', in Kasper, G. (ed.), *Learning, Teaching and Communication in the Foreign Language Classroom*, Aarhus University Press, Aarhus.

Gipps, C. *et al.* 1986, *The GCSE: an Uncommon Examination*, Bedford Way Papers no. 29, University of London, Institute of Education, London.

Grant, M. 1989, *GCSE in Practice*, NFER-Nelson, Windsor.

Howatt, A.P.R. 1984, *A History of English Language Teaching*, OUP, Oxford.

Krashen, S. and Terrell, T. 1983, *The Natural Approach*, Pergamon, Oxford.

LINC (n.d.), *Grammar in Action*, unpublished mimeo, Language in the National Curriculum Project, University of Nottingham.

Midlands Examining Group (n.d.), *English, English Literature: GCSE Examination Syllabuses 1988*, Midlands Examining Group.

Milroy, J. and Milroy, L. 1985, *Authority in Language*, Routledge, London.

Mitchell, R. 1988, *Communicative Language Teaching in Practice*, CILT, London.

National Curriculum Council 1992, *National Curriculum English: The Case for Revising the Order*, NCC, York.

Northern Examining Association (n.d.), *General Certificate of Secondary Education: French Syllabus for the 1990 Examination*, NEA, Manchester.

O'Malley, J.M. and Chamot, A.U. 1990, *Learning Strategies in Second Language Acquisition*, CUP, Cambridge.

Peck, A. 1988, *Language Teachers at Work*, Prentice Hall International, Hemel Hempstead.

Rutherford, W. 1987, *Second Language Grammar: Learning and Teaching*, Longman, Harlow.

Southern Examining Group (n.d.), *German*, SEG.

Stephens, C. 1989, *Metalanguage Set in Context*, MA (Ed) dissertation, University of Southampton.

van Ek, J. 1976, *The Threshold Level for Language Learning in Schools*, Longman, Harlow.

White, R. 1988, *The ELT Curriculum*, Blackwell, Oxford.

Widdowson, H.G. 1989, 'Knowledge of language and ability for use', *Applied Linguistics*, vol. 10, no. 2, 128–37.

English Grammar and the Views of English Teachers

EDDIE WILLIAMS

'The improvements that have been introduced in the education of youth, within the last century, have been great and important, and among them an attention to correctness and elegance in speaking and writing holds a distinguished place. ... But though many excellent Grammars have been composed for persons of all ages, and degrees of capacity, from the babe to the hoary philosopher, yet they have by no means reached that point of perfection beyond which our limited abilities cannot carry them.' (Preface to *Pinnock's Improved Edition of Murray's Grammar*, 1848)

'When a subject is thus hotly debated, and when it is difficult to discover a general consensus of opinion among practitioners upon any aspect of the matter, it is legitimate to suspect that the problem has hitherto not been sufficiently analysed or envisaged, and that the confusion of tongues arises from confusion of thought.' (*The Problem of Grammar*, The English Association, 1923: 2)

1. Introduction

The purpose of the study

All Master's level courses intended for teachers of English as a foreign/second language in the UK contain a component which deals with English grammar (variously entitled 'Grammar', 'Description of English', 'English in Use', etc.). Acquaintance with English grammar seems to be considered a necessary part of an English language teacher's development, and has long been so, as the above quotations indicate. However, as they also indicate (and there are intervals of some 70 years between the first, the second and the present volume), the view that grammar is needed has been accompanied by a certain lack of confidence in the approaches to grammar that have been proposed. As one of the course providers on an MA course grammar component, I was concerned as to whether what was offered was perceived by the students to be relevant. This paper documents an attempt to answer that question. It first considers interpretations of the terms 'competence' and 'grammar' in the context of EFL teaching (by way of a review for those not familiar with the area), then gives an account of a simple ethnomethodologically oriented survey of the views of practising teachers on an MA course. The paper concludes with a discussion of what appear to be the most important issues arising from the survey.

Competence and grammar

Linguistic competence refers to the ability of an individual to produce and understand the sentences of a language. Any native speaker of a language will by definition have such competence. Linguistic competence does not imply any awareness of language systematicity, nor any ability in language analysis, nor indeed any pre-eminence in language performance. Obviously, it does not imply particular ability with respect to a standard language variety. One may be linguistically competent in any variety. Judgements made upon those who use non-standard varieties (or standard varieties) are matters of social psychology, and concerned with status and prestige. The term '(linguistic) competence' in this definition refers to the latent psycholinguistic ability of an individual.

Because 'competence' is a term with specialised meaning within the psychology of language, its use does not normally evoke misunderstanding in a language-learning context, although the validity of the concept may be challenged (e.g. Leech, this volume). The same is not true of the term 'grammar' however, where even within the English language teaching community there are differing interpretations. Incoming MA students have, in the course of their experiences, become aware of various concepts of grammar, not all of which they necessarily agree with. For the sake of clarity an outline of these concepts is provided:

1. The view of grammar as a collection of shibbolethic rules, ubiquitous in English society, is widely discredited within the ELT community (although not entirely extinct). These are rules of the type that proscribe *It's me*, or *Me and Chris left early* and prescribe *different from*. They have not been randomly selected, but usually target forms where non-standard varieties differ from standard varieties (e.g. non-standard negative concord: *I didn't think nothing of it* or nouns of measurement in the singular: *two pound*); these forms are indicators of social group membership, and are stigmatised by the more powerful social groups. These prescriptive rules tend to give rise to insecurity and hypercorrection, such as *They spoke to Chris and I.* (In passing, it may be observed that this hypercorrection has in recent years become so frequent that a 'democratic description of standard English' would probably accept such instances of *I* as an alternative to *me* in such cases.)

2. A more developed view of grammar which has received a rather more sympathetic reaction from linguists is what might be termed 'traditional school grammar'. This refers to grammar as it was taught – and sometimes still is taught – in British schools. It consists of rules for identifying parts of speech, and for analysing sentences (parsing). For a nineteenth-century example of teaching material see Pinnock (1848) with his quaintly labelled 'Promiscuous Exercises in Parsing'.

3. A narrow linguistic view of grammar is that it consists of rules characterising 'well-formed' sentences. 'Well-formedness' here refers to the acceptability of the word order, morphology and structural elements of the given variety of language, without reference to their meaning. (It does not, of course, imply

that 'well-formed' means 'elegant' or 'standard'. Non-standard sentences are also 'well formed' in terms of their own grammar, while 'elegance' in this context is a subjective matter.) Grammar in this narrow sense is within a structuralist tradition, whether the 'static' structuralism of immediate constituent analysis (cf. Bloomfield, 1933) or the 'dynamic' structuralism of a transformational generative approach where the once notorious *Colourless green ideas sleep furiously* was devised to represent the grammatically well-formed but otherwise anomalous sentence (cf. Chomsky, 1957).

4. A broader conception of grammar includes not only a description of the rules for 'well-formedness' (in terms of word order, morphology and structural elements, operating in isolation or in combination), but also rules specifying the relationship between grammatical forms (or structures) and the 'real world'. This may be termed 'pragmatic' grammar, or 'communicative' grammar in the sense in which it is used by Leech and Svartvik (1975) and Leech (this volume). This concern with grammar as communication in terms of 'what structure X means', has a long tradition in EFL. ('Communicative grammar' in this sense is, of course, to be distinguished from 'the communicative approach' to language teaching, which in its most popular manifestations eschewed explicit addressing of language issues in favour of an acquisitional approach; e.g. Allwright, 1976.)

Constitutive and communicative grammar rules

The view of grammar which would seem to be most useful to EFL teachers is 4 above, where attention is given to structures and their meaning. EFL material over the last 25 years has varied in the emphasis it has given to accuracy of forms as opposed to the meanings of the forms. In structuralist–behaviourist teaching material a great deal of attention was given to accuracy of form, with some exercise types (e.g. structural transformation and substitution), paying no attention to structural meaning. On the other hand, some early functionally oriented books focus on meaning rather than form. Obviously, in language teaching the form and meaning of structures should not be dealt with separately – the form represents the meaning and the meaning is embodied in the form. Most teachers would no more envisage presenting a structure one day and its meaning the next, than presenting a vocabulary list one day, and the meaning of the items the next. Likewise in a form-defocus model (see Johnson, this volume) automisation of form is clearly of little value unless the form so automised is used with appropriate meaning. Having made that point, it is nonetheless the case that form and meaning may be – and often have been – treated separately.

Although meaning cannot be 'measured', different English structures or forms vary with respect to the degree of meaning they carry. Thus there is no meaning carried in word order in cases where it is 'fixed', such as *determiner + noun* in noun phrases. In *My name's X* (the favourite unit 1 sentence in many TEFL courses), the order of *My* and *name* is 'given'. The meaning of this particular word order does not arise, for it has no meaning in the sense that there is no contrasting possibility. If you are speaking English, that is what you must produce. A sentence with the order *Name my is X* is simply not English. A rule of this type is a constitutive rule of English, in that if it is not observed the result does not constitute an instance of English. Rogers (this volume) deals with similar constitutive rules for word order in German subordinate clauses.

Constitutive rules also apply to structures or forms which carry a readily identifiable semantic function, for these can, of course, be described as constituting acceptable instances of English without reference to their meanings. Thus one could deal with *be* + *-ing*, or third person *-s* (or indeed any rule of concord), in terms of formal correctness without referring to the meaning of the present progressive or the present simple. Constitutive rules are rules that emerge from a 'narrow' view of grammar mentioned in 3 above. On a formal level, the difference between *I am eating* and *I am eat* is a matter of acceptability as standard English – the former constitutes an example of it, the latter does not. The question of the difference in meaning therefore does not arise. However, *I didn't eat at midday* and *I don't eat at midday* are formally correct (both obey constitutive rules), but each structure expresses a different meaning. The difference between the sentences is thus a matter of communicative grammar rules. In language teaching constitutive rules arise typically in response to such learner enquiries as *Can you say (form A) in (language Y)?* Communicative rules come up typically in response to such enquiries as *What's the difference between (form A) and (form B)?*

Fuzziness and rules in EFL

In EFL constitutive rules and communicative rules are generally not distinguished, although exercises may occasionally deal exclusively with the former. Although communicative rules are more difficult to formulate than constitutive rules, the features of 'good' communicative rules generally receive little attention in TEFL (but see Swan, this volume). Rules that cover simple cases and can be expressed with clarity predictably attract less attention in terms of teachers' queries than do rules that are fuzzy. The notion of 'fuzziness' should not, however, be used as a convenient bin for disposing of difficulties without considering the nature of the fuzziness. There are at least two sources of fuzziness in grammatical rules.

1. Although language is, in Durkheim's terms, a 'social fact' – being a product and an instrument of the collective group – there may nonetheless be a few areas where rules tend to be idiosyncratic. Usage concerning negative and interrogative forms of marginal modals provide instances. Thus while everyone would accept *Oughtn't he to go?* some would not accept *Usedn't he to go?* Note that this is a constitutive issue. Disagreement about communicative rules may also occur. There might be disagreement, for example, as to whether *They shouldn't go* (which certainly constitutes English) could mean *They*

weren't allowed to go (in addition to the readily acceptable meaning of *They ought not to go*).

2. Fuzziness can also arise from the complex nature of some communicative rules. Thus a pedagogically justifiable rule is not always followed in practice; for example the rule that the stative verb *prefer* is not normally used with progressive aspect is not followed in cases such as *Most shareholders are preferring to take their profits this week* (which is a perfectly normal use). Introducing further explanatory concepts (cf. Richards, 1981) may result in a more comprehensive rule which is more difficult to apprehend (i.e. 'fuzzy'). Rules accounting for the use of the present perfect are again notoriously prone to fuzziness (see Swan, this volume). Such points are subject to the law of diminishing returns where longer explanations cover fewer instances.

Further examples of such complications arise from lack of consistent one-to-one form–function relations. Thus we may have two forms where one partially covers the semantic range of the other:

(a) *She pulled the coat round herself.*
   She pulled the coat round her.

(Here the first sentence can only be used where *she* and *herself* are co-referential, whereas the second can be used whether or not we have co-referentiality.) Further, we may have alternative forms with no perceptible difference in meaning at all:

(b) *He cleared up the mess.*
   He cleared the mess up.

From the theoretical standpoint, case (b) is unsatisfactory, because contrasts in meaning in language derive from contrasts in form, and to have contrasting form (in this case word order) with no discernible contrast in meaning (even if only at the level of informal versus formal register) violates this principle.

Grammar for native and non-native speakers

The nature of constitutive and communicative grammar rules suggests that there will be a considerable difference between teaching grammar to non-native speakers and teaching grammar to native speakers. Native speakers are by definition competent in their variety. They know the forms and the meanings of *didn't go* and *doesn't go* – indeed, there is a form/function fusion for them, such that many find it difficult to dissociate the two (which is probably why one incoming British MA student was able to say 'There are no rules of grammar. People just say what they mean.'). In teaching grammar to a native speaker of standard English, then, this communicative rule would not have to be taught – whether one wished to ensure awareness of it is another question.

The position of non-native speakers, however, is different. They would have to be taught the meaning associated with the structures. If learners are not taught (using the term in its widest sense of 'given the opportunity to learn'), they will never know – for the relationship between syntactic form and meaning is as arbitrary as that between lexis and meaning. Thus – to cite an attested instance – a group of pupils in the fourth year of a good state secondary school in Lima did not know the difference between *She didn't go* and *She doesn't go*. This is an important rule in communicative grammar, possession of which helps people to 'say what they mean'; however, analysis of the coursebooks used in the previous three years revealed that there was no overt treatment of *did* as past auxiliary with the negative, and only some three tokens of it.

Since the communicative rules of language variety X are by definition known to native speakers of X, teaching the communicative rules to them is pointless. Teaching grammar to non-native speakers should therefore have different aims from teaching grammar to native speakers – and indeed it generally does. (Notice here that what is at issue is not teaching a standard variety to speakers of non-standard varieties; nor are we dealing with teaching situationally 'appropriate' communication or improving communicative skills. These are different objectives which raise different questions from those of teaching the grammar of a language to people who are already linguistically competent in the language.)

2. The survey of MA students' views

'Stuff what students ask for! Give 'em what we've got!' (Landlord to barman in a Reading pub)

The view of grammar embodied in the 'Grammar' section which I taught on our MA course was primarily one of communicative grammar with respect to the verb phrase in English (other colleagues looked at other topics). After outlining the systematicity of the verb phrase with particular reference to markers of aspect and tense, we then investigated the meanings of selected forms. The methodological procedures varied over time but included plenary lectures, small and large group discussion, discovery tasks, critical reading of the standard descriptive grammars and learners' grammar books, and comparison of these with authentic spoken and written texts. Although end-of-term participant feedback usually suggested the course was well received, I was concerned as to whether it was what participants actually wanted. In particular, I was concerned at the apparent disjunction between the 'acquisition-oriented' pedagogy which successive MA participants overwhelmingly espoused and the demand from the same participants for information on specific grammatical points.

I therefore decided to investigate the participants' views of what the course should contain, and how it should be taught. The problems with collecting reliable data of this kind are well known. First, there is the question of whether the group which provides the data is representative of the population being investigated.

Second, there is the issue of identifying valid categories for enquiry, and third, that of appropriate instruments for eliciting reliable data on the categories identified.

Group representativeness did not pose problems. The nature of the groups does not vary greatly from intake to intake, partly because all are subject to the same entry qualifications. These are that applicants should normally have a first degree, some sort of ELT formation (RSA Diploma, PGCE) and at least three years' experience of teaching EFL/ESL. Approximately 50 per cent of the intake is composed of native speakers of English, with the remainder being non-native speakers from a wide variety of countries. The presentation of the results of the questionnaire separates English native-speaker from non-native-speaker teachers, as the latter seemed generally in our experience to have a higher awareness of grammar and in many cases a more extensive academic background in it.

As far as establishing the categories for enquiry is concerned, this was done in three stages with different groups at each stage (the MA TEFL at Reading has a new intake three times per year). I also decided in advance that the primary data collection instrument would be a structured questionnaire, since this was by far the most economic method in terms of time. The stages of the survey were as follows:

1. The purpose of the exercise was explained to the first group, and they were asked to identify relevant points (which were recorded) for a questionnaire aimed at ensuring the relevance of the grammar course. Inevitably this led to them discussing the points they had identified but no comprehensive record of the latter was made.
2. Some months later a second group was asked to complete an open-ended questionnaire based on the points identified by the first group. This was followed up by a general group discussion.
3. The answers provided by the second group were analysed and consolidated by me to form the options for a structured questionnaire (a copy of the questionnaire is provided in the appendix). This was then administered to subsequent groups at the beginning of their MA course. The major constraint here was that the questionnaire should not occupy more than one side of A4 paper. This was necessary because there is usually a trade-off between the proportion of returns of voluntarily completed questionnaires and their length. Over time the questionnaire was slightly amended, but the results described here are drawn from substantially the same versions.

The questionnaire construction procedure as outlined above is of course liable to be influenced at various times by the presence of the investigator (who was also the course provider) either in terms of the actual points made by the participants, or in terms of decisions on consolidating participant responses which the investigator makes when constructing the questionnaire (for a discussion on data collection instruments see Weir and Roberts, forthcoming).

The investigation is ethnomethodological in the sense that the categories are derived from the population under investigation. In this case the investigative process was facilitated (one assumes) by the fact that the investigator was also familiar with the concepts generally, although not entirely sure of the perceptions (e.g. of 'grammar') nor of the distribution of attitudes of the population.

Results and discussion

The results of the questionnaires are presented in percentage terms below. The questionnaire was given out for students to complete in their own time and return anonymously. The present results are based on administrations between 1990 and 1992, which resulted in 81 returns (36 native speakers, 45 non-native speakers) out of approximately 100 distributed.

Question 1

This was the only question where a free response was asked for (options were provided for other questions). Each response was allocated to one of four categories as follows:

What does 'knowing English grammar' mean to you?

	NS (%)	NNS (%)
'awareness' orientation to answer	75	67
'competence' orientation to answer	11	27
other	8	7
no response	6	0

Note: NS = native speaker; NNS = non-native speaker; rounding up means that totals do not come to 100%.

Answers which made any allusion to conscious awareness (e.g. 'being able to explain the rules') were allocated to the 'awareness' orientation. Answers which made no such reference but simply mentioned being proficient in the language (e.g. 'being able to speak and write correct English') were allocated to the 'competence' orientation. It is noticeable that there is a tendency on the part of non-native-speaker teachers to give more competence-oriented answers; presumably their own experience makes them more aware of the difficulties associated with fluent and appropriate production.

Question 2

Description of English looms larger with native speakers, many of whom have a weak background in descriptive grammar of English (cf. Andrews, this volume). They also tend to see grammar as more of a 'technical' operation, to do with labelling and analysing. The NNSs have a more pragmatic approach, and are less concerned with description and technique (which many are familiar with from their university training) and more with teaching grammar.

What grammar issues do you consider appropriate for an MA in TEFL?

	NS (%)	NNS (%)
(a) the description of English grammar	50	33
(b) grammatical terminology	19	2
(c) analysis of sentence structure	47	7
(d) how to teach grammar	50	73
(e) other (specify)	6	0

Note: respondents were allowed to indicate more than one response, so column totals exceed 100%.

Question 3

Would you like explicit negotiation with the course providers on the grammar component of the MA on:

		NS (%)	NNS (%)
(a) course content?	Yes	69	87
	No	22	9
(b) course methodology?	Yes	83	67
	No	14	20

Overwhelmingly, participants state that they want content and methodology to be the subject of negotiation. Note that (contrary to the stereotypical view) a higher percentage of NNSs want to negotiate content than NSs – possibly because they are generally more familiar with the field and know what they would like to know, while a not uncommon response from NSs is 'I don't know enough to be able to say anything'.

However, on the two occasions when attempts were made to negotiate course content no consensus emerged within the time allotted (30 minutes). This is partly because participants' interests are so diverse. Subjects raised included 'why there are rules', 'universal grammar', 'how to learn grammar myself', 'oral grammar', 'Chomsky's government and binding', 'the difference between Chomsky and Quirk', 'how grammar can help my students to write better'. Specific topics in English grammar featured heavily in negotiation on content but again there was little agreement on topics which should be covered. Those proposed included tenses, the present perfect, prepositions, contrastive analysis, reference and the passive. Given that this was only a 20-hour course it would not have been possible to cover all topics.

On the other hand, perhaps more predictably, the NSs had a greater desire to negotiate methodology than the NNSs. In practice, the negotiation of methodology in broad outline has not given rise to disagreement, with a mixture of lecture, small group and plenary discussion based on articles and authentic data. (There has however been a fairly consistent trickle of individuals opposed to group discussion and favouring lectures.)

Question 4

What should EFL learners learn when they learn 'English grammar'?

	NS (%)	NNS (%)
(a) how to produce correct and appropriate sentences	83	67
(b) to be familiar with categories of grammatical description	11	24
(c) other	17	9

Again there is a large measure of agreement, although, given that more NS than NNS speakers focused on awareness than on competence in question 1 (what 'knowing grammar' means), it is noticeable that those views are not reflected in answer to this question, where twice as many NNSs as NSs see overt linguistic awareness as a goal for their learners. The category 'other' included the responses: 'How not to worry about correct sentences', 'What they need and want', 'That grammar is only a part of English' and simply 'It depends'.

Question 5

What do you think is the role of grammatical terminology in the EFL classroom?

	NS (%)	NNS (%)
(a) to facilitate explanation	42	44
(b) it should not have a role	6	2
(c) its role depends on the teaching/learning situation	67	64

Again there is a high degree of uniformity, with only a small minority of the view that grammatical terminology should have no role. A number of respondents specified that the terminology should not be used with very young learners; others that terminology should be kept to a basic minimum (e.g. singular, plural; present, past).

Question 6

There is a wide spread of options provided here, testimony to the range of methods introduced into EFL in the last 30 years, although it is not clear exactly what the students meant by these terms.

Again there is a broad measure of agreement, with – perhaps surprisingly – the same proportion of both NS and NNS teachers choosing mother-tongue explanation (I have no data on whether all the NSs who chose it are actually capable of

What do you feel are the most effective methods for FL learners to learn grammar?

	NS (%)	NNS (%)
(a) situational methods	56	67
(b) discovery methods	69	56
(c) explanation by teacher in learner's L1	19	18
(d) contrastive analysis of L1 and target language	8	29
(e) explanation by teacher in target language	33	40
(f) meaningful practice	78	71
(g) no specific method, but 'unconscious acquisition'	36	29
(h) other	2	0

carrying it out). Relying on acquisition with no specific attention to grammar is considered an effective method by only about one third of participants, with, as might be expected, a tendency for NSs to be more in favour of it. The most striking difference is in the attitude towards contrastive analysis as a method (see James, this volume), where about one third of NNSs, as opposed to one tenth of NSs, see it as effective. We can only speculate as to why far more NS teachers see L1 explanation as effective while not having the same view of contrastive analysis. Possibly this is due to the prevailing spirit of the times which has hitherto been opposed to contrastive analysis.

3. Concluding observations

1. No question was asked about whether MA courses should or should not contain a grammar component, for the reason that participants took for granted that there should be one. At no point in discussion or in the open sections of the questionnaire did respondents suggest that there should be no grammar component (even those very few who were individually sceptical of it). EFL teachers on the Reading MA TEFL plainly feel that they need an overt knowledge of grammar (they may not, of course, be representative of teachers not on the course). However, only a minority (see question 4) regard an overt knowledge of grammar for their pupils as an end in itself, and the inference that may be drawn from this is that teachers feel that they, the teachers, need overt knowledge in order to bring about competence without overt knowledge in their pupils. The relationship teachers perceive between their own need for overt knowledge and the pupils' learning of grammar is revealed when we consider the answers to question 6. It seems that teachers see 'covert' but grammatically systematic instruction in the form of targeted activities (situational methods, discovery methods, meaningful practice) as the principal techniques for bringing about grammatical competence. They wish to know about grammar in order to guide pedagogic activities.
2. If it is true that teachers believe linguistic competence can result from covert instruction, then their readiness to resort to grammatical terminology (see re-

sponses to question 4) appears at first sight inconsistent. Discussion with individuals suggests that the use of grammatical terminology is in most cases seen as a resort of expediency, repair, remediation or revision, rather than as a principle in initial teaching of a grammar point. Nonetheless, I suspect this would be an area worth looking into further.

3. Although this informal questionnaire survey revealed something of the attitudes of teachers, it was not particularly helpful in one of its main purposes, which was to help us decide on relevant content. The reasons were quite simple: those who had some knowledge had different interests which could not be reconciled in the time available, while those who had little knowledge did not know what to select. Discussion tended to produce inconclusive stalemate, with a number of participants who had no strong views of their own unwilling to agree with the preferences of their colleagues. Negotiation where participants have non-congruent background knowledge is difficult. In the event, it was clearly my responsibility as course provider to address what I felt were the most useful areas within the discipline – but in the final analysis I was addressing the discipline and not the students.

4. One could ask oneself what would be the consequences of denying that a knowledge of grammar is useful to language teachers. The teachers who answered this questionnaire had all embarked on MAs, evidence that they are serious and committed about their careers. In that sense they are professionals and a part of being professional is possession of specialised knowledge. Denying specialisation is denying to some extent professional status. (It might be anecdotally observed here that the small number of MA participants who reject grammar tend to lay heavy stress on pedagogic skill as an alternative and stronger validating feature of an English teacher; however, the claim that no special capacity is needed to be an English teacher is rarely heard on MA courses.)

5. I am not aware of any research that has attempted to compare the results of English language teaching carried out by grammatically 'naive' teachers with those of grammatically 'sophisticated' teachers. It is likely, however, that a teacher who has little awareness of grammar rules is capable of causing confusion through correcting inappropriately (defective negative evidence). An example with respect to a mainstream English teacher is provided in Williams (1989: 196), who quotes from the corrected written work (over two terms) of a native non-standard-English child:

> *My brother done* a jigsaw* (* teacher corrected to: *did*)
> *We done* a bit more dancing* (* pupil corrected to: *did*)
> *When we had done* some work* (* pupil corrected to: *did*)

We might hypothesise that the pupil has concluded on the basis of teacher correction that *done* is always wrong, and *did* is always right. Unless this pupil is on a U-shaped learning curve (Skehan, this volume) with respect to standard grammar, then she may well become one of those whose 'intuitions have proved wrong in so many instances that sounding wrong is a sign of being right' (Shaughnessy, 1977: 99). The teacher's 'one-off' correction has not addressed *done/did* full verb use in standard English. Possibly the teacher was unaware of the standard paradigm, and was almost certainly unaware of the *done/did* full verb paradigm in the child's non-standard variety where *done* is the past tense and past participle of the full verb *do* (with *did* as the past tense of auxiliary *do*). One suspects that no correction would have been a better teacher response than simple word-level correction in this case.

6. The MA student quoted above as pronouncing: 'There are no rules of grammar. People just say what they mean' would, hopefully, by the end of the course, have revised his opinion to: 'People can say what they mean because there are rules of grammar.' The function of grammar is to enable language to deal economically with frequently recurring meanings (such as singularity, plurality, past, present, definiteness, indefiniteness, continuity, etc.). One might speculate on the parallel here between grammaticisation in an individual's language development and grammaticisation in the evolutionary development of a language. Aitchison provides examples of the latter from the creolisation of New Guinea Tok Pisin where *save* ('know how to' from *savvy*) changed to *sa* (with the meaning 'do often') and then became a marker of habituality (Aitchison, 1992). Likewise, Tok Pisin *baimbai*, originally used as an optional adverb (from *by and by*), has been reduced to *bai* and become a marker of futurity, even in contexts where future reference is clear (Aitchison, 1981). Since grammatical structures encode meanings, there is no more reason to disregard grammar than there would be to disregard vocabulary. While there are some EFL teachers who are prepared to disregard both, the majority prefer to have knowledge of grammar so that they can better understand what they are teaching, and also so that they are in a position to decide for themselves when and how to use this knowledge.

References

Aitchison, J. 1981, *Language Change: Progress or Decay?*, Fontana, London.

Aitchison, J. 1992, *Pidgins and Creoles*, unpublished lecture delivered at University of Reading.

Allwright, R.L. 1976, 'Language learning through communication practice', *ELT Documents*, vol. 76, no. 3, British Council, London.

Bloomfield, L. 1933, *Language*, Holt, Rinehart and Winston, New York.

Chomsky, N. 1957, *Syntactic Structures*, Mouton, The Hague.

(The) English Association 1923, *The Problem of Grammar*, printed by OUP, Oxford, published by the English Association as Pamphlet No. 56.

Leech, G. and Svartvik, J. 1975, *A Communicative Grammar of English*, Longman, London.

Pinnock (no initial) 1848, *Pinnock's Improved Edition of Murray's English Grammar*, W.S. Orr & Company, London.

Richards, J.C. 1981, 'Introducing the progressive', *TESOL Quarterly*, vol. 15, no. 4.

Shaughnessy, M. 1977, *Errors and Expectations: A Guide for the Teacher of Basic Writing*, OUP, New York.

Weir, C.J. and Roberts, J.R. (forthcoming 1994), *ELT Evaluation in Practice* (provisional title), Blackwell, Oxford.

Williams, A. 1989, 'Dialect in school written work', in Cheshire, J., Edwards, V., Munsterman, H. and Weltens, B. (eds.), *Dialect and Education: Some European Perspectives*, Multilingual Matters, Clevedon.

Appendix

Questionnaire: Grammar and EFL Teachers

Please tick your answers. You may tick several answers to the same question if you wish.

Are you a native speaker of English?   YES ...   NO ...

1. What does 'knowing English grammar' mean to you?

2. What issues related to grammar do you consider appropriate for an MA in TEFL, aimed at experienced teachers?

   a) the description of English grammar
   b) grammatical terminology
   c) the analysis of sentence structure
   d) how to teach grammar
   e) other (specify)

3. If you were a participant in a course on English grammar for EFL teachers, would you like explicit negotiation between participants and course providers on:

   a) course content?   YES ...   NO ...
   b) course methodology?   YES ...   NO ...
   Comment if you wish:

4. What exactly should EFL learners learn when they learn 'English grammar'?

   a) how to produce correct sentences
   b) be familiar with categories of grammatical description
   c) other (specify)

5. What do you think is the role of grammatical terminology in the EFL class?

   a) to facilitate explanation
   b) it should not have a role
   c) its role depends on the teaching/learning situation

6. What do you feel are the most effective methods for FL learners to learn grammar?

   a) situational presentation
   b) discovery methods
   c) explanation by teacher in L1
   d) contrastive analysis of L1 and target language
   e) explanation by teacher in target language
   f) meaningful practice
   g) 'unconscious acquisition'
   h) other (specify)

7. Other comments?

                              Thank you!

Section 3

GRAMMAR AND LEARNING

Teaching Declarative and Procedural Knowledge

KEITH JOHNSON

1. Introduction

This paper will consider how best to present *knowledge about* grammar to students, then how to convert this into *knowledge how to* use that grammar. We shall consider these issues in relation to what are in fact two models of learning: Anderson (1982) and Neves and Anderson (1981). These two models are very similar, and will here be regarded as one single model. To an extent, what is here being attempted is a restatement of certain familiar issues in language teaching in terms of this model.

Underlying the approach is a view that language learning is comparable to other types of cognitive skill acquisition, and that foreign language teaching may fruitfully be seen as a type of skill training. An advantage of considering language learning in this light is that it permits one to utilise insights from other sorts of learning. It is in keeping with this approach that we here utilise the Anderson/ Neves and Anderson model, which was initially developed to account, not for language learning, but for the learning of geometry.

The model will not here be outlined; only two points about it are central to the argument of this paper:

(a) It utilises the distinction between *declarative* and *procedural* knowledge (henceforth DK and PK). The distinction is related (though not identical) to others made in applied linguistic discussion: the traditional one is *knowledge about* (DK) and *knowledge how to* (PK). There is also Bialystok's (1982) *knowledge/control* distinction. For general discussion of the declarative/procedural distinction, see Winograd (1975).

(b) The model uses *productions*. These are rules of an *IF ... THEN* sort, developed to describe procedures. In Figure 1, P1 and P2 exemplify general productions, P3 a specific one.

In the Anderson/Neves and Anderson model the learner begins by referring to general rules like P1 and P2, and relates them to knowledge held in a memory data base. This procedure ('consciously applying the rules') is laborious. With time, the learner develops PK (that is, proceduralises the knowledge), until finally it is held in a form like P3, which can be applied with speed.

Figure 1: Examples of a production

P1   IF the goal is to form the present perfect of a verb and the person is third singular, THEN form the third singular of *have*.

P2   IF the goal is to form the present perfect of a verb and the appropriate form of *have* has just been formed, THEN form the past participle of the verb.

P3   IF the goal is to form the third singular, present perfect of the verb *change*, THEN form *has changed*.

2. The importance of procedural and declarative knowledge

It is by now well accepted that there is a role for PK (*knowledge how to*) in all language learning, the teaching of grammar included, and the general case no longer needs rehearsing. Bialystok (1982) argues that the specific role of PK depends on the nature of the language task. Her paper uses different terms and has a slightly different conceptual framework from that used here. Using our, not her, terms: for tasks such as spontaneous conversation where immediate access to knowledge is required, PK is important; it will be less so in tasks like writing where speed of production (and hence rapid access to knowledge) is often not required.

What does perhaps need to be established is that there is an equally important role for DK. There are two sorts of reason for this importance. The first has to do with deployment of knowledge in use. There is the general argument which claims that the student who has a series of specific productions of the P3 type above (but no generalised ones of the P1 or P2 sort) cannot generate present perfect tenses for verbs not met before. This student has learned a series of individual present perfects (*has changed* for *change*, *has worked* for *work*, and so on) but possesses no rule. There is no data base or set of rules for generating the tense, and hence the system cannot easily go beyond data already met. The need for 'generativity' is hence a strong argument in favour of DK. Once again, Bialystok (1982) pinpoints a specific role. While DK may have little part to play in spontaneous conversation, for example, it will be crucial in many writing tasks, where having a DK data base of rules to refer to and manipulate will be an advantage.

The second sort of reason why DK is important concerns learning. There is some evidence from the general skills literature that having *knowledge about* is a useful first step to developing PK *how to*. Fitts and Posner (1967), for example, report that time taken to lead novice pilots to their first solo flight is reduced from ten hours for a control group, to three and a half for an experimental group where some initial explanation was given.

Both DK and PK are, then, important for the language user. How may they be developed? We now consider two sorts of general strategy, referred to as Paths 1 and 2. We suggest that these two paths correspond to the two strategies commonly recognised by many (not only Krashen) under the names of 'learning' and 'acquisition'. We here outline the two paths, and identify for each what needs to be done to meet the established aim of providing both DK and PK.

3. Two paths to declarative and procedural knowledge

Path 1

Path 1 is the learning path, and it moves from DK to PK. Teaching provides DK; through a process of automisation this knowledge becomes proceduralised, and so automatic that it is eventually indistinguishable in performance from knowledge internalised by that pathway which Krashen (1982) calls 'acquisition'. Hence the model is what Ellis (1990) refers to as an 'interface' one, where (in loose terminology) learning becomes acquisition.

The two most obvious problems which this path poses are how best to present DK to the learner in the first place, and how to help the learner convert it into PK; both these issues will be considered later. But there is a third. A danger with this path is that the DK will disappear once the procedural has been developed; that P1 and 2 will be unavailable for further use once a set of P3s has been developed. Examples of how PK replaces DK abound in the literature: a car route becomes so familiar that you follow it unconsciously, losing the ability to represent it in map form; a much-used phone number sometimes can only be remembered by dialling; changing gear in a car becomes so automatic that you are unable to explain to another person how to do it.

Bialystok and Sharwood Smith (1985) distance themselves from Anderson, because, recognising the importance of DK, they feel that in Anderson's model the declarative is replaced by the procedural. But Anderson certainly recognises that it is important to maintain declarative representation, and indeed a section of Neves and Anderson (1981) is entitled 'Getting the Best of Both Encodings' (the declarative and the procedural). Anderson concedes that DK may disappear, but regards this as detrimental; something requiring remedial action. The problems with Path 1 are, therefore: initial forming of DK; maintaining DK; proceduralising DK.

Path 2

Path 2 is the acquisition path (in Krashen's sense), and it moves from PK to DK. In the first instance the learner 'directly proceduralises' ('acquires') knowledge. In other words, the learner goes straight to P3, without passing from P1 and P2, and over time develops a number of P3 type constructs. On this path, proceduralising is not an issue – learners do it for themselves in the first place. But Path 2 involves the very great danger that DK will never be achieved. The learner has a set of individual rules; she or he needs to develop the 'cognitive map'. Note that if this *is* achieved, this model is also an 'interface' one, this time with 'acquisition becoming learning'.

This strategy of acquiring procedural rules directly (without moving from the declarative) is dubbed by Anderson as 'high risk' because productions once formed are, if wrong, exceedingly difficult to change. A comparison with learning a musical instrument: once a wrong fingering has been acquired and is well embedded, it is exceedingly difficult to eradicate. Hence, presumably, in second language learning the phenomenon called fossilisation (and part of the reason why pidgins, once acquired, fossilise early).

Two further observations on this problem:

(a) It is difficult not just to 'unproceduralise' the wrong rules (like the wrong fingerings referred to above), but also to declarativise the right ones as well.

(b) Declarativisation, though difficult, is possible. The L1 situation is one in which learners at school declarativise acquired knowledge as part of the process of learning how to write (among other things). This is achieved partly through tuition, and partly simply in confrontation with tasks that require it. One writes a composition, and in the process recognises, for example, incomplete understanding of a word; so one looks it up.

It is not our aim to arbitrate between the two paths (between 'learning' and 'acquisition'). But perhaps viewing these constructs in the light of a general cognitive learning model may provide a framework in which arbitration becomes more possible than at present. Specifically, we might view the learning acquisition issue as part of the more general debate in cognitive science, referred to earlier (Section 1 of this paper), regarding knowledge in data base versus knowledge in productions.

The remainder of this paper will concentrate on Path 1, and will look in more detail at the problems it poses in relation to the development of DK and PK. During the discussion we shall make reference to the traditional presentation – practice – production (P P P) teaching model, beginning by looking at the presentation stage.

4. Forming declarative knowledge

We here briefly consider issues related to the question of how language may best be presented to students. In Section 2 of this paper it is argued that there are two types of motivation for providing and maintaining DK, one related to 'deployment in use', and the other to 'learning'. For deployment in use, the learner requires a set of rules that are generalisable enough to apply overall. In the case of the present perfect, for example, the learner has to know how the participle is formed.

The learning motivation relates to the fact that DK acts as the first stage in the process of proceduralisation. The requirement here is that the knowledge representation should be readily translatable into PK: it should be 'proceduralisable'. We have already seen that providing overviews is useful, but there are two qualifications:

(a) Holding (1965) notes that a little prior teaching is better than a lot, observing that feedback (after rather than before practice) plays an important role in providing assistance for proceduralisation. See Johnson (1986) for discussion.

(b) Explanation (for a language point in the form of linguistic description of 'how it works') is possibly not the best form of guidance to be given. Certainly elaborateness needs to be avoided. Holding (1965): 'It is possible to disrupt the operator's performance in a quite lasting way by the over-elaboration of instructions'. He goes on to suggest that figurative or emotive description is often better than scientific, and speaks of the 'science of hints' which, he admits, is as yet relatively undeveloped.

An issue of recent applied linguistic interest is the relationship between the initial declarative representation of a rule and the internal representation which a student eventually develops. Some imply that the two sorts of representation should resemble each other. Prabhu (1985) argues that since they cannot, we should not offer an external representation. Pienemann (1985 and elsewhere) argues that the sequence of exposure (to grammatical items) provided for learners should relate to some internal sequence, revealed by research (e.g. morpheme acquisition studies).

Presumably, however, external rules can be internalised and can change form. An anecdotal example: my car cassette player has complex rules regarding how to rewind/fast-forward according to which side is uppermost in the machine. My initial set of (learned) rules came from the instruction booklet, and follow the familiar pattern for such sets of instructions. My final representation, which I now use, is quite different, and involves such personal instructions as 'press the button near the fire extinguisher to rewind side A' and 'to fast-forward side B press the button on my wife's side'. If one accepts Rutherford's (1987: 18) point that 'pedagogic descriptions are *aids* to learning, not the *object* of learning', then there is no necessity that such descriptions should initially attempt to replicate in any way any internal representation.

5. Maintaining declarative knowledge

It has been noted in relation to Path 1 that DK may disappear with proceduralisation, and why this disappearance needs to be avoided has been discussed in Section 2 of this paper. This might be done by ensuring that explicit mention of rules regularly occurs, perhaps by consciousness-raising techniques and through exercises that in one way or another 'draw notice' (in Schmidt's 1990 terminology) to rules. What is important is to note the danger, and to recognise that remedial action needs to be taken; the teacher needs regularly to return to rules covered earlier.

6. Proceduralising declarative knowledge

Automisation

The process of proceduralisation is one of automisation: making automatic. P3 in Figure 1 is quicker to use than Ps 1 and 2. Automisation is generally recognised as important in skill learning; indeed Schiffrin and Dumais (1981) dub it 'a fundamental component of skill development'. The reason for its importance is that it releases conscious attention for the higher-order activities that require it. To use a standard example: we automate changing gear in a car so that it no longer takes our conscious attention; we can then concentrate attention on watching and anticipating traffic movement. The importance of automisation to language has already been touched on above in reference to Bialystok (1982) and in relation to different areas of language use.

A characterisation of automisation is: 'getting a skill right when minimal attention is available for getting it right'. To interpret this in terms of grammar: a novice learner can usually only get structures right when there is full attention on them; there is, in other words, full *form focus*. But in much natural language use there is full *message focus*. Thus, to restate the characterisation above in terms of the form/ message focus distinction (much used in recent applied linguistic discussion), automisation is: 'getting the grammar right when there is message focus, and no attention is available for form focus'. Note how well this characterisation relates to some contemporary issues in language teaching. For example, Prabhu's (1987) hypothesis is that form is best acquired when focus is on meaning. This may easily be reconceptualised, in the framework used here, as a statement (with which we do not necessarily agree) that 'form is best learned when no attention is available for getting it right'.

How not to automise: the failed audio-lingual model

For many, automisation implies the type of drilling activity associated with audio-lingual (AL) teaching. Why did AL fail, and what lessons are to be learned from its failure?

In AL the view was that practice alone was sufficient for learning to occur. Hence AL practised the present perfect in the language laboratory, then expected the learner to produce it properly in natural communicative (message-focused) situations. The belief was that there would be transfer from class to life, and the actual failure of this strategy to work may be regarded as a failure of transfer of training. In terms of the P P P model, we may say that AL omitted the final P; it expected transfer from the first two Ps to the third, and hence the production stage was seen as unnecessary.

AL's failure can be regarded in terms of remoteness of practice conditions to the real skill required. Holding (1965) makes the point in relation to swimming: 'practising the arm movements of the breast stroke on land, may not be the same thing as using them to swim in co-ordination with the legs'. The conditions of practice are so remote from what actually happens as to be useless; the expected transfer from practice to production does not occur because the practice offered in class is so unlike the production of real life.

In terms of our earlier characterisation, we may say that language laboratory practice is in 'getting it right when all attention is available for getting it right'. This is highly remote from the actual target behaviour ('getting it right when minimal attention is available . . .'). Hence the failure is not surprising – the skills, in class practice and natural production, are simply not the same ones.

What conclusions may be drawn? An important general one would be that the task of automisation is more complex than hitherto thought. The P P _ model (presentation and practice without production) as conceived of in AL is simply inadequate. It might be argued that a major task of applied linguistics is to consider activation techniques which will ensure transfer from practice to real language use.

More detailed conclusions in relation to the traditional P P P model may be specified. One is that any practice must meet minimum conditions in terms of its relation to the terminal behaviour. In other words, it must not be so remote as to constitute practising a different skill. In terms of Holding's swimming example, one might set a minimum condition that it take place in water. The parallel in language practice terms might be to ensure that certain communicative elements are present, even in the most form-focused practice. One such condition might be to insist on at least a degree of message focus at all stages; another, that there should be an information gap, ensuring at least a degree of information transfer in interactions. A second conclusion is that because the best way of simulating important aspects of communication is through communication, it follows that the final P should be restored; a production stage is necessary.

A form-defocus model of automisation

One possible strategy for the facilitation of automisation would be gradually to 'deprive' the learner of the attention he/she requires to produce a given structure. We would do this by gradually increasing the burden to be placed on the learner's attention, leaving less attention available for focus on the form being practised. Hence when first introduced to the present perfect (for example), a good deal of attention would be available to the learner to focus on the form. Gradually different conditions would be added to make the task more difficult. More language would be required of the learner (making, as it were, less attention available for each 'piece of language'), and more message focus would be demanded. Faster production could also be required, and one notes in passing that computer-assisted exercises would well manipulate the variable of required speed in production.

This idea is discussed in Johnson (forthcoming) where comparison with an aircraft simulator is made. In that learning situation the novice pilot first practises landing in a clear sky. As she/he improves, 'complications' are added by pressing buttons; one button creates fog conditions, another a faulty engine, a third faulty landing gear. By increasing the complexity of the processing conditions, we correspondingly decrease the 'amount of attention available for getting it right' and hence hopefully assist automisation to take place. Johnson (forthcoming) argues that what is needed in language teaching is a 'present perfect simulator' which can vary processing conditions in the same way. He regards the question of how to achieve this as a central methodological issue of the present time. A number of people (some working within the area of task-based learning) have developed taxonomies of operating conditions relevant to what is outlined here; examples are Brown *et al.*

(1984), Nunan (1989), Candlin (1987) and Skehan (1994) where variables like cognitive complexity, cognitive load and affect, are considered.

Communicative methodology and automisation

It is possible to reinterpret what occurs in communicative methodology in terms of automisation. Two examples follow. Figure 2 exemplifies a drill intended for young

Figure 2: Conventional drill

Fred's picture
Look for one minute.

Number one. Is it a bicycle?
No, it isn't.

(from Johnson, 1982, Workbook, p. 11)

learners. The original version did not include the words 'Look for one minute', and was a straightforward (and exceedingly boring!) drill done around the class (Teacher: *Number one. Is it a bicycle?* Pupil: *No, it isn't*, etc.). The instruction 'Look for one minute' turns the exercise into a memory game. Pupils now have a minute to memorise objects and their corresponding numbers. Then they put away the picture, and the teacher's questions (as above) become more meaningful, essentially having the underlying form: *Can you remember whether number one was a bicycle?* The reason for adding the memory element was motivational, to make the exercise more interesting. But the effect has been to achieve 'form defocus'. That is, a memory element has been introduced which deflects the attention away from focus on form and onto the task of remembering. Such an exercise may be seen as a step towards automisation.

The second example (Figure 3) is a conventional information gap exercise. Student A conceals the answers and asks the questions; Student B looks at the

Figure 3: Conventional information gap exercise

---

2. Pairwork

Student A
You'd like to go out, but you've got a sore throat, and you'd better stay at home. Ask your partner for details of radio programmes, and fill in the table. Ask:
What time. . . .?
What's on at. . . .?
Which station. . . .?

Time	*Programme*	*Station*
_____	Late Night Pop	Radio 1
9.00	The World This Weekend	Radio ___
10.00	_____	Radio 3
_____	Schumann's 3rd Symphony	Radio 4
10.15	Interview with Colin Davis	Radio ___
9.00	_____	Radio 2

Student B
Your partner is not very well, and has to stay at home for the evening. He will ask you for information on radio programmes. Tell him, using the programme guide below.

Radio 1

7.30– 9.00	**The Top Thirty Show**
9.00–11.00	**Jimmy Savile's Request Show**
11.00–12.00	**Late Night Pop** The best of the new L.P.s

Radio 2

7.00– 9.00	**Your Hundred Best Tunes**
9.00–10.00	**Waltz Times** A programme of waltz music
10.00–12.00	**Sounds of Jazz**

Radio 3

7.00– 7.30	**News**
7.30– 9.00	**The Evening Concert** (Beethoven's 3rd Symphony, and 2nd Piano Concerto)
9.00–10.00	**Bartok's String Quartets** (This week: Nos 3 and 4)
10.00–10.15	**News**
10.15–12.00	**Music Now** An Interview with Colin Davis

Radio 4

7.00– 8.30	**Play of the Week** ('The Robot' by Andrew Jameson)
8.30– 9.00	**Letter from Japan** Some thoughts on contemporary Japanese life
9.00–10.00	**The World This Weekend**
10.00–11.00	**The Drama of T.S. Eliot** (Talk by Paul Sinclair)
11.00–12.00	**Schumann's Symphony No 3**

(from Johnson and Morrow, 1979: 91–2)

answers but not the questions. Such exercises are often justified in terms of a degree of message focus. It is argued that since the questioner does not have the answers sought, all her/his attention will be turned towards the message (*what* the interlocutor will say). But it may be claimed that such exercises are in fact no more than pseudo-communication; students are not *really* interested in radio programmes and are merely playing what they know to be the language teacher's game, of practising English while pretending to do something else. There is no real message focus, just disguised form focus.

This criticism does indeed have a degree of justification. A much more honest way of justifying such exercises might be that they offer, not message focus, but 'form defocus'. In this conceptualisation, what the information gap achieves is a complication to the task, a complexity of operating condition which absorbs an amount of the learner's attention, thus preventing a narrow focus on the form of what she or he is saying. As such, one might imagine this to be an aid to automisation.

This reconceptualisation would, if accepted, rather change the face of communicative methodology. The standard justification for message focus in communicative methodology is that this is what happens in real communication (being message focused), and communicative methodology is in the business of simulating real communication. The altered justification is that we are helping the student towards a situation of total form defocus, which is another way of looking at what occurs in real communication.

References

Anderson, J.R. (ed.) 1981, *Cognitive Skills and their Acquisition*, Lawrence Erlbaum Associates, Hillsdale.
Anderson, J.R. 1982, 'Acquisition of cognitive skills', *Psychological Review*, vol. 89, no. 4.
Bialystok, E. 1982, 'On the relationship between knowing and using linguistic forms', *Applied Linguistics*, vol. 3.
Bialystok, E. and Sharwood Smith, M. 1985, 'Interlanguage is not a state of mind: an evaluation of the construct for second-language acquisition', *Applied Linguistics*, vol. 6, no. 2.
Brown, G., Anderson, A., Shillcock, R. and Yule, G. 1984, *Teaching Talk*, CUP, Cambridge.
Candlin, C.N. 1987, 'Towards task-based language learning', in Candlin, C.N. and Murphy, D. (eds.), *Language Learning Tasks*, Prentice Hall, Englewood Cliffs, NJ.
Ellis, R. 1990, *Instructed Second Language Acquisition*, Blackwell, Oxford.
Fitts, P.M. and Posner, M.I. 1967, *Human Performance*, Brooks Cole, Belmont, Calif.
Holding, D.H. 1965, *Principles of Training*, Pergamon Press, Oxford.
Johnson, K. 1982, *Now for English 1*, Thomas Nelson, Walton-on-Thames.
Johnson, K. 1986, 'Language teaching as skill training', Centre for Applied Language Studies, University of Reading, colloquium paper.
Johnson, K. forthcoming, *Language Teaching and Skill Learning*, Blackwell, Oxford.
Johnson, K. and Morrow, K. 1979, *Approaches*, CUP, Cambridge.
Krashen, S.D. 1982, *Principles and Practice in Second Language Acquisition*, Pergamon Press, Oxford.
Neves, D.M. and Anderson, J.R. 1981, 'Knowledge compilation: mechanisms for the automization of cognitive skills', in Anderson (ed.), *Cognitive Skills and their Acquisition*.
Nunan, D. 1989, *Designing Tasks for the Communicative Classroom*, CUP, Cambridge.
Pienemann, M. 1985, 'Learnability and syllabus construction', in Hyltenstam, K. and Pienemann (eds.) 1985, *Modelling and Assessing Second Language Acquisition*, Multilingual Matters, Clevedon.

Prabhu, N.S. 1985, 'Guided and unguided grammar construction', paper delivered at BAAL seminar on grammar teaching, Bath, 1985.

Prabhu, N.S. 1987, *Second Language Pedagogy*, OUP, Oxford.

Rutherford, W.E. 1987, *Second Language Grammar: Learning and Teaching*, Longman, Harlow.

Schiffrin, R.M. and Dumais, S.T. 1981, 'The development of automatism', in Anderson (ed.), *Cognitive Skills and their Acquisition*.

Schmidt, R.W. 1990, 'Consciousness in second language learning', *Applied Linguistics*, vol. 11, no. 2.

Skehan, P. 1994, 'Second language acquisition strategies, interlanguage development and task-based learning', this volume.

Winograd, T. 1975, 'Frame representations and the declarative–procedural controversy', in Bobrow, D.G. and Collins, A.M. (eds.) 1975, *Representation and Understanding: Studies in Cognitive Science*, Academic Press, New York.

German Word Order: A Role for Developmental and Linguistic Factors in L2 Pedagogy[1]

MARGARET ROGERS

1. Introduction

To date, surprisingly little research is available to indicate how developmental evidence on learning can be systematically related to pedagogical practice. Indeed, it is only in the last two decades that language learning has begun to emerge from its confusion with language teaching (cf. Selinker, 1972: 209–10). Research in linguistic theory demonstrates an even more tenuous link with the foreign language classroom. In recognition of the feeling that foreign language pedagogy might be missing something worthwhile, the present paper explores how some findings from the study of language learning and from linguistic theory may be related to two aspects of pedagogical practice in the teaching of grammar. The area of grammar with which we are concerned here is German word order. And the two pedagogical issues which are explored are syllabus grading and instructional strategies.

The article starts by describing the German word order rules which are at issue, at the same time considering what is meant by the notion 'rule' (Section 2). Following this linguistic description, we go on to consider some psycholinguistic evidence about how both instructed and naturalistic learners progress in their acquisition of these rules (Section 3). Section 4 of the article moves on to pedagogic issues and is divided into three parts. The first part outlines a recent attempt to relate developmental evidence to pedagogical practice in the German foreign language classroom: Pienemann's teachability hypothesis. The second part considers how Pienemann's hypothesis might be applied to the question of syllabus grading. And the third part discusses a suggestion to accelerate classroom learning by focusing the learner's attention on selected grammatical forms. (Rutherford and Sharwood Smith's pedagogical grammar hypothesis). Section 5 attempts to synthesise the linguistic, psycholinguistic and pedagogical views discussed so far by proposing an ordered syllabus for selected German word order rules for a target group of learners with English as L1. The syllabus also incorporates at each stage outline recommendations for teaching strategies. Finally, in Section 6, some conclusions are drawn and suggestions are made for future research work.

2. Word order in German

Word order in German has long received considerable attention as a central feature of German syntax (Eisenberg, 1986: 300), the position of the verb being considered crucial (Hopper, 1975: 15; Lockwood, 1968: 256). Hence it has been of interest theoretically, pedagogically and, more recently, acquisitionally. Theoretical interest in German word order arises mainly from its typologically mixed nature as an SVO/SOV[2] language. This interest has in turn been reflected in pedagogical interest (cf. for instance, Schneiderbauer, 1966; Esau, 1972; Ebert, 1975; Griesbach, 1978). Finally, during the late 1970s and the 1980s studies began to emerge on word order in naturalistic L2 acquisition (Klein and Dittmar, 1979: 150; Clahsen, Meisel and Pienemann, 1983: 86).

The aspects of word order which will be considered in this paper are those which have formed the principal focus of attention in the research outlined above, namely: the second position of the tensed verb in declarative main clauses (with and without fronting); the final position of the untensed verb in main clauses; and the final position of the tensed verb in subordinate clauses. The notion 'verb-final' incorporates many possibilities, as we will see from the examples below, particularly in main clauses, where the final position in the clause may be occupied by the infinitive, the past participle, or the verbal particle. Examples illustrating these aspects of word order are shown in Table 1, where a structural description is given in terms of the principal clause constituents: S (Subject), V (lexical verb), Aux (auxiliary), Mod (modal), Adv (adverbial phrase) and O (object of the verb).

The rules which are linked with the structures shown in Table 1 are referred to in many different ways in the literature. One common view is presented in Table 2 (based on Clahsen, Meisel and Pienemann, 1983; Pienemann, 1985):

Pedagogically, there are a number of decisions to be made in handling these aspects of word order. Two questions are addressed in this paper in the pedagogical context of English learners of German:

1. In what order should these rules be presented in the teaching syllabus?
2. What instructional strategies would be optimal for promoting the acquisition of each rule?

However, before exploring these questions further, let us consider briefly the notion 'rule'. Concerned as we are with the acquisition of grammatical rules, then, it seems reasonable to require that our understanding of what a rule actually *is* should at least be explicit, and preferably have some theoretical motivation. If this is not the case, then I suggest that we are in danger of producing *ad hoc* interpretations of L2 data which are themselves poorly motivated and potentially inconsistent.

In this article, I have chosen to take my notion of rule from a theoretical description of word order in Germanic languages (Travis, 1984) which has already been applied and discussed in the study of German L2 acquisition (duPlessis, Solin, Travis and White, 1987; Clahsen and Muysken, 1989). For our present purposes it

Table 1: The position of the verb in German main
and subordinate clauses

Verb-second (tensed verb) in a declarative main clause

---

a) Die Kinder <u>essen</u> den Kuchen
    S   V   X
    the children eat the cake

b) Heute <u>essen</u> die Kinder den Kuchen
    Adv. V   S   X
    today eat the children the cake

Verb-final (untensed verb) in a main clause

---

a) Die Kinder essen den Kuchen <u>auf</u>
    S   V   X $V_{particle}$
    the children eat the cake up

b) Die Kinder müssen den Kuchen <u>essen</u>
    S   Mod   X   V
    the children must the cake eat

c) Die Kinder haben den Kuchen <u>gegessen</u>
    S   Aux   X   V
    the children have the cake eaten

Verb-final (tensed verb) in subordinate clauses

---

a) Ich weiß, daß die Kinder den Kuchen <u>essen</u>
    sub.conj. S   X   V
    I know that the children the cake eat

Table 2: Word order rules in German

Verb-second (tensed verb) in a declarative main clause

---

a) Basic order
b) (Subject-verb) inversion

Verb-final (untensed verb) in a main clause

---

a) Verb separation
b) Verb separation
c) Verb separation

Verb-final (tensed verb) in subordinate clauses

---

a) Verb-end

---

has the advantage that it can be used to describe not only the target language, German, but also the native language of our intended learner group, namely English, by reference to the same set of rules. We describe these rules, which are considered to be part of 'universal grammar', below. A further related advantage for our present purpose is that a model of this kind is required if we are to explore Rutherford and Sharwood Smith's pedagogical grammar hypothesis (1985), since that too is expressed in terms of rules which are shared between two or more languages. And finally, the model is broadly consistent with recent generative thinking on German as a characteristically verb-final language (cf. den Besten, 1983; Platzack, 1985; Haider, 1986; Fanselow, 1987).

Travis's description of word order in Germanic languages is what is known as a 'parameterised' model. Parameters can be understood as limited options which need to be learnt within the grammar of natural languages. The options are normally limited to a binary choice, and the way in which the parameters are 'set' determines similarities and differences between the structures in languages. In this approach, one of the main tasks in syntax acquisition (whether L1 or L2) is said to be determining the value of given parameters for the language in question. A well-known example is the head-complement parameter, for which the two options are: head-initial, i.e. head-complement ordering, or head-final, i.e. complement-head ordering. English, for example, has head-initial ordering in the verb phrase (e.g. *read a book*), whereas German has head-final ordering (e.g. *ein Buch lesen*). Similarly, in the adjective phrase, German is head-final (e.g. *aller Achtung wert*) whereas English is head-initial (e.g. *worth the attention*). What are compared in this model of grammar are not constructions, but the principles which are exemplified by those constructions.

More specifically, I have chosen to interpret the notion 'rule' as a particular setting of a parameter, as defined in Travis (1984). German and English exhibit a number of word order contrasts, some of which are shared by other Germanic languages and can also be described within Travis's model. The principal differences are outlined in simplified form below, before we go on to sketch the three parameters which, according to Travis, underlie these contrasts. The contrasts can be seen in main clauses with complex verbs (examples 1 and 2), in main clauses in which a non-subject element has been 'fronted' (examples 3 and 4), and in a comparison of main and subordinate clauses (examples 5 to 7).

In main clauses, complex verbs are split in German, as in 1(a), with the object always preceding the lexical verb; this is not possible in English, as shown in 1(b):

S Aux O V

   1(a) *Das Kind hat den Kuchen gegessen*
   1(b) **The child has the cake eaten*

In English, the object must follow the verb, as in 2(a); this is not possible in German[3], as shown in 2(b):

S Aux V O

   2(a) *The child has eaten the cake*
   2(b) **Das Kind hat gegessen den Kuchen*

A further difference in main clauses concerns the effects of placing an element which is not the grammatical subject at the beginning of the clause, i.e. 'fronting'. In English, it is possible to front a non-subject element without affecting the position of the tensed verb in relation to the grammatical subject, as in 3(a), but this is not possible in German, as example 3(b) shows:

Adv S V O

    3(a) *Yesterday the child ate the cake*
    3(b) **Gestern das Kind aß den Kuchen*

In German, if a non-subject element is fronted, the order of the subject and the verb is 'reversed', as in 4(a); in English, this leads to an ungrammatical structure, as shown in 4(b):

Adv V S O

    4(a) *Gestern aß das Kind den Kuchen*
    4(b) **Yesterday ate the child the cake*

The correct English structure is termed 'fronting by adjunction' (see below).

    A third difference concerns the position of the verb in subordinate clauses. In German, subordinate clauses are verb-final, i.e. the tensed verb appears in clause-final position as in 5(a), in contrast to second position in main clauses; the clause-final position is not possible for the verb in English, as shown in 5(b):

sub conj S O V

    5(a) *Ich weiß, daß das Kind den Kuchen aß*
    5(b) **I know that the child the cake ate*

In English, subordinate clauses behave like main clauses, with the verb appearing in post-subject position, as in 6(a) and 6(b):

sub conj S V O

    6(a) *I know that the child ate the cake*
    6(b) *The child ate the cake*

In German, the verb appears in a different position in subordinate (example 7(a)) and main clauses (example 7(b)), namely final and second positions respectively. Verb-second order is not possible in subordinate clauses with a subordinating conjunction (example 7(c)):

SVO/sub conj S O V

    7(a) *Ich weiß, daß das Kind den Kuchen aß*
    7(b) *Das Kind aß den Kuchen*
    7(c) **Ich weiß, daß das Kind aß den Kuchen*

Having reviewed the structural contrasts in word order between English and German, let us now turn to the issue of parameters and see how parameters and structures can be related. The differences shown between German and English in examples 1 to 7 can be viewed as the outcome of different parameter settings or of 'parametric variation' in the respective grammars of German and English. In other words, certain parameters are said to be active in both German and English, but in each case, the value of the parameter is set differently. What are these parameters and what are the possible settings?

Travis (1984) has proposed three parameters to account for a number of word order phenomena in Germanic languages (cf. also duPlessis *et al.*, 1987, for a summary).[4] These parameters, together with a rule of verb movement whereby the tensed or finite verb is moved into post-subject position, are said to interact to produce the surface properties of German verb placement, and, given different settings and combinations of settings, the surface properties of other Germanic languages, including English.

The first parameter relates to the ordering of the verb and its complements within the verb phrase (VP), i.e. OV or VO, as in examples 1 and 2 respectively. The second parameter concerns alternative methods of fronting non-subject elements, either by adjunction to the left of the grammatical subject or not, as in examples 3 and 4 respectively. Finally, the third parameter relates to the possibility of blocking movement of the tensed verb from its clause-final position in German subordinate clauses with a complementiser or subordinating conjunction (cf. example 7(a)). (Recall that the order of verb and object has been set at OV by the first parameter, giving a base order of SOV for German.) Failure to block this movement of the tensed verb would result in the verb-second structure in example 7(c), which is not well formed in German.[5]

Table 3 presents a summary of the differences between English and German in this parametric model of word order.

Table 3: Differences between English and German in three parametric settings after Travis (1984)

Parameter	English	German
VP order	V-initial (VO)	V-final (OV)
Fronting by or not by adjunction	+ (by adjunction)	− (not by adjunction)
Sub cl order: verb movement blocked or not blocked	− (not blocked)	+ (blocked)

Since English and German do not share any settings for the three proposed parameters, we can assume that English learners of German have to 'reset' all three parameters if they are successfully to produce structures which are well formed in

German. We return to how they might achieve this in a classroom setting in Section 3 below.

Having described in linguistic terms the three word order rules of German which are of interest in this paper by reference to a parameter-setting view of grammar, we can now move on to look at some findings on how learners actually acquire these aspects of German word order. Later we consider what implications these linguistic and developmental descriptions may have for certain decisions in the classroom.

3. A developmental perspective

This section presents some psycholinguistic evidence on the development of German as L2. Firstly, some evidence concerning the naturalistic or untutored acquisition of L2 German word order is discussed (Clahsen, Meisel and Pienemann, 1983). The second part considers some evidence on the instructed or classroom acquisition of L2 German word order (Ellis, 1989). This brief survey is intended to offer a perspective on learner development with a view to considering its relevance to organising a syllabus on grammatical lines. If naturalistic and instructed development coincide, then the case for a particular developmental order will be strengthened. If there is no coincidence, then we have to decide which order is more relevant. However, even if a clear developmental path emerges, we still have to decide precisely what its relationship is to classroom practice, in terms, for instance, of syllabus grading. We return to this question in the following section.

Acquisition in a natural setting

The most well-known and widely quoted study of German L2 word order acquisition is that of Clahsen, Meisel and Pienemann (1983), namely the ZISA study (*Zweitspracherwerb italienischer und spanischer Arbeiter*). Clahsen *et al.*'s study of 45 adult Romance learners of German is cross-sectional in design, surveying subjects with a wide range of proficiency, and is based largely on spontaneously elicited data collected by interviewing subjects in familiar surroundings. The project concentrates on problems of syntactic development. Clahsen *et al.*'s model is said to be 'multidimensional', consisting of a cognitively determined developmental dimension, and a variational dimension which reflects learner type. (Word order acquisition is said to be part of the developmental dimension.)

Clahsen *et al.*'s results indicate the following sequence (1983: 158),[6] which is said to be independent of learner type. The model of grammar on which they draw is said to be Chomsky's Standard Theory (1965), not a parametric model. (The glosses in parentheses are mine, not the authors'.)

    I single constituent phase
    II multiple constituent phase   (*fixed SVX order*)
    III ADV-VOR   (*adverb preposing*)

IV VERB SEPARATION[7]   (*clause-final placement of untensed verbal elements*)

V INVERSION   (*subject-verb inversion*)

VI DV-VP   (*clause-internal adverbial placement*)

VII V-ENDE   (*verb-final order in subordinate clauses*)

Each stage of development can be illustrated by the following examples taken from Clahsen *et al.* (1983) (my glosses):

I nich guck (p. 98)
NEG look

II die Leute arbeiten hier (p. 101)
the people work here

III und dann er sagen (p. 135)
and then he say

IV ich kann nix bezahle (p. 139)
I can NEG pay

V jetzt kann sie mir eine frage machen (p. 141)
now can she to-me a question make

VI da is' immer schwierigkeit (p. 152)
there is always difficulty

VII kann die nich merken, ne, wenn ich in schule war (p. 335)
can she NEG notice if I in school was

For present purposes, Stage IV (verb separation), Stage V (inversion) and Stage VII (verb-end) are of interest. The structures shown for each of these stages correspond to those described in the previous section – see examples 1(a), 4(a) and 7(a) – although the grammatical rules which are said to underlie these structures are differently conceived.

The ZISA results show that in main clauses the naturalistic learners studied find the clause-final position of the non-finite part of the verb easier to acquire than the V-S order after a fronted element. The clause-final position of the finite verb in subordinate clauses seems to be the hardest of all.

In the second part of this section, we consider the acquisition of these word order rules in a classroom setting, since the issue of whether naturalistic and instructed learning share any common features is an intriguing one. Precisely this question has been addressed by Ellis (1989) in connection with German word order, and so it is to his study that we now turn.

Acquisition in a classroom setting

Ellis (1989) reports on an empirical investigation of whether classroom and natural-istic acquisition are the same for adult learners. The results of the study suggest that this is indeed the case, providing support for Ellis's hypothesis that formal instruc-tion – 'the external manipulation of the input' (p. 305) – does not affect the sequence of acquisition.

The structures investigated by Ellis are the three pivotal ones of German word order identified in the previous section. Ellis adopts the same terminology and (presumably) grammatical framework as the ZISA study, since this is the basis of his comparison, and so the rules with which he is dealing are verb separation (particle), inversion and verb-end (p. 308). As we have seen, the implicational order of development for naturalistic adult Romance learners (i.e. for learners with an SVO language) for these three rules is (Clahsen *et al.*, 1983: 156):

Verb-end (finite verb)   > Inversion (of S and V   > Verb separation (of finite
                                after fronting)   and non-finite parts)
(in subordinate clauses)   (in main clauses)   (in main clauses)

In other words, if the verb-end rule has been acquired, so have inversion and verb separation; if inversion has been acquired, so has the verb separation rule, but not necessarily the verb-end rule. And so on.

Ellis's study reports on 39 *ab initio* adult students of German as a foreign language taking German as part of their undergraduate degree programme in the UK. L1s included Spanish, English, French, Mauritian Creole and Arabic. Ellis reports that all learners were experienced and successful language learners with substantial experience of classroom foreign language learning, and were totally reliant on classroom learning for input. Subjects were taught in five groups. No uniformity in instruction was received, but 'similarities in instructional practices outweighed the differences' (p. 313), according to Ellis. Data were collected on two occasions, once after 11 weeks (Time 1) and once after 22 weeks (Time 2) by means of a speech elicitation task. The data from Time 2 were analysed by implicational scaling as a basis for inferring developmental sequences.

Ellis suggests that three possible factors may influence the sequence of develop-ment: the order of instruction; instructional emphasis (number of explicit refer-ences to structures requiring each of the three word order rules in the textbook, teachers' records, homework); and the naturalistic developmental order. What influence would we predict for each of these factors?

Firstly, the order of instruction for the three selected rules is reported for all five groups to be:

1. inversion
2. particle
3. verb-end

If the order of learning follows the order of instruction, then inversion would be learnt first of the three rules. However, considering the second factor, that of instructional emphasis, according to Ellis's report of the teaching of the three rules, we can expect verb separation and verb-end to be acquired before inversion, which received less 'emphasis' than the other two rules. The third factor, that of developmental evidence, suggests that the verb separation rule will be the first to be learnt. These three predictions are summarised in Table 4 (where 1 indicates the first rule predicted to be acquired):

Table 4: Acquisition sequences predicted

Order of instruction	*Instructional emphasis*	*Developmental order*
1. inversion	1. verb separation	1. verb separation
2. verb separation	2. verb-end	2. inversion
3. verb-end	3. inversion	3. verb-end

The results of Ellis's study indicate little influence for instructional factors, with regard either to order of instruction or to instructional emphasis, suggesting instead that classroom learners follow the same developmental route as learners in a naturalistic context, namely:

1. verb separation
2. inversion
3. verb-end

Ellis's conclusion that formal instruction does not affect the sequence of acquisition is a strong one, given the amount of relevant data which was eventually available from his subjects (only 17 subjects produced three or more occasions for each of the rules investigated at Time 2). The data is, nevertheless, clearly suggestive, particularly given the comparable results for naturalistic adult learners. He proposes that there is an acquisitional 'syllabus' for learners of German word order which is 'the same for both tutored and untutored learners' (p. 320), although he does not make clear what pedagogical decisions follow from such a conclusion.

What Ellis claims his research does show is a role for instruction in accelerating development. For instance, in Ellis's study nearly all the classroom learners acquired[8] the verb separation rule, whereas many of the ZISA learners are said not to have acquired this rule. Similarly, many of the ZISA learners failed to acquire inversion or verb-end after several years of living in the Federal Republic of Germany, whereas 28 of the 39 foreign language learners 'succeeded correctly in producing one or more utterances requiring verb-end' (pp. 321–2).

In this section we have reviewed some evidence about how learners of German as a second and foreign language develop with respect to three German word order structures. Based on a comparison of naturalistic and instructed learners, it may be that the influence of instruction is limited to accelerating the rate of learning, having no influence on the path of development. But, as we have seen, the conditions under which tuition may exercise this influence remain unclear. In the following section, we look at two hypotheses which have attempted to clarify what these conditions might be.

4. A pedagogical perspective

The two hypotheses which are presented in this section are Pienemann's teachability hypothesis (Pienemann, 1985, 1989) and Rutherford and Sharwood Smith's pedagogical grammar hypothesis (Rutherford and Sharwood Smith, 1985). Pienemann is concerned with the assumptions which underlie the grading of syllabuses and attempts to link developmental evidence with pedagogical decisions. Rutherford and Sharwood Smith direct their attention to the kind of instruction offered and the linguistic conditions which determine decisions about this. Both hypotheses will be related to German word order. Let us look first at Pienemann's teachability hypothesis.

Pienemann's teachability hypothesis

Pienemann's approach attempts to link classroom decisions on the use of instruction with developmental evidence. This runs contrary to traditional views of the power of instruction as the principal way for teachers to 'model' (i.e. 'steer' and 'shape') language learning. He suggests that 'teaching itself is subject to some of the constraints which determine the course of natural acquisition' (1989: 57) which he refers to as the 'teachability hypothesis'. This asserts that the acquisition of a certain structure can only be promoted by instruction if the learner's interlanguage is 'close to the point' (p. 60) when that structure would be acquired in a natural setting. In other words, Pienemann is proposing a kind of minimal critical period for instruction, before which it is likely to be ineffective.

Pienemann's hypothesis is mainly based on a study which he conducted with ten Italian children learning German as a second language, i.e. in a German-speaking environment (Pienemann, 1985: 35–7, 1989: 58–60). The ten subjects were selected from a larger group of 100 according to whether they were at either of the following developmental stages: adverb-preposing without inversion (cf. Stage III of ZISA) or verb separation (cf. Stage IV of ZISA). An attempt was then made to teach[9] the subjects as a group, i.e. regardless of whether they were at Stage III or Stage IV, a new word order rule, namely inversion (cf. Stage V of ZISA). Pienemann claims that it was possible for learners from both stages of development to master the formal learning tasks in the instruction, but that only those from the more advanced stage were able to use this structure correctly in their speech production. He suggests that the different responses of the learners to the identical instruction offered can be explained by their different stages of development: the less advanced group was, according to Pienemann, simply not ready to incorporate the new rule into their interlanguage system. Hence it makes little sense, according to this view, for the teacher to spend time instructing learners on a particular rule if their grammar has not developed to the relevant stage in the 'natural' order of development. We return to the possible implications of this below.

The explanation underlying the teachability hypothesis is, according to Pienemann, that the learner needs to acquire certain processing strategies before moving on to the next stage of development. In other words, each stage of development represents mastery of a further processing difficulty. Pienemann argues that since the difficulty is cumulative, no stage can be omitted and no changes in order can occur. To illustrate what is meant, let us look at the sequencing of some of the rules discussed in Pienemann's study and the reasons suggested for their developmental ordering (cf. Clahsen *et al.*, 1983: 162–4; Pienemann, 1989: 54–5).[10]

Of the three rules, adverb-preposing without inversion (Stage III) is said to be the simplest in processing terms, since the adverb is moved to a salient position at the front of the sentence and the canonical SVO order remains undisturbed (Adv+S+V+O). The claim that this rule is the simplest rests on the assumption that the canonical order reflects underlying grammatical and semantic relations in the simplest way, i.e. underlying semantic units such as verb-object structures, verbal elements, and so on, are not separated.[11] But rules such as verb separation (Stage IV) and inversion (Stage V) do precisely this: verb separation separates two verbal elements (e.g. S+Aux+X+V) and inversion separates the finite lexical verb and its object (Adv+V+S+O) and so, the argument goes, they develop later than adverb-preposing. The ZISA researchers (who include Pienemann) argue that verb separation precedes inversion because the separation of the two parts of the verb allows the object and the untensed verb to remain adjacent (in OV order) while the subject and the tensed verb are inverted (Adv+Aux+S+O+V). In their terms, the processing prerequisite for inversion is fulfilled once verb separation has been acquired.

The implication for syllabus grading which Pienemann draws from his study is that the teaching syllabus should optimally follow the natural order of development. This strong view is not uncontroversial[12] and has been challenged in particular by Lightbown (1985: 109) who argues that our knowledge about L2 development is best used to inform teachers, testers and programme planners what to expect, not what to do. She suggests that Pienemann's proposal for grading should be treated more as a proposal for future research than as a proposal for direct pedagogical action. And it is in this spirit that we now turn to consider some specific proposals for the grading of word order rules in syllabuses of German as a foreign language.

Teachability and syllabus grading

In the light of his teachability hypothesis, Pienemann has critically evaluated a grammatically based syllabus taken from a 'popular' textbook for German as a foreign/second language used for migrant children (Pienemann, 1985). Pienemann's evaluation is based on the degree of match between the teaching objectives in the textbook and the developmental stages for naturalistic learners established in the ZISA study. He suggests that where word order is concerned, the textbook syllabus contains some 'fairly good guesses' about the order in which word order rules are handled, but that it has what he assumes to be shortcomings in its 'teaching objectives',[13] to which we return below. In his analysis, teaching objectives are distinguished from 'general input', i.e. input which is not intended for production by the learner. Hence, 'teaching' here has the narrow sense of providing form-focused instruction with the objective of introducing the said form into the learner's productive use.

Pienemann's analysis of the chosen textbook (*Wir sind dabei*, Gradewald, 1971) is shown in modified form in Table 5.

Table 5: Grading of German word order rules in a textbook (modified after Pienemann, 1985: 62)

General input	Teaching objectives	
	Word order rule	*Developmental stage*
SVO inversion verb separation	SVO	Stage II
SVO inversion verb separation adverb-preposing	adverb-preposing inversion	Stage III Stage V
as above	modal verbs *(without verb separation)*	
as above	inversion with Mod + V	Stage V
as above	inversion *(implicitly verb separation)*	Stage V Stage IV

We can see from this table that the teaching objectives in the chosen textbook are not ordered entirely in accordance with the developmental order proposed in the ZISA study, leading Pienemann to suggest that one rule is introduced 'much too early' (inversion) and that one is missing altogether as a teaching objective (verb separation) (1985: 63). Pienemann suggests that this sample syllabus illustrates 'the discrepancy between what is learnable and what the students are expected to learn in a language course' (1985: 61).

In the light of his criticisms, Pienemann goes on to propose what he calls a 'naturally graded' syllabus (presented in Table 6 below). In so doing, he encounters what he considers to be a problem to his approach in connection with the inversion rule. The reader will recall from earlier descriptions of the ZISA developmental order that inversion is acquired in two stages: the learner first fronts adverbials without inverting subject and verb (Stage III) and then with inversion (Stage V). At Stage III a non-target structure is produced (e.g. *und dann er sagen*); at Stage V, the word order is target-like (e.g. *jetzt kann sie mir eine Frage machen*). The pedagogical dilemma here concerns the treatment of the earlier non-target *Adv+S+V+(O) structure. Clearly, to input non-target structures to the learner would be counter-intuitive; Pienemann accordingly proscribes this solution, pointing out that it could even be counter-productive (1989: 72–6). But according to the teachability hypothesis, there is no point in teaching Stage V (inversion) before learners have passed through Stage III (adverb-preposing) and Stage IV (verb separation), since the processing prerequisites for Stage V are not yet available. Recall that Pienemann argues that the prior acquisition of the adverb-preposing and verb separation rules facilitates acquisition of inversion.

Given this processing prerequisite (i.e. that the inversion stage presupposes the non-target adverb-preposing stage and the verb separation stage), how is the problem of non-target interim structures to be solved pedagogically? Pienemann's proposed solution (1985: 64–5) exploits the distinction between general input and teaching objectives described above. He proposes a time delay between the use of target structures in the general input on the one hand, and a focus on the target structure as a teaching objective on the other hand. Hence, in the general input, target-like structures with preposed adverbs and inversion are introduced simultaneously with the appearance of the adverb-preposing rule as a teaching objective. However, no explicit attention is drawn to the inversion rule which is triggered by the preposed adverb. So, for instance, learners' Adv+S+V+O errors are not corrected at this stage. In fact, this time lag between a structure appearing in the general input and the expectation of learners' correct production is already a common strategy in many textbooks, although the rationale is normally not explicit.

We can now turn to Pienemann's proposal for a 'naturally graded' syllabus in Table 6. This table shows that Pienemann's own proposal is indeed consistent with the ZISA developmental order, given the classification of Stage V (inversion) as part of the general input rather than as a teaching objective. But we have no way of judging the representativeness of the textbook criticised by Pienemann (as he himself acknowledges), and therefore no way of judging how necessary his proposal might be in practice.

To this end, I undertook a broader survey based on six textbooks[14] representing a range of pedagogical approaches. The purpose of the survey was to establish if there is any consensus about the sequencing of word order rules in a sample of textbooks for German as a foreign language, and to ask what relationship this bears, if any, to the developmental order. Table 7 presents a summary of the ordering of word order rules based on the teaching objectives for production, as indicated by chapter headings, grammar notes and explanations, and exercises in the textbooks investigated. It should be noted that 'adverb-preposing' (ZISA Stage III) is subsumed under 'inversion' (ZISA Stage V), since non-target rules are not taught. Three environments are distinguished for verb separation (ZISA stage IV): separable verbs; modal + infinitive; auxiliary + past participle. And the verb-end rule (ZISA Stage VII) is also included.

Table 6: A proposal for a 'naturally graded' syllabus of German word order rules
(modified after Pienemann, 1985: 64)

General input	Teaching objectives	
	Word order rule	*Developmental stage*
SVO	–	
SVO	SVO	Stage II
SVO adverb-preposing inversion	adverb-preposing	Stage III
SVO adverb-preposing inversion verb separation	*(modals and auxiliaries introduced at this point)*	
as above	verb separation	Stage IV
as above	inversion	Stage V

A number of patterns can be discerned in this broader survey:

• The clearest mismatch between pedagogical and developmental order is the introduction in all textbooks of inversion before verb separation as a teaching objective; this is inconsistent with the developmental order and hence also with Pienemann's teachability hypothesis.
• With regard to the three linguistic contexts for the verb separation rule, with the exception of Textbook A, the last linguistic context to be introduced is Aux. By contrast, developmental evidence indicates an implicational order of: verbal particle ($V_{particle}$) > Aux/Mod (Clahsen *et al.*, 1983: 172). In other words, Aux (together with Mod) is the first environment in which the verb separation rule is applied in a naturalistic environment, not the last.
• In all textbooks except E, some kind of subordinate clause structure is introduced before the third environment for the application of verb separation, usually Aux, as we have seen. Hence, students are supposed to learn how to produce a subordinate clause before they have learnt the complex form of the perfect tense (*haben/sein* + past participle), or, less likely, the future tense (*werden* + infinitive). Developmental evidence tells us, however, that subordinate clause production is relatively late (Klein and Dittmar, 1979: 165) and that target production of verb-final structures in subordinate clauses is usually the last stage in word order development (Clahsen *et al.*, 1983).

Simply put, the survey reveals the following broad consensus outlined in Table 8. As this table shows, the consensual order of teaching objectives is not consistent with the developmental order proposed in the ZISA study. Two main discrepancies emerge. The first is the introduction of the inversion rule at an early stage in the syllabus. The second is the alternation of various linguistic contexts for verb separ-

Table 7: A survey of seven textbooks of German showing the ordering of teaching objectives for word order rules

Textbook/date of publication	*Basic* *SVX*	*Verb separation* *SVXV$_{particle}$* *S Mod XV* *S Aux XV*	*Inversion* *Adv VSX*	*Verb-end* *daß SXV*
		Order of teaching objectives		
A. 1907	1	6 (V$_{particle}$) 4 (Mod) 3 (Aux) *all rules covered by Lesson 9 of 30 lessons*	2	5
B. 1955	1	4 (V$_{particle}$) 3 (Mod) 6 (Aux) *all rules covered by Lesson 19 of 21 lessons*	2	5 (rel. clauses) 7 (other sub cl)
C. 1968	1	3 (V$_{particle}$) 4 (Mod) 6 (Aux) *all rules covered by Lesson 12 of 20 lessons*	1	5
D. 1972	1	3 (V$_{particle}$) 4 (Mod) 6 (Aux) *all rules covered by Lesson 18 of 24 lessons*	2	5 (weil) 7 (other)
E. 1974	1	4 (V$_{particle}$) 3 (Mod) 5 (Aux) *subordinate clause rule not covered in 28 lessons*	2	
F. 1979	1	3 (V$_{particle}$) 4 (Mod) 6 (Aux) *all rules covered by Lesson 11 of 12 lessons*	2	5 (rel. clauses) 7 (other)

ation and verb-end. If Pienemann's claims about processing prerequisites are correct, then inversion is the teaching objective which is the least likely to succeed, since it is introduced at an early stage. The alternation of Stage IV (verb separation) and Stage VII (verb-end) according to linguistic context should be of less importance, since there is evidence to suggest that a number of learners do not in any case acquire all contexts of a rule before moving on to the next developmental stage (Clahsen *et al.*, 1983; Ellis, 1989).[15] However, if these rules are to alternate, then Aux or Mod should be introduced as the first context for verb separation.

Having looked at a range of textbooks, we now have a sounder basis on which to explore further implications of Pienemann's teachability hypothesis for syllabus grading, although as yet no means of actually testing it. Having considered the question of syllabus grading for German word order rules, we now go on to

Table 8: A comparison of the order of teaching objectives in six selected textbooks
of German and developmental order after ZISA (Clahsen *et al.*, 1983)

Order of teaching objectives	*Developmental order (after ZISA)*
1 Basic SVO	II
2 Inversion	V
3/4 Verb separation[a] (separable verbs; modular + infinitive)	IV
5 Verb-end[b] (all clause types, or a selected type)	VII
6 Verb separation (Auxiliary + past participle)	IV
7 Verb-end (for remaining subordinate clause types not covered under 5)	VII

Notes:
a. except textbook A (1907)
b. except textbook E (1974)

consider a further aspect of instruction, namely, the type of instruction which is
recommended for particular rules.

The pedagogical grammar hypothesis

In any discussion of classroom practice, the efficient use of the teacher's time must
be a consideration. Rutherford and Sharwood Smith's 'pedagogical grammar hypothesis' (PGH) can be seen as an attempt to provide a means for effective distribution of tuition effort. The PGH suggests that formed-focused instruction may
'under certain conditions significantly increase the rate of acquisition over and
above the rate expected from learners acquiring that language under natural circumstances where attention to form may be minimal and sporadic' (Rutherford and
Sharwood Smith, 1985: 275). As Rutherford and Sharwood Smith acknowledge,
their hypothesis is tentative, since little empirical work has been carried out. Other
researchers have, however, also proposed that form-focused instruction may accelerate learning (e.g. Ellis, 1989, discussed in an earlier section). In a summary of
classroom studies on the effect of formal instruction, Chaudron (1988: 164–7)
tentatively suggests that 'a focus on form or explicit talk about grammar' may
contribute to the learning process. Assuming then that a focus on form does in
some way accelerate learning in the classroom, what remains outstanding is to
establish what kind of instruction for what kind of rules and for which learner
groups.

In attempting to define the conditions under which form-focused instruction may
accelerate learning, Rutherford and Sharwood Smith refer to formal similarities
and contrasts between the L1 and L2. Later in this section we return to how their
proposal might be applied to our German word order rules.

Rutherford and Sharwood Smith's PGH is based on a contrastive analysis of L1 and L2, and so it can have no direct implications for the grading of rules in a syllabus. On the other hand, since Pienemann is concerned with L2 development from a processing perspective, his teachability hypothesis can more legitimately be used to formulate hypotheses about the optimal sequencing of syntactic rules in the teaching syllabus, although it has little if anything to say about the kind of input which learners need in order to progress from one developmental stage to the next. In fact, it would make little sense for a hypothesis such as the PGH, which is based on formal rather than processing considerations, to make predictions about real-time development. Neither would it make much sense to expect the teachability hypothesis, which makes no reference to linguistic contrasts/similarities, to make predictions about the kind of formal tuition which might optimally accelerate learning for particular groups. Both hypotheses are therefore being explored in the current article, since the two aspects of tuition which we are considering, syllabus grading and instructional strategy, can reasonably be assumed to be based on different kinds of evidence. This assumption is lacking in some earlier studies of foreign language pedagogy where a contrastive linguistic analysis was taken to indicate an optimal order of tuition, as well as certain teaching strategies. In connection with German word order, for instance, this led Esau (1972) to propose – quite counter-intuitively – that subordinate clauses be introduced before main clauses, since this sequencing reflected the theoretical argument that SOV was the base order and SVO the derived order.

Let us examine Rutherford and Sharwood Smith's approach in more detail. They propose that where the structural properties of the L1 and the L2 differ, the rate of acquisition can be accelerated by drawing the learner's attention to those differences. This is referred to as 'consciousness-raising' (C-R): 'the deliberate attempt to draw the learner's attention specifically to the formal properties of the target language' (1985: 274).[16] Two questions need to be asked when considering whether to use C-R in connection with a particular rule of grammar, according to the PGH:

1. Can C-R accelerate learning of this rule?
2. If so, what kind of C-R is recommended?

The decision whether C-R can accelerate learning rests on a formal structural comparison of the learner's L1 and the target L2 for the rules concerned. Where there is what Rutherford and Sharwood Smith call 'identity' between L1 and L2, C-R is not thought to be helpful in accelerating learning ('zero C-R'). If there is no formal identity (we return to this notion shortly), then C-R should be considered in one of two forms ('implicit C-R' or 'explicit C-R'), depending on the nature of the contrast.

In sum, C-R can be represented as points on a 'continuum' (pp. 276–7). As the term 'continuum' implies, some of the concepts in the PGH remain rather fuzzy, especially 'zero C-R' and 'implicit C-R'. And in order to test the PGH, clearer operational definitions of these concepts would need to be developed.

Where there is identity between L1 and L2:

- **zero C-R**: neither suppress nor give prominence to a grammatical feature.

Where there is no identity between L1 and L2:

- **implicit C-R**: implicitly call attention to a grammatical feature through calculated exposure of the learner to crucial pre-selected data;
- **explicit C-R**: explicitly call attention to a grammatical feature, e.g. by typographical means, and even articulate an instruction rule.

Formal 'identity' between L1 and L2 is measured in the PGH by reference to parameters, so formal identity is understood as 'universal grammar' (UG) identity: the same setting for a given parameter. Difference is defined as a different setting for a given parameter. Applying this now to our language pair of English as the learners' L1 and German as the target L2, we can recall from our earlier description of German word order in terms of a parametric model of grammar, that German differs from English in the setting of all three parameters discussed. So there is no 'UG identity'. Consequently, according to the PGH, some kind of C-R is recommended in all three cases to help the learners assign a new value to each of the parameters. But what kind of C-R: implicit or explicit?

The decision whether to use implicit or explicit C-R depends, so the PGH suggests, on the nature of the evidence available to the learner about the structural differences (i.e. different parametric values) between L1 and L2. So what is the nature of the evidence available to the English learner of German? In the case of English learners of German, the (a) examples below show what the target structures of German are and what might occur in natural input to the learner; the (b) examples show what the learner might incorrectly assume to be the case in German, based on English.

Verb phrase order: L1: VO; L2: OV

8(a) Das Kind hat den Kuchen gegessen
      the child has the cake eaten
8(b) *Das Kind hat gegessen den Kuchen
      the child has eaten the cake

Fronting by (or not by) adjunction: L1: yes; L2: no

9(a) Gestern hat das Kind den Kuchen gegessen
      yesterday has the child the cake eaten
9(b) *Gestern das Kind hat den Kuchen gegessen
      yesterday the child has the cake eaten

Subordinate clause: verb movement blocked or not blocked: L1: no; L2: yes

10(a) (Ich habe ihm gesagt) daß das Kind den Kuchen gegessen hat
       I have to him said that the child the cake eaten has

10(b) (Ich habe ihm gesagt) daß das Kind hat den Kuchen gegessen
       I have to him said that the child has the cake eaten

The idea of the PGH regarding evidence to the learner is in principle a simple one and is based on the so-called 'logical problem of [first] language acquisition'.[17] The key word here is 'logical'. Let us assume that the L2 learner has a hypothesis about a particular rule in the L2, and, as already suggested, that this hypothesis is based on the learner's L1. In a parametric model of grammar, each 'rule' is expressed in a binary form, e.g. does the rule apply or not apply? Logically, so the argument goes, it is easier to learn that a rule does apply rather than that it doesn't apply. Consider the reasons for this. One occurrence of an utterance in which the rule is applied provides sufficient evidence for the learner to reject an incorrect hypothesis that the rule does not apply in the L2. In other words, the learner has positive evidence that something does occur. If, however, the learner starts from the incorrect assumption that the rule does apply in the L2, then the problem is of a different order. No matter how many times the learner encounters examples of the rule *not* being applied in L2 utterances, the original hypothesis cannot logically be rejected, since the evidence is of a negative kind. How can the learner know that the rule is never applied in L2? Perhaps he/she simply hasn't encountered an example yet.

Returning to the PGH, and to our question whether implicit or explicit C-R is called for where L1 and L2 contrast, we can now offer an answer in terms of positive evidence (that something must be done) and negative evidence (that something must not be done). If the learner has positive evidence about the application of a rule in natural input, then implicit C-R is said, according to the PGH, to be sufficient to accelerate learning. But, if the natural input only provides negative evidence about the non-application of a rule, then explicit C-R is said to be required to provide the learner with what is called 'direct' negative evidence from the teacher, such as error correction or rule explanation.

Let us consider how this applies specifically to the three word order rules in German, as described in our chosen grammatical model. While other interpretations or models are indeed possible, I intend to pursue the model chosen here in a consistent way in accordance with my original intention to explore how linguistic theory may be related to language teaching. *Ad hoc* changes to the chosen exemplar, in our case a parametric model of word order in Germanic languages, would clearly not be helpful in exploring this idea. Consistent with the chosen model of grammar, the nature of evidence available in natural input to the English L2 learner of German can be represented as in Table 9. Let us consider each of the three rules in turn.

The English learner of German has positive evidence in the natural input that German is OV in subordinate clauses in the context of both finite and non-finite verbs, and in main clauses where the verb has two or more parts (e.g. *hat ... gegessen*). It seems reasonable to assume that the evidence for OV outweighs that for VO, since evidence of VO order is restricted to simplex finite verbs in main

Table 9: Evidence available to English learners of L2 German on word order rules, and appropriate consciousness-raising (C-R) according to the PGH

Parameter	English (L1)	German (L2)	Evidence available to L2 learner (English as L1)	Type of C-R
VP order	V-initial	V-final	positive	implicit
Fronting by adjunction	+	−	negative	explicit
Sub cl order: verb movement blocked	−	+	positive	implicit

clauses. Moreover, modern German has only retained two simplex verb forms, the present and the preterite. While the choice for the learner is still a binary one in the case of the VP rule, what the learner has to decide is not whether the rule applies or not, but in which way it applies – VO or OV. In the case of the other two rules discussed here, namely the adverbial fronting rule and the subordinate clause rule, our grammatical model indicates that the learner's task is to establish whether the rule applies (as in the case of the subordinate clause rule) or does not apply (as in the case of the adverbial fronting rule). Let us start with the adverbial fronting rule.

The English learner of German has to understand, according to the model of grammar which we have selected here, that non-subject elements such as adverbials may not be fronted in the same way in German as in English. In other words, they have to learn a negative: that the order Adv+S+V+O does *not* occur in German. The occurrence of structures such as 9(a) demonstrates that Adv+V+S+O is possible, but it can never be directly demonstrated from the language input that Adv+S+V+O order (the assumption from which English learners of German are said to start) *never* occurs. Put another way, the English learner's original hypothesis of Adv+S+V+O cannot be rejected because the only evidence available is of a negative kind. Learners do not receive any direct evidence from the language input that Adv+S+V+O structures never occur. The only way in which learners can establish that this is the case is by 'direct' negative evidence, i.e. by having their mistakes corrected or by having the rule explained to them; that is, through what Rutherford and Sharwood Smith refer to as explicit C-R.

In the case of our third rule, where the learner has to choose whether or not verb movement is blocked in subordinate clauses with a complementiser, our English learner's task is logically easier than in the case of fronting, according to the assumptions of the positive/negative evidence distinction. Structures such as 10(a) show that there is a difference between main and subordinate clause word order in German, and that a rule is operative in subordinate clauses which is not operative in main clauses. So, according to the PGH, only implicit C-R is called for, since the learner's hypothesis that there is no difference can be rejected on the basis of positive evidence in the natural input.

As already indicated, no predictions about the grading of a syllabus can be derived directly from the PGH. But it can be argued that the varying degrees of C-R may be viewed as parallel to Pienemann's distinction between 'general input' in the classroom and 'teaching objectives'. The reader will recall that in the case of general input, no attention is focused on the structure in question, either in use by the teacher or through correction of the learner's errors. By contrast, in the case of teaching objectives, explicit attention is paid to the structure by the teacher. Hence, Pienemann's 'general input' can be seen as broadly equivalent to Rutherford and Sharwood Smith's 'zero C-R' and 'implicit C-R', while Pienemann's 'teaching objective' is broadly equivalent to Rutherford and Sharwood Smith's 'explicit C-R'. However, as well as being differently motivated, these distinctions are further differentiated by the fact that for Pienemann all rules at some point become teaching objectives, whereas for Rutherford and Sharwood Smith some rules do not require this status, since the L2 learner in a sense already 'knows' the rule from the L1 or can work it out from positive evidence in the input data.

The PGH therefore arguably provides a way of fine-tuning the way in which input is presented for particular learner groups, defined by their L1, and can be viewed as complementary to Pienemann's teachability hypothesis which has more to contribute in terms of sequencing.

5. Teaching word order in German: an integrated approach

Having considered in the previous sections the three perspectives on German word order which I set out to describe, namely, linguistic, developmental and pedagogic, we are now in a position to make some recommendations for teaching German word order to learners with English as their L1. These recommendations would, of course, form only a part of a more fully elaborated syllabus in any classroom.

Table 10 shows a proposed order for the introduction of the word order rules under discussion. The order of presentation is divided into three main 'steps', one for each of the three rules discussed. Each step is then further sub-divided according to the range of linguistic contexts for the application of each rule. The table also contains a suggestion for the appropriate type of C-R, and a comparison with the developmental stages proposed in Clahsen *et al.* (1983).

A number of aspects of this proposal require comment. These are: the early inclusion of a developmentally late structure in Step 1, which apparently runs counter to Pienemann's teachability hypothesis; the conflation of two stages at Step 2 (ZISA Stages III and V), for which Pienemann proposed two separate steps; and the motivation for the ordering of linguistic contexts within each step, on which Pienemann provides little information.

Rules and structures

The first point concerns the way in which we view the relationship between the notion 'rule' and particular structures. In the grammatical grading of foreign language syllabuses, grading takes place according to the assumed relative complexity of various rules, and the notion of 'rule' itself is usually closely linked with particular structures and illustrated by actual examples of those structures. For example,

Table 10: A proposal for the ordering of selected word order rules in a syllabus for German as L2 (L1 English)

	Linguistic context	*Type of C-R*	*Developmental stage after Clahsen et al. (1983)*
Step 0 – Basic			
	main clause with simplex verb (e.g. *Laura ißt viel Brot*)	zero	Stage II (multiple constituent phase)
Step 1 – VP order: OV			
Step 1(a)	main clause with complex verb: Mod + V (e.g. *Laura muß viel Brot essen*)	implicit	Stage IV (verb separation)
Step 1(b)	main clause with complex verb: Aux + V (e.g. *Laura hat das Brot gegessen*)	implicit	Stage IV (verb separation)
Step 1(c)	main clause with particle (e.g. *Laura ißt das Brot auf*)	implicit	Stage IV (verb separation)
Step 1(d)	subordinate clause with simplex verb (e.g. *Ich weiß, daß Laura viel Brot ißt*)	zero	Stage VII (verb-end)
Step 2 – Fronting not by adjunction to subject			
Step 2(a)	main clause with complex verb (e.g. *Gestern hat Laura viel Brot gegessen*)	explicit	Stage V (inversion)
Step 2(b)	main clause with simplex verb (e.g. *Heute ißt Laura viel Brot*)	explicit	Stage V (inversion)
Step 3 – Subordinate clause order different from main clause order			
Step 3(a)	subordinate clause with simplex verb (e.g. *Ich weiß, daß Laura viel Brot ißt*)	implicit	Stage VII (verb-end)
Step 3(b)	subordinate clause with complex verb (e.g. *Ich weiß, daß Laura viel Brot essen muß*) (e.g. *Ich weiß, daß Laura viel Brot gegessen hat*) (e.g. *Ich weiß, daß Laura viel Brot aufißt*)	implicit	Stage VII (verb-end)

the 'verb-final rule' in German is traditionally regarded as the distinguishing characteristic of subordinate clauses as opposed to main clauses, and is therefore normally associated uniquely with subordinate clauses. Hence, in this kind of approach, the 'verb-final rule' is often called the 'subordinate clause rule'. But in the descriptive model of word order which I have adopted here, the OV order which is characteristic of German is realised in main clauses with complex verbs as well as in subordinate clauses. So in a parametric model, the relationship between 'rule' and structure is more abstract: a rule is not necessarily associated uniquely with one particular structure.

What complicates the issue for our present purpose of syllabus grading is not only that a parameter may be operative in more than one structure, but also that parameters interact, and that structures may be the outcome of two parameters, not just one. Take the example of subordinate clauses again. Recall that the objective of Step 1 in Table 10 is to introduce the learner to evidence that German is OV. Such evidence comes from both main and subordinate clauses, so it can be argued that both structures should be present in the input to the learner. But subordinate clause structures are also the outcome of the operation of a parameter which is not dealt with until Step 3.[18] One solution to the problem would be to delay introduction of subordinate clauses, as most traditional syllabuses do, until Step 3. But I have rejected this solution, since it implies that OV order is a rule peculiar to subordinate clauses, rather than characteristic of German as a whole. It might also imply that the main clause order S+Aux/Mod+O+V is a deviation from (S)VO order rather than what is *left* of (S)OV order after the finite verb has been moved. It is really a question of whether German is viewed as basically VO or OV. In this article I have tried to pursue some pedagogical implications of regarding German as OV, and so my preferred solution is to introduce subordinate clauses as well as main clauses with complex verbs as illustrations of the verb-final order in the German VP at Step 1, but to provide zero C-R for subordinate clauses. The treatment is analogous to Pienemann's recommendation for dealing with adverb-preposing as a necessary prerequisite for inversion.

Grading and the fronting rule

The second point about Table 10 concerns fronting in main clauses. In this case, a different solution from that of Pienemann is proposed, namely to delay any evidence of fronting in input to the learner until the rule becomes a teaching objective in Step 2. This allows attention to be focused during Step 1 on a single parameter setting which in any case operates in a wide range of linguistic contexts. It is still possible that learners will try in their own production to front certain elements during Step 1, particularly adverbs, with resulting errors (*AdvSVO). However, such errors can be passed over, i.e. not corrected or discussed.

Grading of linguistic contexts for rules

The third point about Table 10 concerns the ordering of structures within each step according to linguistic context. At Step 1 (OV), Mod + V and Aux + V are introduced before V + V$_{particle}$, since the developmental evidence indicates that the Mod and Aux contexts are acquired before separable verbs consisting of verb and particle (i.e. V + V$_{particle}$) (Clahsen *et al.*, 1983: 172). Furthermore, Mod + V is introduced before Aux + V since Mod appears with the basic infinitive form (*Das Kind muß den Kuchen essen*), whereas the most common realisations of Aux (*sein, haben*) appear with the morphologically modified past participle (*Das Kind hat den Kuchen gegessen*).

At Step 2, the sequencing of Step 2(a) (fronting in main clauses with a complex verb) before Step 2(b) (fronting in main clauses with a simplex verb) is intended to facilitate the learner's task in processing terms. As noted earlier, inversion is easier in main clauses with a complex verb because the object and the (lexical) verb are unaffected in their adjacency by any fronting operation in this context (cf. *Das Kind hat den Kuchen gegessen* and *Gestern hat das Kind den Kuchen gegessen*). By contrast, in main clauses with a simplex verb, the subject intervenes between the object and the 'lexical' verb after fronting (cf. *Das Kind aß den Kuchen* and *Gestern aß das Kind den Kuchen*).

At Step 3, the passively familiar subordinate clause structure with a simplex verb (cf. Step 1(d)) is introduced before the range of contexts required for complex verbs, so far only familiar from a main clause context.

6. Conclusion

In this article, an attempt has been made to show how pedagogical decisions on the teaching of grammar may be systematically related to both linguistic and developmental factors. The approach has been illustrated in relation to syntactic rules, using the example of word order in German. Two hypotheses are central to the integrated approach described: Pienemann's teachability hypothesis, and Rutherford and Sharwood Smith's pedagogical grammar hypothesis. Interpreting these hypotheses in the pedagogical context of English learners of German as L2, proposals have been made for the sequencing of rules (also taking into account the various linguistic contexts for these rules), as well as for the apparently most efficient type of form-focused pedagogical strategy. It remains to be seen whether such an approach can offer any advantages over more traditional approaches, and whether it can be generalised to other areas of grammar and to other language pairs.

It has been suggested here that the teachability hypothesis and the PGH are complementary in terms of their respective relevance to the L2 learner's path of development and rate of development.[19] Nevertheless, as the originators of these hypotheses acknowledge, they are to be regarded as tentative, particularly the PGH, as we have seen. Empirical investigations of key issues on which the PGH depends, particularly those relating to claims about the role of evidence in L2 acquisition, are, however, beginning to emerge (see, for instance, White, 1991; Felix and Weigl, 1991). Of special interest in this regard are claims regarding negative evidence in the classroom. Key issues include the effect on learning of direct negative evidence, for instance, in the form of corrective feedback and contrastive rule exposition, as well as the sufficiency of positive evidence. So far, results are ambivalent.

To my knowledge, no work has yet been carried out on these questions with English learners of German. The proposals made in this paper could be used as the basis for an investigation of some of these important questions. The resulting data would be of potential value not only to the theoretical issue of negative evidence and second language acquisition, but also to any discussion of the validity of the teachability hypothesis and the pedagogical grammar hypothesis.

Notes

1. I am very grateful to Martin Bygate for his detailed and helpful comments on an earlier version of this paper. Any remaining shortcomings are, of course, entirely my own. I would also like to thank the participants at the BAAL conference in July 1991 who contributed many useful ideas during the discussion of this paper in its original form, particularly Walter Grauberg, Richard Ingham and Bill Littlewood.
2. These abbreviations refer to the 'basic' ordering of the principal sentence constituents S: Subject; V: Verb; and O: Object. Logically there are six 'types' of basic word order, but SVO and SOV account for the majority of known languages. Mixed-type languages such as German are highly unusual. Hawkins (1979), for instance, identifies only three such languages: German, Mandarin Chinese and Homeric Greek.
3. This analysis assumes that German is basically OV, or verb-final. The SVO structure *Das Kind aß den Kuchen*, although a relatively common structure, is said to be derived from a base SOV structure by movement of the tensed or finite verb into the position immediately following the subject. Note that VO order only occurs with simplex verb forms of the finite verb in main clauses. It is not a possible order in any other context: **Das Kind hat gegessen den Kuchen*; **Das Kind muß essen den Kuchen*; **daß das Kind aß den Kuchen*; **daß das Kind gegessen hat den Kuchen*; **daß das Kind essen den Kuchen muß*; and so on. Another way of looking at this is to say that the verb-second order only occurs with finite verbs in main clauses, whereas the verb-final order occurs with non-finite parts of the verb (main clauses) as well as with finite verbs (subordinate clauses).
4. These parameters are referred to in Travis (1984) as the 'Headedness' parameter, the 'Adjunction' parameter, and the 'COMP as Proper Governor' parameter. The PS-configuration for word order in Germanic languages as in duPlessis *et al.* (1987) after Travis (1984) is:

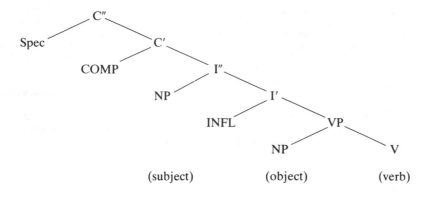

5. English does not block verb movement into the post-subject position in subordinate clauses with a complementiser, but the relative ordering of the constituents is not altered, because English is VO in the verb phrase ('t' indicates the 'trace' left of the verb after movement):
   (a) [$_{CP}$ that [$_{IP}$ the children [$_{INFL}$e] ate the cake]]
   (b) [$_{CP}$ that [$_{IP}$ the children [$_{INFL}$ ate$_i$] t$_i$ the cake]]
   In German, where the order in the verb phrase is OV, movement of the tensed verb does alter the relative order of constituents:
   (c) [$_{CP}$ daß [$_{IP}$ die Kinder [$_{INFL}$e] den Kuchen aßen]]
   (d) *[$_{CP}$ daß [$_{IP}$ die Kinder [$_{INFL}$ aßen$_i$] den Kuchen t$_i$]]
6. This order is based on cross-sectional, not longitudinal data, analysed by implicational scaling. This method of data analysis allows the researcher to see how learners progress in their acquisition of structures by comparing individual performances. If these individuals represent a range of pro-

ficiencies, then it may be possible to infer a developmental order if certain structures can be seen to be always acquired before others. Clahsen and Muysken (1986: 107) report that a preliminary study by Clahsen (1984) based on longitudinal ZISA data shows that 'the supposed stages can be confirmed in the majority of cases'.

7. The term used here by Clahsen *et al.* (1983) is *Partikel*. I have chosen *verb separation* (Pienemann, 1985) as the more transparent term, and will use this term throughout.

8. Ellis's (1989: 317) operational definition of 'acquisition' is three correct applications of a particular rule in an obligatory context.

9. Few details are given about how the subjects were taught. Pienemann simply says that specially designed materials were used (1985: 36) and that 'a variety of materials and activities were used' (1989: 58).

10. For a critique of the processing orientation of the ZISA study, see Zobl, 1985.

11. These suggestions go back to Slobin's universal processing strategies which were proposed for children learning their first language (Slobin, 1973). See in particular Slobin's Operating Principle D.

12. It also presupposes that information about natural orders is available for a wide range of grammatical rules and languages. This is, however, not the case.

13. Pienemann also uses the term 'learning objective' (see, for instance, his Table 5, 1985: 62) in apparently the same sense as 'teaching objective'.

14. The textbooks surveyed in Table 7 are as follows:
    Textbook A: Joerg, J.B. and Joerg, J.A. 1907, *A First German Course*, Cassell, London.
    Textbook B: Anderson, W.E. 1955 (revised edition 1960), *Das schöne Deutschland*, Harrap, London.
    Textbook C: Braun, K., Nieder, L. and Schmöe, F. 1968, *Deutsch als Fremdsprache*, Klett, Stuttgart.
    Textbook D: Schäpers, R. 1972, *Deutsch 2000*, Band I, Hueber, München.
    Textbook E: Nuffield Foundation 1974, *Vorwärts*, Kurzfassung.
    Textbook F: Neuner, G., Schmidt, R., Wilms, H. and Zirkel, M. 1979, *Deutsch aktiv*, Band 1, Langenscheidt, Berlin.

15. Ellis (1989) distinguishes between 'communicators', who move on to the next stage of development without seeking to master a rule across a full range of contexts, and 'error avoiders', who do not move on to the next stage until the current rule has been mastered across the range of contexts. In the ZISA study, this variational aspect of learner behaviour is related to learner type.

16. The term 'consciousness' is conceptually unclear, as Schmidt (1990) has pointed out. I understand Rutherford and Sharwood Smith to be using the term in the sense of 'awareness' rather than 'intention' or 'knowledge' (Schmidt, 1990: 131–4).

17. A very readable account can be found in Cook, 1988: 59–62.

18. For a re-analysis of Clahsen *et al.*'s (1983) developmental stages in a parametric framework, cf. duPleissis *et al.* (1987: 67–8).

19. It has been pointed out to me that not only rate of acquisition but also relative success is at issue here. One of the major tasks of L2 acquisition studies is to explain why some learners fail to progress beyond certain developmental levels.

References

den Besten, H. 1983, 'On the interaction of root transformations and lexical deletive rules', in Abraham, W. (ed.), *On the Formal Syntax of Westgermania*, John Benjamins, Amsterdam/Philadelphia.

Chaudron, C. 1988, *Second Language Classrooms*, CUP, Cambridge.

Chomsky, N. 1965 *Aspects of the Theory of Syntax*, MIT Press, Cambridge, Mass.

Clahsen, H. 1984, 'The acquisition of German word order: a test case for cognitive approaches to L2 development', in Anderson, R.W. (ed.), *Second Languages: A Cross-Linguistic Perspective*, Newbury House, Rowley, Mass.

Clahsen, H., Meisel, J. and Pienemann, M. 1983, *Deutsch als Zweitsprache. Der Spracherwerb ausländischer Arbeiter*, Gunter Narr, Tübingen.

Clahsen, H. and Muysken, H. 1986, 'The availability of universal grammar to adult and child learners: a study of the acquisition of German word order', *Second Language Research*, vol. 2, no. 2, 93–119.

Clahsen, H. and Muysken, H. 1989, 'The UG paradox in L2 acquisition', *Second Language Research*, vol. 5, no. 1, 1–29.

Cook, V. 1988, *Chomsky's Universal Grammar. An Introduction*, Blackwell, Oxford.

duPlessis, J., Solin, D., Travis, L. and White, L. 1987, 'UG or not UG, that is the question: a reply to Clahsen & Muysken', *Second Language Research*, vol. 3, no. 1, 56–75.

Ebert, R.P. 1975, 'A note on the analysis and teaching of German word order', *Die Unterrichtspraxis*, vol. 1, 60–6.

Eisenberg, P. 1986, *Grundriß der deutschen Grammatik*, J.B. Metzlersche Verlagsbuchhandlung, Stuttgart.

Ellis, R. 1989, 'Are classroom and naturalistic acquisition the same?: A study of the classroom acquisition of German word order rules', *Studies in Second Language Acquisition*, vol. 11, 305–28.

Esau, H. 1972, 'A new approach to the teaching of word order in elementary German', *Die Unterrichtspraxis*, vol. 5, no. 2, 127–39.

Fanselow, G. 1987, *Konfigurationalität: Untersuchungen zur Universalgrammatik am Beispiel des Deutschen*, Gunter Narr, Tübingen.

Felix, S. and Weigl, W. 1991, 'Universal grammar in the classroom: the effects of formal instruction on second language acquisition', *Second Language Research*, vol. 7, no. 2, 162–80.

Griesbach, H. 1978, 'Die Stellung der Satzglieder im Satz – ein Unterrichtsproblem', *Zielsprache Deutsch*, vol. 1, 2–9.

Haider, H. 1986, 'V-second in German', in Haider, H. and Prinzhorn, M. (eds.), *Verb Second Phenomena in Germanic Languages*, Foris Publications, Dordrecht/Holland, Riverton/USA.

Hawkins, J.A. 1979, 'Implicational universals as predictors of word order change', *Language*, vol. 55, no. 3, 618–48.

Hopper, P.J. 1975, *The Syntax of the Simple Sentence in Proto-Germanic*, Mouton, The Hague.

Klein, W. and Dittmar, N. 1979, *Developing Grammars. The Acquisition of German Syntax by Foreign Workers*, Springer, Berlin.

Lightbown, P. 1985, 'Can language acquisition be altered by instruction?', in Hyltenstam, K. and Pienemann, M. (eds.), *Modelling and Assessing Second Language Acquisition*, Multilingual Matters, Clevedon.

Lockwood, W. 1968, *Historical German Syntax*, Clarendon Press, Oxford.

Pienemann, M. 1985, 'Learnability and syllabus construction', in Hyltenstam, K. and Pienemann, M. (eds.), *Modelling and Assessing Second Language Acquisition*, Multilingual Matters, Clevedon.

Pienemann, M. 1989, 'Is language teachable? Psycholinguistic experiments and hypotheses', *Applied Linguistics*, vol. 10, no. 1, 52–79.

Platzack, C. 1985, 'A survey of generative analyses of the verb second phenomenon in Germanic', *Nordic Journal of Linguistics*, vol. 8, 49–73.

Rutherford, W. and Sharwood Smith, M. 1985, 'Consciousness-raising and universal grammar', *Applied Linguistics*, vol. 6, no. 3, 274–82.

Schmidt, R.W. 1990, 'The role of consciousness in second language learning', *Applied Linguistics*, vol. 11, no. 2, 129–58.

Schneiderbauer, A.M. 1966, 'Schwierigkeiten der deutschen Wortstellung für Englischsprechende', *Deutschunterricht für Ausländer*, vol. 5, no. 6, 153–67.

Selinker, L. 1972, 'Interlanguage', *International Review of Applied Linguistics*, vol. 10, 209–31.

Slobin, D.I. 1973, 'Cognitive prerequisites for the development of grammar', in Ferguson, C.A. and Slobin, D.I. (eds.), *Studies of Child Language Development*, Holt, Rinehart & Winston, New York.

Travis, L. 1984, *Parameters and effects of word order variation*, PhD dissertation, MIT, Cambridge, Mass.

White, L. 1991, 'Adverb placement in second language acquisition: some effects of positive and negative evidence in the classroom', *Second Language Research*, vol. 7, no. 2, 133–61.

Zobl, H. 1985, 'Review of H. Clahsen, J. Meisel and M. Pienemann 1983', *Studies in Second Language Acquisition*, vol. 7, no. 1, 125–8.

Articles of Faith: The Acquisition, Learning and Teaching of a and the

MIKE BEAUMONT and CLARE GALLAWAY

1. Introduction

'Articles of faith are sometimes subtle, pervasive, unrecognised, and therefore very powerful. They also frequently have a certain amount of emotion attached to them.' (Stevick, 1990: 17–18)

The title of this paper is inspired by this observation by Stevick. Although made in an entirely different context, it seems to have a certain relevance to the definite and indefinite articles of English. It is an engaging paradox that these small words, which occur so frequently, carry such subtleties of meaning, and are often barely audible in a stream of speech, nonetheless require highly complex grammatical explanations to account for their use. In the context of second language learning, they also seem to generate a good deal of passionate conviction about the way they should be taught.

The article system of English provides an excellent context for bringing both theoretical and pedagogic issues together, and attempting to rationalise work in a number of fields related to the description, acquisition, learning and teaching of grammar. Using the article as a case study, we argue that the teaching of grammar must integrate insights from three broad theoretical areas: language description, language processing, and language acquisition.

Until quite recently, theories of language description have been the dominant influence on the teaching of grammar. However, much of that description is of limited use to the second language teacher, and therefore learner, because the kinds of 'rules' that underpin much classroom practice are based either on native-speaker intuition or on generalisations from written language. With the current interest in the teaching of the spoken language, the ever-growing corpus of spoken data should be examined to establish how spoken and written usage differ. By so doing, we might also gain insights into how fluent speakers cope with the real-time language processing demands of encoding and decoding complex areas of grammar. Finally, it is unwise to extrapolate approaches to teaching directly from descriptions of a grammatical area (the intended product, if you like, of teaching) without also taking into account what we now know about the language learning process, in the form of both first and second language acquisition studies. As Rutherford (1987: 17) points out: 'Theories of grammar, though highly important to language pedagogy for other reasons, are not theories of language acquisition.'

It is only within such a broad theoretical perspective, we would argue, that the teacher can begin to make informed judgements about appropriate classroom strategies relating to the teaching and learning of grammar. Accordingly, we set out here to consider four domains:

1. existing theoretical and pedagogic descriptions of the article system
2. article use in the spoken language of adult native speakers
3. first and second language acquisition of the article system
4. implications for the classroom teacher of English as a second language.

First, however, let us examine one example of the kind of 'rule of thumb' that learners are often presented with in the classroom. It is commonly referred to as 'first/second mention'. One popular grammar describes the rule as follows:

The use of 'a/an' when something is mentioned for the first time
A/an is used before a countable noun mentioned for the first time: the speaker assumes the listener does not know what is referred to:
   *I looked up and saw **a plane**.* (Mentioned for the first time – you don't know which plane I mean.) ***The plane** flew low over the trees.* (You know exactly which plane I mean and the plane is, in that sense, identified.) (Alexander, 1988: 60)

Specifying by means of back-reference . . .
Something that has been mentioned is referred to again.
   *Singleton is a **quiet village** near Chichester. **The village** has a population of a few hundred people.* (Alexander, 1988: 62)

Some grammarians recognise that this generalisation needs qualifying:

   It is not true, as is sometimes stated, that the indefinite article is always used for 'first mention' and that the definite article is used subsequently for reference back . . . *The* can in fact be used for first mention . . . or indefiniteness may persist in second and subsequent mentions. (Chalker, 1984: 53)

Unfortunately, instances of article use which 'break' this 'first/second mention' rule are widespread in spoken language, and are not infrequent in written language. Therefore an L2 learner who attempts to operate the rule on anything other than highly controlled 'model' texts is likely to suffer considerable confusion. The reason for this is that the conditions dictating whether a referent is classified as identifiable or not identifiable in discourse are essentially pragmatic ones; that is, identifiability is not an absolute notion and is determined by the needs of the current context. Many examples, therefore, will not be satisfactorily explained to the learner by the unknown/known distinction as they understand it. The following examples illustrate this point.

   1 (a) A: *Where's June?*
         B: *She's gone to a party.*

   (b) A: *Where's June?*
         B: *She's gone to the pub.*

In examples 1(a) and 1(b), there might be no difference between the identifiability status of the respective noun phrases *a party* and *the pub*; the listener in each case may not be able to identify either of them. The difference is that there is a loose assumption that one's local environment includes a pub, and one can therefore refer to it without introducing it first, whereas the same does not hold for a party.

Secondly, first-mention *the* is not at all uncommon at the beginning of written texts. The following is the first sentence of David Lodge's novel *Nice Work*:

   2. *Monday, January 13th, 1986. Victor Wilcox lies awake, in **the** dark bedroom, waiting for his Quark alarm clock to bleep.* (our emphasis)

There are more examples in the following text from a newspaper:

   3. *The RAF telegraphist at the centre of the recent 'Mata Hari' spying trial has been dismissed from the service for falling short of required standards and failing to conform to the military way of life.*

Thirdly, in some contexts, particularly where noun phrases are predominantly abstract, it often seems to make no difference which article is used. One of the authors has informally tested this by taking a short extract from a newspaper article, deleting all the articles, and giving it as a cloze test to native speakers. They were unanimous in restoring the original article in only 70 per cent of cases. Example 3 is the first paragraph of the article. The last noun phrase is an example of a context where either article is acceptable.

Finally, in many cases the syntactic–semantic context totally predicts the article because it forms part of some idiom or collocation; for example:

   4. *What's the time?*

The important point here is that a meaning contrast between *a* and *the* is not always available or relevant. Although the choice of *the* in this case may have its roots in semantics, the sequence has become fixed and part of a native speaker's stock repertoire, rather than processed afresh on each occasion – what Pawley and Syder (1983: 205) refer to as 'familiar, memorized sequences'. Such fixed uses exist for both *a* and *the*.

These examples do not constitute 'exceptions' to the 'rule'. On the contrary, they are uncontroversial examples of everyday article use, but they are quite difficult to account for unless a sophisticated and comprehensive framework is used. We argue that it is possible to account for them if we first reach an understanding of key terms such as 'identifiability and 'referentiality'. As teachers, we need to understand the article system before deciding what information to pass on to learners, and whether that information should, to use Harmer's terms (1987: 3), be overt or covert.

The following discussion centres chiefly on the concepts of identifiability and referentiality. Therefore we do not deal with choices which depend on the countable/uncountable (e.g. *a* versus 0) and singular/plural (e.g. *a* versus *some*) distinctions. There are other reasons for concentrating on tangible instances of *a* and *the*, some of which are implied by Thomas's (1989) discussion.

2. Existing theoretical and pedagogic descriptions of the article system

Theoretical descriptions

There have been numerous attempts by linguists to capture the essential meaning and use of the articles (e.g. Karttunen, 1968; Christophersen, 1939; Hawkins, 1978, 1980; Givón, 1978; DuBois, 1980). Such discussions depend on a number of binary oppositions which are said to be relevant in accounting for the way the articles work:

definite/indefinite
referential/non-referential
specific/non-specific
identifiable/non-identifiable
general/particular
countable/uncountable
singular/plural.

Problems arise with some of these terms which are not always used with the same meanings. In particular, the contrast definite/indefinite can cause confusion. Since it is the traditional (pre-theoretic) way of describing the articles, some (e.g. DuBois) use these terms to signal the formal or surface distinction only, while using other terms to account for the meaning difference. Some (e.g. Givón) use the term 'non-definite' as well as 'indefinite'.

The classic distinction of identifiable versus non-identifiable referents is perfectly adequate if it is properly related to the demands of a conversational setting. Quirk *et al.* (1985: 272) give this definition:

> The indefinite article is notionally the 'unmarked' article in the sense that it is used (for singular count nouns) where the conditions for the use of *the* do not obtain. That is, *a/an X* will be used where the reference of *X* is not uniquely identifiable in the shared knowledge of speaker and hearer.

A more process-oriented definition is that the definite article acts as an instruction to the listener to identify the referent of the noun phrase (Hawkins, 1978). The indefinite article acts as an instruction to the listener not to bother to search for that referent – for a variety of reasons (see Gallaway, 1987).

It has already been pointed out that real-world identifiability and linguistic identifiability are not equivalent. In fact, the word 'identifiable' can best be understood within a pragmatic framework such as Grice's conversational maxims (1975). The point is, referents have to be identifiable only as far as required for the purposes of conversation (DuBois, 1980). This alters the notion of identifiability and goes a long way towards explaining why some instances of *the* mark referents which are not unambiguously identifiable (e.g. example 1 above).

If unambiguous identification is not required for comprehension of the message, then we get weak referentiality. Weakly referential noun phrases often cannot be identified in any meaningful sense. The definite article just indicates that the hearer does not need to know any more about it in order to decode the message. Typically, these weakly referential noun phrases will occur in non-topicalised sentence constituents such as locative phrases and certain kinds of object (e.g. *on the beach*, *to the pub*, *doing the washing*).

That point also reminds us that, to add further to the complications, syntax plays a role in determining whether a referent is encoded by using a definite or indefinite noun phrase. Consider the following (attested) example:

5. *I've got a wife who's doing a Ph.D. in Linguistics.*

In the following alternative version, which appears semantically (but not pragmatically) equivalent, the underlined noun phrase would be definite:

6. *My wife is doing a Ph.D. in Linguistics.*

To go into this issue comprehensively would require discussions of a depth far beyond the scope of this article but, in brief, it appears that the difference lies in the speaker's preferred topic–comment structure, i.e. the choice of syntactic 'packaging' for the information (see Rutherford, 1987: Ch. 6).

To sum up, these apparent complications, though not difficult to explain in an appropriate linguistic framework, do present problems for teachers and learners, who may be operating with a simplified notion of what the articles mean.

Pedagogic descriptions

In an area of such agreed complexity, setting up a working basis for teaching articles is clearly difficult. Not surprisingly, those who have attempted to do so have come up with radically different proposals. The studies we discuss here may all be described as pedagogic grammars in at least one of three senses. First, they offer the teacher a simplified picture of article usage. Second, they provide advice on sequencing different uses within a syllabus. Third, they offer some kind of teaching methodology. However, we can observe significant differences in the relationship of each to linguistic, and, in the case of the later studies, psycholinguistic, theory.

One early study (Grannis, 1972) argued that the linguistic theory available at the time was of little use to teachers and advised them to step outside existing theoretical frameworks and to handle articles in 'non-formal terms'. This rejection of theory may be representative of the attitude of a number of teachers. Its dangers are eloquently described by Widdowson (1984). To be fair to Grannis, however, it is certainly the case that linguistic theory alone is an inadequate base for making decisions about teaching grammar. Whitman (1974: 253), in response to what he sees as a 'misconception ... preserved by many transformational linguists', provides his own analysis of the article, based on the concepts of quantification and determination. He then sets out 'an appropriate organization for the presentation of the article in an EFL course' in six steps. Both these studies illustrate a frustration that many teachers felt at the time, namely that exciting developments in linguistic theory were not resulting in clear implications for second language classroom practice.

McEldowney (1977) also offers a simplified grammar of the article system, although there is no overt reference to a particular grammatical theory. Rather, the study is framed within the 'common errors' tradition of French (1949) and George (1972). Viewed in retrospect, the observation that learners worldwide appear to make the same kinds of error can be seen as a phenomenon for which second language acquisition theory now offers some explanations. However, in keeping with the times, McEldowney's four 'stages of learning' represent a refinement of the structural approach to syllabus design, taking the avoidance of learner error as the guiding methodological principle.

Lindstromberg's (1986) suggestion is different again. His approach is not to simplify the system, but to make the complexity 'manageable' by simplifying the terminology. To this end he produces a 'decision sheet', extending over two pages, which resolves the article system 'into some twenty low-level teaching points such that they 1) can be clearly related to examples of use and 2) direct the learner toward eventual, higher level understanding of what the system does' (Lindstromberg, 1986: 35). Lindstromberg's sheet has the merit of not oversimplifying the article system, but he does make it clear that it is designed for teachers of intermediate and advanced students. He also attempts to relate his pedagogic stance to acquisition studies. He argues strongly for the interface position in the learning/acquisition debate (see, for example, Ellis, 1984, for a summary of this), namely that teaching the rules of article usage can make a difference to learners' understanding and use of the system.

Berry (1991: 256) recommends using 'a principled descriptive account' as the basis for a classroom approach to the articles. His main source for this account is Quirk *et al.* (1985), which in turn incorporates insights from Hawkins (1978). This enables Berry to recognise, like us, the inadequacy of concepts such as second mention, and to derive a set of principles for materials design. However, he takes no account of acquisition studies, rejecting Pica's (1985) study as 'fundamentally flawed' (1991: 253). This may be the case, but there are questions raised by studies such as Pica's which need to be addressed. We shall return in Sections 3 and 4 to some of these questions.

Master (1990) produces the most simplified framework, reducing article use to a meaning contrast between classification (signalled by *a* or 0) and identification (signalled by *the*). As a contribution to the learning/acquisition debate, he also offers evidence from one of his own studies that a systematic approach to teaching the article system can result in a significant improvement in test performance. He admits, however, that this improvement might have arisen from 'the focusing of students' attention on the need for articles in English rather than from any explicit method for choosing the articles correctly' (Master, 1990: 465).

To sum up, then, the prevailing approach to the production of a framework for the teaching of the article system is to derive a simplified grammar from a more complex linguistic description. Some of the more recent studies recognise the relevance of second language acquisition theory to teaching grammar, but none addresses the issue of how rules might be applied in language processing, either by fluent speakers of the language or by learners. We turn in Section 3, therefore, to an examination of article use in a small corpus of spontaneous spoken language.

3. Article use in the spoken language of adult native speakers

As we have argued, theoretical and pedagogic descriptions of a particular grammatical area may not be adequately specified to account for everyday examples of language (particularly spoken language) use. With articles, our investigation of spoken language data suggests that their use is not as contrastive as has been indicated in the past.

Gallaway (1987) took a small corpus of spoken English (ten extracts including over 400 instances of *a* and *the*) and analysed these using a linguistic framework taken chiefly from Givón (1978), Hawkins (1978 and 1980) and DuBois (1980). The hypothesis was that article use is less creative, less semantically motivated and more closely linked with the syntactic structure of sentences and phrases than is generally supposed. In other words, much article use can be predicted from the syntactic context and is not based on the speaker making any obvious semantic choice. In some cases, choice of the other article often would not have made any difference to the interpretation of the meaning. In others, the use of fixed phrases meant that there was no choice anyway.

The first finding was that instances of *the* outnumber those of *a* by about three to two. This can be explained by the fact that the majority of referents in a discourse are given, or else packaged as sufficiently known for the purposes of the current discourse. In fact, once the proportion of indefinite noun phrases within a discourse rises above a certain number, it becomes impossible for the hearer to process it.

The defining characteristics of each article, based on their distribution in the data, were as follows.

a

First-mention indefinites accounted for only a relatively small proportion of uses (about 25 per cent). Most of the remaining instances of *a* were entailed in some way by the syntactic context. These were commonly:

  a) within idioms (e.g. *a bit*)
  b) within the scope of negation – non-specific *a* (e.g. *I haven't got a x*)
  c) in naming or existential utterances (e.g. *It's a x, There's a x*).

Even for first-mention uses, the syntactic context was often predictable – in object position after a limited number of common verbs (e.g. *I've got a x*, *We saw a x*, *Yesterday I met a x*). Indefinite sentence subjects rarely occur (and indeed are ungrammatical in some languages).

the

Perhaps the most noticeable feature was that definiteness was very rarely justified by first mention (only 22 instances out of 250 occurrences; that is, less than 10 per cent). Generally, anaphoric reference is more likely to be achieved by a proform than by *the* + N, an observation also made by Pica (1983) referred to by Master (1990, *TESOL Quarterly*). Consider:

7. *A gardener called yesterday. He seemed very knowledgeable.*
8. *A gardener called yesterday. The gardener seemed very knowledgeable.*

Unfortunately, whereas first/second mention is easy to explain, the other, overwhelmingly more frequent, types of justification for using *the* are much more difficult to explain, which may account for what gets taught and what does not. Syntactically, the contexts where *the* occurred most frequently were in the subject noun phrase and within prepositional phrases. The characteristics of sentence subject (generally given, topicalised material) mean it is usually definite. In the case of prepositional (and particularly locative) phrases, only low identifiability tends to be required in the context and so we get phrases like *on the beach*, *to the butcher's*, *on the line*, etc. Finally, as with *a*, there was a substantial number of fixed contexts where *the* occurred, such as with particular adjectives (e.g. *the first*, *the next*, *the same*) or in idioms such as *the thing is*.

The following extract from a telephone conversation (from Beattie, 1983: 90–2) illustrates a number of our conclusions. The conversation is between the operator (Op) and a subscriber (Sub). Occurrences of *a* and *the* are underlined.

Op 1	Directory Enquiries, for which town please?
Sub 1	Woburn Sands.
Op 2	Woburn Sands. Yes.
Sub 2	And the name is Anyname.
Op 3	The name of the person is Anyname?
Sub 3	Anyname, yes . . .
Sub 7	. . . there's not been any change of coding or anything like that about that number?
Op 8	Just checking for you. I've got a list of changed numbers but I don't think that's one of them. No that's not on the changed numbers list. It should be alright.
Sub 8	Well, I can't get it. I've just tried it.
Op 9	Have you? Well I should dial 100 and ask the operator to help you.
Sub 9	Yeah.
Sub 10	Err well I see. Who will know if there is any change of ah exchange um and all the rest of it?
Op 10	Well you know I've got the changed number list for Woburn Sands so it um

Sub 11	And it's definitely not one of them?
Op 11	No it isn't. No.
Sub 12	Ah the thing is this. Bit of a mystery. I've been trying this number for two days. Um yesterday somebody told me to put 58 in front of it which got me a very unusual dialling situation. I haven't been able to get through and I'm you know. I have a letter from a large company saying he's there waiting for me to phone, and I can't get through.
Op 12	Yes.
Op 13	Yes, well, 58 should be put in front of some numbers but these these um let me just read this. You've tried it with 58 in front?
Sub 13	Yes.
Op 14	Oh, I should dial 100 and ask the operator to help you then because um you know if you dial it with 58 in front it should certainly be alright.
Sub 14	But I should be able to dial it without the 58 in front?
Op 15	Just a moment let me read this list here properly. No, you should have the 58 in front of it.
Sub 15	I should have a $\big\{$ 58 in front.
Op 16	$\big\{$ Yes yes and
	I'll just check the code for you while you're on the line.
	Perhaps it's the code you see. Your code should be 0908.
Sub 16	Yes, that's what I've been dialling.
Op 17	And then 58 and then the number. That should definitely be alright.
Sub 17	Yes, I I've got a feeling there's something going on, on the exchange there, because it gives a very funny, very sort of, you know, it dials, then it stops.
Op 18	Oh $\big\{$ that sounds like
Sub 18	$\big\{$ and then it
	goes on again
Op 19	That sounds like a fault on the phone itself not on, not on any dialling. If you're actually getting a ringing tone it should be alright. It's a $\big\{$ faul-
Sub 19	$\big\{$ who do
	I get on to about fault enquiries anyway?
Op 20	Fault enquiries, or or eh dial 100 and ask the operator to help you and she'll report it.
Sub 20	Yes. O.K., then.
Op 21	One or the other.

The extract confirms much of what we observed in the survey.

(a) There are substantially more definites than indefinites, even though the interlocutors have a minimal degree of shared knowledge. Most of the definite articles are entailed by the immediate context (*the name, the person, the operator*, etc.).

(b) Definite noun phrases with *the* appear in subject position, object position and prepositional phrases in almost equal proportion, whereas instances of *a* are chiefly in object position after common verbs (*get, have, give*).

(c) There are fixed, or idiomatic, uses of both *a* and *the* (*bit of a mystery, all the rest*).

(d) There is only one example of first/second mention (*a list of changed numbers, the changed numbers list*).

Consider also the extraordinary case of *58*, of which there are eight occurrences.

Articles are attached, or not attached, in a manner which is seemingly random. The first four occurrences have no article. Then we have two with *the*, followed by one with *a*. The final occurrence reverts to no article. It seems to us that this kind of variation cannot be explained without recourse to some of the pragmatic and syntactic factors we have highlighted.

Our examination of article use in spoken language has two main implications. Firstly, it suggests that, in many contexts, pragmatic demands and syntactic predictability play a more significant role than meaning in the choice of article use. Second, it offers tentative support to Pawley and Syder's (1983) view that fluent linguistic encoding is not an entirely creative process but relies partly on a repertoire of highly predictable sequences and structures. Both these observations must cast doubt on the usefulness to L2 learners of English of pedagogic frameworks that concentrate solely on establishing meaning contrasts between the definite and indefinite articles.

Our next move is to see what we can learn from acquisition studies of the article system of English.

4. First and second language acquisition of the article system

Brown (1973) was the first to investigate article acquisition, in an observational study, followed by Maratsos (1976), Warden (1976, 1981), Karmiloff-Smith (1979) and Emslie and Stevenson (1981), which were all experimental studies. Gallaway (1987) examined the data from these studies, reassessing their possible significance and adding a new longitudinal study of four children aged between 1; 10 and 2; 6 (i.e. from non-article use to apparently competent article use). Looking at the syntactic and general contextual reasons for choosing one or the other article, rather than concentrating solely on semantic motivation, was a new perspective for article studies.

The findings from this study were, in brief, that the children's earliest uses of articles in many ways mirrored the adult use observed in the corpus. The first articles appeared within what seemed to be learned chunks or 'memorised sequences' in the kind of syntactic context we have outlined, for example, *do the washing, got a tortoise, cross the road, it's a x, that's a x, there's a x, where's the x, in the x*. Children took longer to produce articles correctly with lone nouns, for example:

9. Mum: *What's that?*
   Child: *Tortoise.*

There was no evidence that the children understood the real significance of *the*. That is, applying the normal tests used in child language research to demonstrate the linguistic productivity of an item by a child showed that there was no evidence of articles ever being used alternately or contrastively within the same or similar syntactic contexts. However, there was evidence that they were sensitive to the syntactic contexts where *the* is typically used, including low identifiability prepositional phrases. By far the commonest context for *the* was locative phrases.

How do children learn to use *a* and *the* appropriately, then? Clearly, they do not approach articles via a strategy of 'core' meanings such as the simplified 'unknown/ known' contrast. In fact, the earliest uses are as far removed from identifiability as they could be. In the earliest stages, use appears to be formulaic rather than rule-based. Children subsequently infer correct uses of *a* and *the* from the language they hear around them, very probably forming a large number of correct hypotheses about article use based on surface phenomena – co-occurrence restrictions with adjectives like *first*, and commonly occurring chunks like *want a x*. Only when they have built up an extensive working repertoire of articles in use can children complete the necessary mental reorganisation which leads to rule-based competence and some kind of metalinguistic awareness of the article system.

Recent second language acquisition studies have produced some interesting results. Tarone (1985), in a study of adult Japanese- and Arabic-speaking learners of English, found to her surprise that both groups demonstrated significantly greater accuracy in their production of articles in oral interview and oral narrative tasks than they did in a grammar test, in other words when they were fluency- rather than accuracy-focused. The results for present simple verb + *s* were, incidentally, exactly the reverse. Furthermore, of the two oral tasks, the accuracy of both groups was greater in the narrative. In a more detailed analysis of the same data Tarone and Parrish (1988) observed firstly that, in both oral tasks, noun phrases with *the* were by far the most frequently produced noun phrase type; second, that in the narrative task, which elicited nearly twice as many definite noun phrases as the interview, accuracy in producing this particular type of noun phrase was greater. It needs to be noted, however, that proper names and idiomatic uses of the article were omitted from the study. Nonetheless, definite article use was better acquired, and accuracy was greater on communicative tasks.

In a longitudinal study of a single Japanese-speaking learner, Parrish (1987) provides further evidence that learners make better progress with the definite article than with the indefinite, although she points out how erratic the progress is in both cases. The study also shows how, in the latter stages, the subject begins to overgeneralise her rule-governed behaviour to proper noun and idiomatic uses, therefore making errors in contexts where she had previously demonstrated correct usage.

Thomas's (1989) study is unusual in that it considers the acquisition of articles by both first and second language learners. From the evidence currently available, she concludes that the first accurate use of articles to appear in both groups is *the* in 'specific reference/identifiable' (i.e. second-mention) environments. In fact in general, accurate use of *the* emerges earlier than that of *a*. One consequence of this, perhaps, is that both groups also share the characteristic of overgeneralising the definite article into specific reference/non-identifiable (i.e. first-mention) contexts. In the case of first language learners, the explanation that has traditionally been offered for this phenomenon is the child's egocentric view of the world. However, if this characteristic is also observed in adult second language learners, Thomas argues, the claim is not tenable. Her proposal, then, is that

> in the course of acquisition of the English article system both L1 and L2 learners may overgeneralise the definite article into first-mention contexts because they initially associate *the* with the feature [+SR] (i.e. specific reference). (Thomas, 1989: 351)

Her claim is that this explanation fits the data better than that offered by other writers, i.e. that learners begin by associating *the* with the concept of identifiability. As we have seen, our own data suggests that noun phrases in first-mention contexts are frequently marked by *the*, where identifiability is assumed. If Thomas has not allowed for this, then her subjects may not be overgeneralising at all, but may be using the definite article quite naturally.

Pica's (1985) study is one of the few that attempt to examine what happens in the second language classroom. She assessed the progress of tutored, untutored and mixed groups of Spanish speakers in three grammatical areas: *a* and *the*, verb + *s*, and verb + *ing*. She concludes that

> for highly complex grammatical morphology such as article *a*, instruction appeared to have little impact, as all three groups followed a similar developmental sequence, unaffected by their conditions of exposure to English L2. (Pica, 1985: 214)

Again, interestingly, the results for verb + *s* were the opposite, Pica claiming that instruction did assist the acquisition of this grammatical item. Berry's criticism, to which we have already referred, is that Pica does not consider the quality of the instruction involved (Berry, 1991: 253). In fact, Pica provides no information about the instructional methods used. However, it seems safe to assume that the teaching approach was consistent across the three grammatical areas. Even if we reject Pica's own conclusion, therefore, on the grounds that other evidence suggests that exposure strongly influences development, the study still leaves us with the interesting implication that the teaching approach was particularly appropriate for verb + *s* but not for articles.

A number of hypotheses for further second language acquisition research suggest themselves from the survey above:

(a) The article system may be an area of grammar where the developmental progress of first and second language learners is very similar, accurate use of *the*, for example, emerging before that of *a*, later rule-based use developing from the early acquisition of memorised sequences.

(b) The article system may be an area of grammar which is less amenable tto classroom instruction than others, or it is an area of grammar which requires a different type of classroom instruction from others.

(c) The article system may be an area of grammar where, paradoxically, communicative tasks produce greater accuracy than tasks which require learners consciously to apply their rule system.

We now turn to some of the questions which these different perspectives on article use raise for the classroom practice of teachers of English as a second language.

5. Implications for the classroom teacher of English as a second language

An important initial point to make is that there is no simple link between the theoretical issues we have been discussing in this paper so far and the classroom behaviour of teachers and learners. We should no more expect linguistic and psycholinguistic theory to provide us with straightforward answers to classroom problems than reject theory altogether. Teachers and learners vary. Some teachers understand grammar better than others, are more interested in it and are better at teaching it, just as others excel at organising role plays. Learners also differ from each other. Celce-Murcia and Hilles (1988) summarise learner variables relevant to the teaching of grammar. They include: analytical versus holistic learners, child versus adult learners, visually oriented versus auditory oriented learners, and learners with varying language learning needs. It is particularly interesting to note, however, that 'many of these students *demand* grammar instruction because it fulfils a cultural expectation of what constitutes a language class' (Celce-Murcia and Hilles, 1988: 7). It is also true that many teachers provide grammar instruction for the same reason.

Readers will, of course, find their own classroom implications in what we have discussed. There are, however, a number of issues raised by our paper which we feel both teachers and learners need to address. These issues relate not only to the teaching and learning of the article system in particular, but also to the more general treatment of grammar in the second language classroom.

First, we may need to accept that information about the different meanings certain grammatical items can carry may be of more interest and use to grammarians than it is to learners. It may be that, in the real-time comprehension and production of spoken language by both native and second language speakers, syntactic context plays a much more fundamental role than we have hitherto recognised. A particularly good example of this is the case of *a* in object or complement position after common verbs such as *be, have* or *got*. As more information becomes available about how articles behave in spoken language, textbook writers will be able to approximate their input texts more closely to authentic language use, and teachers will be able to organise language practice that is consistent with that use. This may be more helpful in the long run than oversimplified 'rules of thumb' about meaning. Furthermore, a semantic approach is of no help in article use that is fixed or idiomatic. Nearly half the uses in our data were of this type. Teachers need to help learners to identify these uses and encourage them to absorb them as item-learnt chunks.

Second, there is an uncertain relationship between frequency of occurrence and ease of learning (or order of acquisition). In the case of articles, it is clear that uses of the definite article considerably outnumber uses of the indefinite. This may or may not account for the fact that both first and second language learners appear to develop accuracy with *the* earlier than they do with *a*. Another reason may be that the one form–function relationship learners do seem to be able to make is that between *the* and the identifiability of a specific referent. Teachers need to understand, however, particularly in spoken language, the wide range of pragmatic conditions under which the shared knowledge assumed by the participants renders a referent identifiable. The concept of first/second mention is almost certainly too simplified and unrepresentative to be helpful here.

Thirdly, although, as Celce-Murcia and Hilles put it (1988: 4), 'the jury is still out' on the effect of formal instruction on the acquisition of grammatical items, there does seem to be some evidence that the article system, in particular indefinite *a*, is amongst the most resistant to instruction. One major problem with the evidence is the interpretation of the term 'formal instruction'. To some it may mean overt teaching, i.e. 'the teacher actually provides the students with grammatical rules and explanations' (Harmer, 1987: 4). To others it may constitute or include covert teaching, i.e. the grammatical control of input texts and student practice without drawing the students' 'conscious attention to the grammatical facts of the language' (Harmer, 1987: 3). In either case, the development of a learner's grasp of the article system seems as good an example as any of what Rutherford (1987: 40) refers to as 'gradual grammaticization' and of a process 'that does not necessarily apply uniformly to all grammatical features of the same rank'. Long and Crookes (1992: 31) support this view:

> When plural *s*, articles, third-person singular *s*, and other morphemes first appear, they tend to do so variably and on certain words or word classes first . . . they are not suddenly supplied correctly across all appropriate nouns and verbs . . . despite teachers' and text-book writers' best instructional efforts.

Fourthly, the general thrust of second language acquisition research suggests that naturalistic and classroom learners of all language backgrounds tend to pass through similar developmental sequences in their acquisition of certain grammatical items. However, it seems intuitively right to predict that, at least in the area of article acquisition, some differences will be observed between learners whose L1 has a comparable article system and those whose L1 does not.

In conclusion, it is our view that a fundamental implication of all current language acquisition research is that teachers would be wise to remain sceptical of the long-term effects of any kind of formal instruction on the grammatical development of their learners.

References

Alexander, L.G. 1988, *Longman English Grammar*, Longman, Harlow.
Beattie, G. 1983, *Talk: An Analysis of Speech and Non-Verbal Behaviour in Conversation*, Open University Press, Milton Keynes.
Berry, R. 1991, 'Re-articulating the articles', *English Language Teaching Journal*, vol. 45, no. 3, 252–9.
Brown, R. 1973, *A First Language*, Allen & Unwin, London.
Celce-Murcia, M. and Hilles, S. 1988, *Techniques and Resources in Teaching Grammar*, OUP, Oxford.
Chalker, S. 1984, *Current English Grammar*, Macmillan, London.
Christophersen P. 1939, *The Articles: a Study of their Theory and Use in English*, Munksgaard, Copenhagen.
DuBois, J.W. 1980, 'Beyond definiteness: the trace of identity in discourse', in Chafe, W. (ed.), *The Pear Stories: Cultural, Cognitive and Linguistic Aspects of Narrative Production*, Ablex, Norwood, NJ.

Ellis, R. 1984, 'Can syntax be taught? A study of the effects of formal instruction on the acquisition of WH questions by children', *Applied Linguistics*, vol. 5, 138–55.

Emslie, H.C. and Stevenson, R.J. 1981, 'Pre-school children's use of the articles in definite and indefinite referring expressions', *Journal of Child Language*, vol. 8, 313–28.

French, F.G. 1949, *Common Errors in English*, OUP, London.

Gallaway, C. 1987, *The emergence of* a *and* the, unpublished Ph.D thesis, University of Lancaster.

George, H.V. 1972, *Common Errors in Language Learning: Insights from English*, Newbury House, Rowley, Mass.

Givón, T. 1978, 'Definiteness and referentiality', in Greenberg, J.H. (ed.), *Universals of Human Language Volume 4: Syntax*, Stanford University Press, Stanford.

Grannis, O.C. 1972, 'The definite article conspiracy in English', *Language Learning*, vol. 22, no. 2, 275–89.

Grice, H. 1975, 'Logic and conversation', in Cole, P. and Morgan, J.L. (eds.), *Syntax and Semantics Volume 3: Speech Acts*, Academic Press, New York.

Harmer, J. 1987, *Teaching and Learning Grammar*, Longman, Harlow.

Hawkins, J.A. 1978, *Definiteness and Indefiniteness*, Croom Helm, London.

Hawkins, J.A. 1980, 'On surface definite articles in English', in van der Auwera, J. (ed.), *The Semantics of D^terminers*, Croom Helm, London.

Karmiloff-Smith, A. 1979, *A Functional Approach to Child Language: a Study of Determiners and Reference*, CUP, Cambridge.

Karttunen, L. 1968, *What Makes Noun Phrases Definite?*, Report p. 3871, The Rand Corporation, Santa Monica.

Lindstromberg, S. 1986, 'Guidelines for teaching the English article system', *Cross Currents*, vol. 13, no. 1, 31–41.

Long, M.H. and Crookes, G. 1992, 'Three approaches to task-based syllabus design', *TESOL Quarterly*, vol. 26, no. 1, 27–56.

Maratsos, M. 1976, *The Use of Definite and Indefinite Reference in Young Children*, CUP, Cambridge.

Master, P. 1990, 'Teaching the English articles as a binary system', *TESOL Quarterly*, vol. 24, no. 3, 461–78.

McEldowney, P.L. 1977, 'A teaching grammar of the English article system', *International Review of Applied Linguistics*, vol. 15, no. 2, 95–112.

Parrish, B. 1987, 'A new look at methodologies in the study of article acquisition for learners of ESL', *Language Learning*, vol. 37, no. 3, 361–83.

Pawley, A. and Syder, F.H. 1983, 'Two puzzles for linguistic theory: native-like selection and native-like fluency', in Richards, J.C. and Schmidt, R.W. (eds.), *Language and Communication*, Longman, Harlow.

Pica, T. 1983, 'The article in American English: what the textbooks don't tell us', in Wolfson, N. and Judd, E. (eds.), *Sociolinguistics and Language Acquisition*, Newbury House, Rowley, Mass.

Pica, T. 1985, 'The selective impact of classroom instruction on second-language acquisition', *Applied Linguistics*, vol. 6, no. 3, 214–22.

Quirk, R., Greenbaum, S., Leech, G. and Svartvik, J. 1985, *A Comprehensive Grammar of the English Language*, Longman, Harlow.

Rutherford, W.E. 1987, *Second Language Grammar: Learning and Teaching*, Longman, Harlow.

Stevick, E.W. 1990, *Humanism in Language Teaching*, OUP, Oxford.

Tarone, E. 1985, 'Variability in interlanguage use: a study of style-shifting in morphology and syntax', *Language Learning*, vol. 35, 373–404.

Tarone, E. and Parrish, B. 1988, 'Task-related variation in interlanguage: the case of articles', *Language Learning*, vol. 38, no. 1, 21–44.

Thomas, M. 1989, 'The acquisition of English articles by first- and second-language learners', *Applied Psycholinguistics*, vol. 10, no. 3, 335–55.

Warden, D.A. 1976, 'The influence of context on children's uses of identifying expressions and references', *British Journal of Psychology*, vol. 67, 101–12.

Warden, D.A. 1981, 'Learning to identify referents', *British Journal of Psychology*, vol. 72, 93–9.

Whitman, R.L. 1974, 'Teaching the article in English', *TESOL Quarterly*, vol. 8, no. 3, 253–62.

Widdowson, H.G. 1984, 'The incentive value of theory in teacher education', *English Language Teaching Journal*, vol. 38, no. 2, 86–90.

Second Language Acquisition Strategies, Interlanguage Development and Task-based Learning

PETER SKEHAN

1. Introduction

Developments in early second language acquisition research have called into question the place of grammar in language teaching. They suggest that direct grammar teaching is, at best, futile, and at worst, even harmful, since such teaching has minor impact in face of more powerful naturalistic processes. More recent developments suggest that grammar still has a role to play in language teaching, but not in a direct manner. Instead, it needs to underlie the syllabuses and method-ologies that are used, so that it provides an organising framework while other goals are simultaneously pursued to ensure balanced development. This article sets out how such a role for grammar, within the context of task-based learning, can be most effectively conceptualised.

2. Strategies in language development

Comprehension-driven learning

Krashen, as is well known, has proposed the comprehensible input hypothesis (Krashen, 1985). He claims that ideal input for language learning, i.e. the sort of input which is most likely to drive the learner's interlanguage forward, is that input which is (a) just beyond the learner's current level of linguistic development, and (b) comprehensible nonetheless because its meaning can be inferred from the context in which it occurs. In this way the input acts as commentary on what is already understood, and so its form can be focused on. The learner is provided with a maximally helpful form–meaning pairing which is most likely to have an impact on the developing interlanguage system. In addition to this general justification for the role of input, Krashen has drawn attention to the supporting evidence provided by the success of comprehension-driven methodologies, in general, and immersion education, in particular. This is because immersion education, which provides ample comprehensible input, has been shown to be significantly more effective than conventional 'drip-feed' approaches to language instruction (Swain and Lapkin, 1982).

The arguments against the comprehensible input hypothesis – and the monitor model – (McLaughlin, 1987; White, 1987; Gregg, 1984) are well known, and will not be repeated in detail here. Two general criticisms only will be made. First, the immersion case, on further examination, has been shown to be not as supportive as Krashen originally claimed. Swain (1985) has shown that immersion-educated children do indeed attain high levels of *comprehension* performance, equivalent, in fact, to that attained by native-speaker children of comparable age (a remarkable feat in itself). However, the children do not attain the same level *productively*. They do not attain the same speaking levels, that is, as they do in comprehension, casting considerable doubt on the original and central claim that comprehensible input is the driving force for language development, and that gains achieved in comprehension are transferred to the developing interlanguage system and thence to production.

This lack of transfer can be understood readily if we turn to a second point and ask how comprehension proceeds under natural circumstances. Studies of native-speaker comprehension suggest that language users do not rely on a deterministic, linguistic model when they are comprehending, but instead are more likely to use comprehension strategies (Clark and Clark, 1977). Micro-strategies operate when, during comprehension, language users make guesses about the probable structure of what they are hearing based on syntactic clues, e.g. when you hear a definite article, start a new constituent; or semantic cues, e.g. try to guess the meanings of sentences using the (more heavily stressed) contact words alone (Clark and Clark, 1977). In each case, the user cannot be certain that the processing strategy is appropriate, but it *probably* will be, and so will be worth using habitually because the greater processing ease will usually outweigh the risk of being wrong. One can also look at comprehension from a macro-level, where users can draw upon a wide range of knowledge sources, in addition to the linguistic, to extract meaning from what is said to them. Anderson and Lynch (1987), for example, discuss the way comprehension is achieved by listeners drawing on background and schematic knowledge, and on contextual knowledge (both textual and situational), as well as linguistic knowledge. In this way, the language user once more risks being wrong in the meaning that is constructed from incoming sound, but, most importantly, he or she is able to handle the pressure of dealing with messages in real time, an issue we will return to later.

So we see that while the comprehensible input approach assumes that input is processed in linguistic ways which facilitate development of the underlying inter-language system, there are actually clear reasons why language users may by-pass an approach to comprehension which requires them to do this (even though they could use the approach if they wanted). Users, instead, are concerned with extracting meaning in real time, and may achieve this without using interlanguage-stretching approaches to language processing.

The role of interaction in interlanguage development

Following this analysis, it is not surprising (in retrospect) that the immersion studies have not turned out to be as supportive as was originally hoped, and that the lack of comprehension–production transfer was shown to be so important. Swain, the researcher who has done most to evaluate immersion education, has proposed (Swain, 1985) that one needs to discuss not just comprehensible input, but also comprehensible *output*. She suggests that output has an essential role in the development of language proficiency. More specifically, and drawing on her detailed analysis, one can propose the following reasons for the importance of output in learning:

- to generate better input
- to force learners into a more syntactic processing mode
- to enable learners to test hypotheses
- to develop automaticity
- to develop discourse skills
- to develop a personal voice.

The first of these, to generate better input, concerns the way in which appropriate level input is obtained. Long (1985) suggests that learners negotiate their way to such input, i.e. output indicates lack of comprehension, and leads interlocutors to provide more finely tuned and useful input. The second function for output is also connected to input. Knowing that they must produce language later may 'force' learners into a more syntactic mode while they are listening, because they know that focusing on meaning extraction during listening will not be enough to enable them to convey meanings themselves. It is as if the thought of having to speak in the future will predispose them to notice how the meaning is conveyed as a better preparation for subsequent speaking.

The remaining reasons for the significance of output concern the role of output itself. Testing hypotheses is important because, in the context of older language learners, it is less likely that their interlocutors will spontaneously provide them with feedback about the incorrectness of their utterances. It may be more useful for such learners to take the initiative, and actively try out syntactic and morphological patterns that they are unsure of and then look for feedback (e.g. incomprehension, rephrasing) to statements that they have made. This will allow them to get indirectly expressed information which will help them to work out how successful they have been in constructing an acceptable interlanguage system.

Output is also important in areas other than language structure. It is important to give learners opportunity to develop fluency, and to be able to produce integrated performance in real time when difficult planning decisions may be involved (articulatory as well as with syntax and the expression of meanings). Output is important also to enable learners to acquire discourse skills, such as conversation management, the use of repair strategies and skill in negotiating meaning. Finally, output is important to enable learners to develop a personal voice, to learn how to say things that are important to them, rather than to be dependent on what has been said to them by others.

The role of communication strategies

So one might evaluate the criticisms of comprehensible input based on Swain's work as suggesting that input has to be balanced judiciously with speaking activities, and that the construction of opportunities for interaction has a vital place in language teaching. In this view, the teacher's role would be one of combining the two skills, listening and speaking, in the most effective manner.

But we saw that one of the major problems for input providing a dynamic for change in the learner's interlanguage system was that a deterministic, syntax-oriented role for comprehension could be by-passed by the use of comprehension strategies. These strategies 'disengaged' the way in which comprehension, even though potentially useful, might impact upon the process of interlanguage change. It is important, therefore, to examine how strategies of *production* might have an impact on the value of speaking/interaction activities.

The study of communication strategies has been an active area for some time. Researchers such as Faerch and Kasper (1983), Tarone (1977), and Bialystok (1990) have investigated the ways in which such strategies operate within a language-processing system, and how they may be classified. Faerch and Kasper (1983) distinguish between achievement and avoidance strategies. The former require the extension of existing resources to enable the original communicative intention to be expressed, while the latter accept the lack of necessary resources and the modification of the intended message. Bialystok (1990) has discussed communication strategies in terms of her psycholinguistic processing model, following Kellerman (1991) in distinguishing between linguistic and cognitive strategies.

So the operation of strategies has been shown to be extensive, and typical of what happens in communicative language situations. Not surprisingly, therefore, they have also had an impact on models of communicative competence that have been proposed. Canale and Swain (1980) proposed that communicative competence has three components, linguistic competence, sociolinguistic competence *and strategic competence*. Bachman (1990) has put forward an extended and revised version of this model, reorganising the interrelationships of component competences. He proposes that they have the structure shown in Figure 1.

The components of language competence have been structured slightly differently here. Textual competence is seen as closer to linguistic competence, both being parts of organisational competence, while pragmatic competence is slightly broadened in scope. Most important for current purposes, strategic competence is seen as a more independent component, fulfilling a more integral function in the nature of language performance. It is seen, that is, as having a vital role in handling the problems when the other competences are lacking in some way, so that resourcefulness and improvising ability are called into play. It is also seen as having a vital role in the way language is related to the situation of language use.

Figure 1: Bachman's model of communicative competence

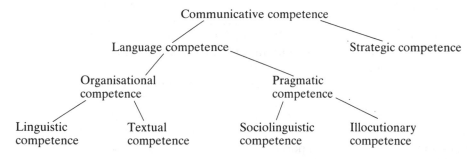

This characterisation of the structure of communicative competence is intended to capture the interrelationships of the different competences at a particular time, but it also implies structural relationships which have implications for the *growth* of language abilities, for we have to ask how the components of language competence change over time. Here, one plausible scenario is that it is the operation of strategic competence (for instance through the use of communication strategies such as Faerch and Kasper's achieving strategies) which is at the cutting edge for language development, and it is the use of such improvising competence to solve problems that constitutes a force for change in the underlying interlanguage. This 'beneficial' interpretation implies that we learn to talk by talking, a viewpoint consistent, at least in part, with the output-driven analysis presented by Swain (1985).

Unfortunately, there are reasons why this beneficial process might not be so certain to occur. For example, the communication strategies which have been studied (Paribakht, 1985; Faerch and Kasper, 1983; Tarone, 1977) seem frequently to involve lexical problems, or to involve simplification strategies. These get the job done, but have no obvious connection with how the underlying system is being driven forward. What is necessary is to link the actual operations involved in the use of strategic competence with the details of sustained language development. And here, it is not clear that dealing with a lexical gap problem connects in any consistent way with the sort of change in the language system which is productive and which might lead to cumulative progress. In contrast, it seems more likely that what may happen is that a solution to a communicative problem is remembered (Schmidt and Frota, 1986), even though the solution does not necessarily contain a system-improving quality. Its success is enough to make it more likely that the 'solution' will be retained and re-used.

There is also the problem, in terms of communication leading to interlanguage development, that the nature of effective native-speaker to native-speaker communication may not be as centrally syntactic and as system stretching as we would like (Faerch and Kasper, 1983). As with comprehension, when we produce language, we operate on a 'least effort' principle, which means that we often say only as much as is necessary to communicate. There is no obligation to be comprehensive or grammatical, only effective. Second language performers, in other words, may operate according to the Gricean maxims of communication, and attempt not to be long-winded! They are considerably aided in this by the way in which conversations involve participants in judging what their interlocutor knows and doesn't need to be told. The obligation on the speaker, in other words, is to add to the unfolding discourse in a way that continues to engage the interest of the interlocutor. And there is nothing which *requires* that conversations of this type should be ideal for the production of language which is interlanguage stretching – they are required only to be effective.

There is some empirical support for the claim that the use of communication strategies compromises the automatic value of speaking activities for interlanguage development. Schmidt (1983) reports the case of Wes, a Japanese learner of English in Hawaii. Wes was studied over an extended period, and his progress in English was monitored in terms of the Canale and Swain model of communicative competence. During this period Wes progressed from an initial level in which he was not regarded as a worthwhile interlocutor at all, to a level at the end of the period investigated where he was accepted as worth talking to by native speakers. What was most interesting, though, is that during this period, when Wes's communicative competence was assessed in relation to the Canale and Swain model, it was revealed that his progress was mainly in terms of his strategic competence and, to a certain extent, discourse competence. His progress in the other domains was not very impressive at all, and his improvement in linguistic competence was negligible. So communicative effectiveness was achieved largely through the use of communication strategies, and this progress did not spill over into the other, more structural domains. Schmidt reports that Wes himself was quite aware of this state of affairs, and content with it, since it matched the goals that he had, which were more communicatively oriented than concerned with the language itself or its correctness. So 'unbalanced' language development was, in this case, associated with fossilisation and a plateaued linguistic competence, with the learner in question being aware of this, and happy with it, so that he did not try to redress the imbalance in his communicative competence in terms of the Canale and Swain model.

Additional evidence comes from research completed within the context of the Foreign Service Institute (FSI) language instruction programme. Higgs and Clifford (1982) report studies which tracked students longitudinally, assessing them in terms of analytic rating scales, including grammar, vocabulary, fluency, etc. They were able to show that learners who, at Level 2 in the FSI framework, were balanced in their analytic profile of skills, or whose grammar was at higher levels than vocabulary and fluency, continued to make progress and to reach significantly higher FSI levels. In contrast, students who at Level 2 had vocabulary and fluency scores which were strong relative to grammar, did not continue to make progress, and plateaued at Level 2 (more precisely at the 2+ level). These students, in other words, seemed to have made early gains in performance in such a way as to compromise later progress, and so seemed destined to become premature fossilisers.

We see, then, that there are dangers with both comprehension- and interaction-driven learning approaches which connect with the use of strategies. Although they hold out the promise of allowing second language acquisition processes to be capitalised upon naturalistically, they both encounter the problem that with mature language learners, there is the possibility that communicating meaning will predominate as an aim, and that learners will achieve this aim by using strategies which by-pass the underlying language system, so that they may not be driven to develop their interlanguage systems. In such cases, the grammar of the target language assumes secondary importance, since it is neither necessary for much communication nor drawn into prominence. Accessibility (and processing) take priority at the expense of analysability (and grammar). In view of this, it is next necessary to examine some alternative approaches to the nature of language, second language performance and learning which provide a better basis for understanding the nature of second language development.

3. Alternative perspectives

Language

Most linguistic analyses take as a starting point the position that their goal is to provide a powerful, parsimonious and elegant account of language, with these qualities being judged by the way in which the rule system proposed generates all and only the correct sentences of the language. The emphasis is on grammar and rules, and lexis is seen as having a subservient, 'fill-the-slot' position. A variety of such accounts has been proposed over the last sixty years or so, and many of them have been influential in language teaching, with many syllabus designers and textbook writers seeming to take the attitude that if something is worthy of description by a linguist, it must be relevant to the poor consumer – the language teaching professional. The assumption, what might be termed the 'linguistic fallacy', is that there is a straightforward relationship between how grammatical systems are described, and how they should be used practically.

Such approaches, then, downgrade the importance of vocabulary, of idiom, of collocation, etc. There have, though, been dissenters to this general view, who have preferred to emphasise precisely what more structurally oriented linguists typically sweep under the carpet as disordered, particular and unsystematisable – the functioning of lexis. Bolinger (1975), for example, proposes that rather than being subserved by a rule system, language is produced on the basis of a large, capacious and redundantly structured memory system. The user, in this view, operates with a more lexical unit of analysis, and achieves communication *in real time* not by the complexities of producing utterances on the basis of a rule system, constructing anew each time, but instead by drawing on ready-made elements and chunks. This avoids the loss of time spent in planning the internal organisation of utterances. Instead, larger units than the word or morpheme are accessed and used as wholes (Widdowson, 1989) as they have been on previous occasions. Language, then, is underpinned by a complex and very large memory system. The same words may be stored in different locations redundantly, since they will form parts of numerous different idiomatic structures. Then, when required, they will be used in performance, with the whole of the relevant unit accessed at once. The duplication in memory structure (as opposed to having one lexical entry per semantic unit) is justified because of the speed of performance that it enables, and takes account of the nature and potential of the underlying retrieval system.

This perspective has been extended by the work of Pawley and Syder (1983), who argue that native speakers achieve the fluency that they do by using an intrinsically improvisatory approach to planning. They produce utterances, Pawley and Syder suggest, by starting with 'lexicalised sentence stems', i.e. chunks, which then become the starting point for improvisations. The speaker, in other words, has not planned the complete utterance at the time when he or she starts to speak. Instead, the speaker embarks upon an utterance, confident that it will be possible to stitch together chunks which will communicate the intended meanings. The utterances may, retrospectively, be analysable. But the speaker's great achievement is to select chunks which combine in such a way that meanings are expressed by acceptable syntactic means.

The implications are that (a) much of the communication is achieved by lexical means, consistent with the claims made by Bolinger (1975), and (b) there are sufficient permissible structural alternatives to enable speakers to proceed in this rather improvisatory manner, without being 'burned' too often by encountering insoluble problems. As a result, speaking in real time and keeping up with the general speed of conversations is given priority over composing more polished and creative utterances. In other words, it is important to distinguish between the *analyst's model*, as represented in the work of many linguists, and the *user's model*, which may have more direct connections with psychological processing of language. The former assumes that the grammatical categories of the linguist can be directly applied to performance, while the latter places such categories within a wider set of influences. Grammatical units, that is, may not be the basis for language processing.

Second language performance

These analyses of what are essentially native-speaker performances connect with research which has been done on second language speaking and which examines the influence of performance conditions on various grammatical systems. Three relevant studies will be reviewed here. First of all, Ellis (1987) investigated the performance of learners on three related tasks, focusing on the use of the different forms of the past tense. In Task 1, learners had to write a story from a picture series. In Task 2, the same learners had to speak a story from the same series of pictures. In Task 3 learners had to speak a story from a new set of pictures. Ellis proposed that the three tasks provided learners with progressively less planning time. He was interested in the performance of the learners on three forms of the simple past tense (which was produced with reasonable frequency, given the way the study was conducted). The three forms were the regular past, the irregular past, and the past of the copula *be*.

Ellis's results demonstrated that average performance across all three past tense morphemes progressively declined. This result is consistent with much research conducted with native speakers within a sociolinguistic framework which links attention to speech to accuracy of performance (e.g. Labov, 1970). In that respect, the Ellis result contains nothing new. But what is more remarkable is the picture that emerges when one looks at the three past tense morphemes singly as a function of the three tasks. Here the most interesting finding is that performance on the regular and irregular past tense forms differs markedly. The regular past is severely affected by task conditions, declining in accuracy from 77 per cent (Task 1), to 57 per cent (Task 2), to 43 per cent (Task 3). In contrast, performance on the irregular past hardly declines at all. The comparable figures are 60, 57 and 55 per cent.

So we see that task and performance conditions influence two past tense morphemes quite differently. The regular past is susceptible to clear influence by the task conditions involved, while the irregular past is impervious to them. Ellis proposes that the reason for this difference is that the irregular past draws upon a lexical basis for its production; i.e. the different irregular past tense forms are, in effect, integrated, self-standing lexical units which are either known or not known. The regular past, in contrast, is constructed morphologically, on a rule basis, and so requires some available on-line processing capacity. Consequently, when planning time is reduced, as is the case when one moves from Task 1 to Task 3, the on-line processing capacity is less available, and accuracy decreases. Since the lexical basis for the irregular past does not require this processing 'overhead', it emerges practically unscathed. This leads to the conclusion that manipulation of task conditions affects planning time, which in turn influences the balance between lexical and syntactic performance.

The Ellis study has been extended on a longitudinal basis by Underwood (1990). Underwood used the same basic experimental design as Ellis but, in addition, he obtained data at two points in time, at the beginning and end of a 100-hour course of intensive instruction at the proficiency level where students are taught the use of the past tense. In this way he was able to calculate gain scores for each cell of a 3 by 3 matrix (i.e. three task conditions by the three past tense morphemes). Underwood discovered that the 'gain score' matrix, reflecting change after 100 hours of instruction, actually showed some decrements in performance, and these, too, involved an interaction between task conditions and morpheme. In particular, although the regular past improved in accuracy level on Task 1, it decreased on Tasks 2 and 3. In other words, instruction seemed to be harmful! It is more likely, however, that what was happening was an example of what Kellerman (1985) has termed U-shaped growth, i.e. in a process of restructuring, what appears to be retrogression is a necessary step backwards while a newer, and ultimately more robust and effective, system is being constructed. Again, the implication is that task conditions can affect the balance between syntactic and lexical processing, but that, this time, there is a longitudinal, learning dimension to add in to the equation.

The final study to be covered here is that of Crookes (1989). Crookes was also interested in the issue of planning time, but from a slightly different perspective. He asked subjects to respond to information-gap tasks by producing some connected speech. In one condition the subjects had no time to plan what they would say while in the other the subjects were given ten minutes to plan their talk. Unlike Ellis, Crookes found that the subjects who operated under the planned condition did not produce language which was any more accurate. On the other hand, they did produce a wider variety of lexis and syntax. He interprets this result to imply that subjects can use planning time to take risks and to incorporate more ambitious language in what they want to say.

The two research designs, that of Ellis and that of Crookes, differ in a number of ways. Ellis (and Underwood) used a design which focused upon one area of syntax, and then investigated what they termed 'planned discourse', but which might also be considered to be monitored language. They then found an accuracy effect. Crookes used a design which did not really cue any one area of syntax in such a constrained way, and he manipulated things so that the planning was done prior to the actual language production. He found no accuracy effect, but one indicating that planning time does have an impact on the complexity and riskiness of language production. The two research designs have in common, therefore, a demonstration of the importance of planning, and of how performance factors may have an important effect on the language which is produced. They also hint that it may be possible to predict systematic influences of performance conditions on the nature of the language used, an issue we will return to in the final section on pedagogy.

Learning

Ellis and Crookes are demonstrating that there is variation in language use *at a given time*. This connects with Widdowson's claim (1979) that variation at a point in time is the precursor of change *over time*. In other words, the variation that exists at one time is the basis for, or at least contains clues for, the process of learning and interlanguage change. Variation, particularly variation influenced by performance conditions, suggests ways in which a balance needs to be struck between the pressures of using a language, on the one hand, and the pressures connected with learning by restructuring interlanguage, on the other. The former has an emphasis on communication, and away from grammar, while the latter brings the form of language, and grammatical development, into clearer focus. The former sees performance conditions producing variability, while the latter leads to more emphasis on the prescriptive norms of grammar.

Within this section on alternative perspectives, it was first claimed that language itself is more memory-based and idiomatic in nature and use than is often realised. Then, in relation to second language performance, it was proposed that there is something of a trade-off between fluency (and real-time pressures), on the one hand, and accuracy (and possibly restructuring processes), on the other. In other words, there seemed to be a balance in second language performance between a lexical mode and a morphological–syntactic mode.

These new perspectives can be linked with more syntactic views if one proposes three stages that are involved in language learning. These are:

lexicalisation
|
syntacticisation
|
relexicalisation

Let us look initially at first language development. It has been proposed (Peters, 1983) that early development is primarily lexical, with young children being less interested in the structure of their utterances, and more interested in expressing meanings directly through lexical elements. These may not correspond to adult words, because the unit of analysis the child uses is not the word but the prefabricated chunk. Subsequently, the child imposes structural analyses on these lexicalised units, as the operation of universal grammar has material to operate upon, and then the child is able to develop the creativity and rule-governed system that many linguists have described. However, this approach to learning language has the disadvantage that it does not equip the child to handle the speed of real-time communication. Consequently, at a later stage, the child learns to by-pass the syntactic mode of communication (creative, flexible, but laborious in terms of information-processing demands) and develops an alternative, and parallel, lexicalised mode (following the analysis of Bolinger's and Pawley and Syder's work; see above under 'Language'). At this time, therefore, the child is *re*lexicalising language units so that they may be combined more quickly during language production. This, then, becomes the default mode of communication unless it encounters problems. In such case the child can 'shift gear' to a more syntactic mode, pay the processing penalties, but use a more principled and syntactic mode of communication.

When we turn to second language acquisition, the situation is similar in terms of general stages (lexicalisation – syntacticisation – relexicalisation), but there are also differences. In terms of the similarities, one might consider the ideal path for second language acquisition to be very similar. Opportunities for lexicalised communication might first be available; followed by a process of operating syntactically on this lexical base, to allow accurate and varied but halting communication; followed finally by the relexicalisation phase where the second language acquirer would produce accurate, native-like and fluent speech. In this respect, the second language learner would be responding to the two pressures identified by Widdowson (1989): analysability (the structural, syntactic phase) and accessibility (the relexicalisation phase). One might also portray the progress of the second language learner in terms of a productive tension between synthesis and analysis. The analytic tendency will operate to preserve openness and capacity for change during the learning process; the synthetic tendency will be to integrate what has just been restructured into more fluent performance.

This view makes it easy to see how second language learners can operate differently in different parts of the language system. In some areas the process of analysis will predominate, as new problems are grappled with. In others, synthesis will predominate: structural insights have occurred, a subsystem of language will have been restructured, but the current task will be to reintegrate this achievement into a wider system so that fluent performance can result. The learner, then, is constantly having to handle the ways in which these different tensions can co-exist, and actual language use nonetheless take place. It may also be possible that what appeared to be ripe for synthesis one day will give way to analysis the next, as the learner is confronted with new insights which demonstrate that an earlier acceptance of the completion of a process of analysis of one subsystem was premature.

First language acquisition, despite using untrained instructors (usually mothers), is associated with near-universal success. Second language learning, even when involving trained teachers, is not (d'Anglejan, 1978). So any attempt to account for second language learning has to explain both success and failure, with the emphasis, unfortunately, often being on the latter. We have already reviewed some of the factors which influence the failure, i.e. the use of comprehension and communication strategies. These have in common the way they remove syntactic pressure for change from the process of language learning, and serve the more pressing need of meaning extraction and expression instead. The emphasis is on the negotiation of meaning concisely and efficiently. As a result, the motive force for change and for restructuring of the interlanguage system is attenuated. We have also seen that performance factors can emphasise a more lexical form of communication amongst second language learners, with pressure for communication causing learners to use reliably what has a more lexical basis.

In themselves, these tendencies in second language learning amongst more mature learners would already account, to some degree, for the way in which fossilisation occurs, for the way in which learners do not straightforwardly improve until they reach native-speaker competence. But it is also important to look at the situational contexts in which languages are learned and identify factors which predispose fossilisation and lack of interlanguage development. For example, very naturalistic learning circumstances where there is a lot of pressure to communicate meanings may well have this effect. Wes would be a good example of this (linked to learner predispositions also). In such cases, it is likely that, in terms of the three-stage model outlined earlier, the learner does not progress beyond the initial lexicalisation stage, but with the qualification that considerable communicative effectiveness is achieved.

There is an alternative scenario where a formal learning situation effectively by-passes the initial possible lexical stage, in the (educational) belief that mature learners can start directly from a syntactic level. Here, possibly, continued development could occur. But it is possible that if the pedagogic, syntactic goals are emphasised, the final process of relexicalisation will not take place. The goal of the learning may then become implicitly only syntactic, preventing the learner from aspiring to native-like fluency, impeding the memory-based performance that would be required to handle the second language effectively in real time.

In effect, these contrasting outcomes indicate that SLA has to consider the goals that are appropriate for different learners and for different learning situations. In the case where instruction is lacking, exemplified by Wes, it may be that achieving communicative effectiveness through strategic competence is satisfactory for the learner. It was for Wes, apparently (Schmidt, 1983), and to impose syntax on him would have been a negation of his right to choose how he wanted to approach language learning. In more formal learning settings, it may well be that the relexicalisation stage, desirable as it may be, is unattainable given the constraints which operate. It might be better to accept as a goal the syntacticisation stage, and provide learners with a basis for communication which will not allow them to be considered native-like, but which will be a practical basis for expressing their meanings, a level of competence which would be better than none at all (Cook, personal communication).

4. Pedagogy

The two positions just described are extreme in their contrast. Most of the time it will be the purpose of teaching to try to realise simultaneously goals which have some degree of mutual tension. In this respect we have seen that the major tensions are between restructuring, accuracy and fluency, with the way these respective goals are handled having a critical influence on the tension between synthesis and analysis. Excessive priority given to analysis will compromise the process of synthesis and the acquisition of a memory-based fluency in performance. Too much emphasis on synthesis may well detract from the learner's ability to be accurate and restructure. It will produce learners who are fluent communicators but who are not sensitive to the need to develop their control of the grammatical system (restructuring) or to the need to conform to its rules and conventions (accuracy). Against the background of these problems, this final section will examine different ways in which a balance can be attained between the various goals in language learning. It will examine, in turn, the roles of individual differences, instruction, syllabus and methodology.

Individual differences

So far in this discussion, all learners have been considered to be the same, and other factors, whether situational or instructional, have been seen as having the most decisive influence on language development. But there is considerable evidence that individual differences exert a strong influence upon language learning success (Skehan, 1989). More particularly, there is evidence that there are learner types who have systematic preferences for different modes of language development. For example, Skehan (1986), using the technique of cluster analysis, identified two types of learner, the memory-driven and the analysis-driven. The former preferred to treat language learning as a memory issue, while the latter were more drawn to the analytic potential of the course they were doing. Wesche (1981) was able to show, using a similar categorisation of learners, that matching learner type with appropriate methodology produced disproportionate success, while mismatching had the opposite effect.

Following this account, it would seem that analytic learners are those learners who are drawn, other things being equal, to emphasising the potential for analysis in learning situations, with memory-oriented learners having the opposite tendency. Referring back to the three-stage model proposed earlier (lexicalisation – syntacticisation – relexicalisation), the analytical learners would seem more likely to reach the syntacticisation stage even when confronted with naturalistic learning opportunities, or functionally-communicatively oriented language teaching materials. In each case, they are likely to look for and impose structure on the less structured situation, and independently make up for the lack of guidance in this area from the learning situation itself. In some ways, the ideal combination for learners whose natural predisposition is towards analysis would be informality of learning situation and the 'natural' pressure it would bring towards fluency, synthesis and integration. In contrast, memory-oriented learners might complement more analytic learning situations. Their tendency to treat language as chunks, and to emphasise fluency in communication would be balanced by the methodology, emphasising the structural organisation of language and making salient for them aspects of language organisation they would otherwise ignore. In each case, the issue would be the balance between the learner's predisposition towards learning, and the influences built into the learning situation. Of course, the ideal would be a methodology which adapted to the predispositions of each learner to provide appropriate instruction in each case. But where this is not possible, it is important to include learner predisposition when one is assessing what sort of balance is likely to be found between fluency, accuracy and restructuring.

Instruction

Attempts to demonstrate the value of instruction have often encountered difficulty, either when methodology comparisons are made or when attempts are made to substantiate the effectiveness of error correction. Two articles by Michael Long (1983, 1988) make the case for its effectiveness most strongly. First, he showed that instruction does make a difference (Long, 1983), leading to more progress than occurs when instruction is absent. More relevant for present purposes is a more recent study (Long, 1988) in which instruction is shown to be associated with higher ultimate attainment in language learning, faster progress and different types of error. This last effect is the most important for present purposes. Instructed learners (Pica, 1983; Lightbown, 1983) tend to make errors of commission, i.e. they over-use the forms which are the current focus of instruction. Uninstructed learners, in contrast, tend to make errors of omission, i.e. they simply do not use certain forms. For example, instructed learners might make mistakes with the definite article such that they use it when it is not necessary, while uninstructed learners tend not to use it when it is required.

Importantly, it is proposed (Long, 1988) that errors of commission are then more likely to approximate target language forms, by becoming less prevalent, while errors of omission are more likely to persist. It is more probable, that is, that learners will notice that they are doing something unnecessary, and even super-fluous, than that they will notice that they are not doing something. It is then more straightforward to stop doing something than to start doing something new.

In a sense we have a paradox here. Studies which attempt to find a direct influence for instruction (e.g. error correction studies) tend to be disappointing. In contrast, studies which take a more indirect approach are more likely to encounter success. The error type issue is a case in point. We have to *infer* how instruction exerts an effect such that it is associated with different types of error, even though explicit focus on errors does not have a direct influence.

One possible intepretation is that instruction has two general influences, neither of which is immediately apparent. First of all, it provides learners with new forms to think about, by focusing explicitly on one aspect of language structure at a time. When this occurs, instruction will make it more likely that some restructuring will occur, which otherwise would be less probable. It will also constitute an influence for the sort of over-use of new forms discussed by Long. So the first function of instruction is to make initial change more likely. But the second function of explicit teaching is that it serves to mark for learners that they have not succeeded in mastering the interlanguage system of the language that they are learning. This signalling of incompletion is important for learners since it is likely to preserve openness in the language system being developed, and it induces learners to persist at a difficult task.

But more relevant for the present discussion, it may be that the general effect of making pedagogic norms salient for learners also has an important effect on the balance between analysis and synthesis. By demonstrating to learners that there is more to be learned, by showing them that they have not finished the process of restructuring their language system, by inducing a more salient type of error, instruction is also exerting an influence to combat unbalanced memory-driven development. Learners are not easily allowed, that is, to forget about structure, when their tendency might be to concentrate on communication and meaning. In this way, instruction pre-emptively reduces the likelihood of inflexibility and fossil-isation in language development (Long, 1988).

Syllabus

In the previous section the characterisation of instruction was left deliberately vague, although by implication it was suggested that some grammar focus would be involved. More recently, approaches to instruction involving task-based learning have become more common (cf. discussion in White, 1988). As represented in the

Bangalore Project, for example, the underlying theory seems to be that development can only proceed by natural acquisitional mechanisms being engaged to drive
the grammatical system forward. Learners, that is, will engage in interaction, and
as a result their underlying language systems will develop. The goal of instruction
may be the same, i.e. the acquisition of a grammatical system (Prabhu, 1987), but
the means to achieve this will be much more process oriented.

The dangers of taking such an approach in unrestrained form should be clear
from the discussion in the previous sections. Requiring learners to engage in task-
based learning, if not balanced by other activities, may well lead to the use of
comprehension and communication strategies, and encourage a performance-
oriented approach to learning, with the result that fluency and synthesis are developed at the expense of accuracy and restructuring. Although it is proposed that
interaction will extend the grammatical system, the reality may be that the engagement of grammatical processes becomes 'unhooked' from communication, because
other resources and strategies, which have a more direct pay-off, are employed. As
a result, the grammatical system is by-passed, rather than extended or effectively
applied, and short-term communicative gain assumes greater importance than
longer-term grammatical development.

Clearly this negative evaluation of task-based learning assumes a worst case, to
the extent that it assumes there is:

- no counterbalancing influence of learner-analytic orientation
- no structure-oriented instruction
- little attention paid to task sequencing
- little attention paid to the methodology of implementing a task-based
  approach.

In the previous two sections, we discussed the general effects of learner orientation and explicit instruction, and how they may exert a moderating influence on
the analysis–synthesis balance. The present section will discuss issues arising out of
task sequencing, and the next section will discuss methodological issues.

The thrust of this entire article has been towards balance in the way second
language learning proceeds, and how this need for balance arises from the competing pressures for mature language users of meaning and structural orientations to
language. One assumes that the purpose of instruction is to make it more likely that
learning will proceed along the right path and with maximum speed. So attempts to
use a task-based approach to language teaching represent the hypotheses that this
interaction-driven perspective will achieve these goals. Yet we have seen that there
are dangers from taking an approach which may be predisposed to a lack of
balance. So the key with task-based learning is how to preserve a controlled
approach to language development and ensure that the acquisition of fluency is not
at the expense of development in structure.

Vital in this regard is the issue of how tasks are sequenced. It would seem likely
that if tasks are pitched at the right level of difficulty, and if they fit into a pedagogic

sequence, then there is more chance that they will drive forward more naturalistic acquisitional processes. In other words, they will discharge a mediating function between the competing pressures of restructuring, accuracy and fluency. On the one hand, they will provide opportunities for synthesis and the more interactive phases of language acquisition; on the other, they should provide some motivation in the learner towards analysis and towards a realisation, implicit or explicit, that attention to language will keep the developing interlanguage system open. The tasks, that is, must represent a worthwhile challenge for the language learner – not too difficult, so that achieving meaning at any cost predominates, and not too simple, in which case nothing is being learned or developed.

This clearly points to the importance of being able to assess task difficulty, and to decide what order tasks should come in. In this regard, Candlin (1987) proposed six features which may be used when tasks are sequenced. They are:

- cognitive load
- communicative stress
- particularity/generalisability
- code complexity and interpretive density
- content continuity
- process continuity

This list is extremely valuable, since it implies that there are six areas in which task variation occurs, potentially independently, and that these six areas may have an impact on the nature of processing and learning that take place when tasks are used.

The approach, however, has three main drawbacks. First, it does not make sufficient connection with research findings which exist, of the sort covered earlier in this article. Second, it is a list, and does not give any clear guidance on how the different elements interrelate or can be combined. Third, and related to the previous point, there is insufficient connection with theory to justify the categories used. As a result, ratings and judgements of task difficulty based upon it would not be very practical.

For that reason a modified scheme is presented here, which obviously is connected with Candlin's list, but which indicates internal organisation a little more clearly, connects with theory and practice and provides a more practical method of decision making about task difficulty. It contains the following elements:

Code complexity

- linguistic complexity and variety
- vocabulary load and variety
- redundancy
- density

Communicative stress

- time limits and time pressure
- speed of presentation
- number of participants
- length of texts used
- type of response
- opportunities to control interaction

Cognitive complexity

Cognitive processing

- information organisation
- amount of 'computation'
- clarity of information given
- sufficiency of information given
- information type

Cognitive familiarity

- familiarity of topic and its predictability
- familiarity of discourse genre
- ease of relationship to background knowledge
- familiarity of task

Of the three superordinate components in this framework, the first is connected with code features, the second with performance conditions, and the third with cognition, each of which has an important part to play in communication. Clearly the first, code complexity, is concerned with the difficulty of the formal language elements that are involved in a task. It is concerned with the actual target (i.e. restructuring and interlanguage development), and also has a task difficulty influence. How these two are related will depend on a range of factors, including the role of performance conditions and cognitive factors.

Communicative stress derives from the research on comprehension and communication strategies which indicated a predisposition to by-pass syntax in the service of achieving current processing of meaning. It concerns the way real-time pressures influence communication, and the extent to which learners are drawn into using language at a speed beyond the one at which they are comfortable. These factors also connect, therefore, with Ellis's work showing a connection between performance conditions and a syntax–lexis processing trade-off. So this area is concerned with *how* the task is transacted, rather than *what* is transacted.

The latter is more the concern of the final general area, cognitive complexity, the area which will be discussed most extensively here. Given that form and structural elements are used to express meanings, the concern here is with how much mental activity is involved in the construction of the underlying meanings that need to be expressed, with the basic idea that the more attention is required in this domain, the less attention can be devoted to the formal elements of the message. In other words, we need to consider how cognitive (and code and performance) demands operate within the context of a limited-capacity information-processing system (Schmidt, 1990; Skehan, forthcoming) where attention paid to one aspect of processing may be at the expense of what can be used elsewhere.

Within this general heading of cognition, two sub-areas are identified. The first of these, cognitive processing, concerns 'on-line' computation, i.e. the extent to which active thinking about new material is involved in doing a task. Imagine learners confronted by one of the tasks from the Cobuild Course, Book 1 (Willis and Willis, 1988):

> Peter, Mary, and John all went away last weekend. One of them went to Birmingham, one to Manchester, and one to London. One of them went to the theatre, one went to see a relative, and one went to buy a computer.
> Who did what?
> <u>Clues</u>: One of them went to London to visit her mother. John bought a computer, but not in Manchester.
> Can you explain how you did the puzzle?

In order to work out the answer to this problem, learners have to think actively, and use language to do so. Above all, they have to reason logically to follow up the consequences of certain proposed solutions. The result is that a considerable amount of attentional resources is devoted to thinking and so is diverted from availability to handle language, either for accuracy or to incorporate new forms.

In contrast, cognitive familiarity concerns how easily a task can be completed by drawing on no more than existing schematic knowledge. Whereas cognitive load concerns the situation when a ready-made solution to a task is not available, cognitive familiarity emphasises the way in which a new task can be solved by using a 'canned' solution. The task may directly use information stored in long-term memory, or it may recall information in long-term memory which can then be adapted to the solution of the current problem.

An example in this area (at a lower level of proficiency) would be another Cobuild Book 1 task: 'In pairs, find out one another's family trees.' In this case, the task requires the participants simply to retrieve discrete and simple items of information from long-term memory which are then used in the transaction of the task. Learners will know (one assumes) the nature of their family trees and so, when questioned by the other member of the pair, will be able to plug this knowledge into the discourse with minimal use of cognitive resources, and with maximum opportunity to devote attention to other things, principally language form.

We see, then, that different task designs will place different processing loads on learners. The greater the cognitive load, the smaller the attention left over for planning in general, and attention to form in particular. This processing burden can be mediated, to some extent, by the way the task designer manipulates the operation of communicative stress features. So the role of the task designer/task selector is to make effective judgements about the balancing of the pressures that come from these different task components. The task designer and task participants may need to explore different ways of 'creating time', so that learners can find a judicious balance between the restructuring, accuracy and fluency goals discussed earlier. Only if this is done can task sequencing lead to the balanced interlanguage development that is desirable.

This discussion, it is clear, is largely speculative, and the analytic frame for assessing task difficulty is clearly a set of hypotheses, the internal organisation and composition of which need research to validate it. It attempts to make clear theoretical and empirical justifications, as they have influenced the construction of the framework. But it is important that the validating research is done. We need, for example, to clarify the respective roles of communicative stress and cognition. In the Ellis study, for example, where there was a decrease in accuracy of past tense use as one moved from Task 1 to Task 3, one can ask what the relative importance was of communicative stress (i.e. writing tasks being less pressured than speaking tasks), or cognitive complexity (i.e. the opportunity to plan, and therefore draw upon more organised ideas as the tasks proceeded). (See Crookes, 1989, for discussion of this point.) We also need to explore, within each general category, which aspects of task design are most influential (Crookes, 1986). Is it, for example, simply time pressure within communicative stress? Or should one also attach great importance to the number of participants (Brown and Yule, 1983)? Similarly, one wonders about the relative importance of cognitive processing versus cognitive familiarity factors. Are they equally important? Do they interact in significant ways?

Clearly research is needed to demonstrate which of these factors is important. Doubtless, such research would demonstrate that some of the hypothesised influences have only a weak impact. But for the moment, the framework is proposed as a starting point to solve what has been identified as a pressing problem.

Methodology

But we can go beyond task-sequencing considerations, and also consider how a task-based approach to teaching can be implemented more or less effectively at the methodological level. Once again the issue is how to achieve balance between the competing requirements of restructuring, accuracy and fluency. This can be addressed either by manipulating the pedagogic sequence, methodologically, or by focusing on the manner in which tasks are done. The former goal is likely to be concerned with highlighting restructuring, accuracy or fluency, while the latter focuses more on how the competing pressures can be balanced in actual task performance. In this respect, one can distinguish between three phases in task-based work which each contain choices which the teacher may make.

Pre-emptive language work

First of all, we can consider the preparatory work the teacher can organise before a task itself is done. The extreme form of task-based learning uses a 'deep-end' strategy: learners have to transact tasks, and it is hoped that these interactions will drive forward the language system. However, it is also possible to consider tasks as the most important, indeed *the* organising principle in language teaching but not use a deep-end approach. One might, that is, predict the language that a task will require and pre-teach that language, in the hope that doing the actual task will allow learners to use that which has just been the focus of explicit instruction (Loschky and Bley-Vroman, 1990). Such use may then allow learners to integrate what is new into the larger interlanguage system that they already have. This would emphasise the need for restructuring and clarify, for the learner, what parts of his or her interlanguage system need to evolve or change. Such a teaching sequence may be difficult to achieve, since it requires fairly accurate prediction, or a dictatorial approach to the language that learners will use, rather than a spontaneous capacity to express meanings. Even so, it may be possible, and would be consistent with a consciousness-raising approach to language learning, in which the learner's attention is directed to formal features of language to maximise the chances that internalisation processes will be triggered.

It has been argued, in fact, that the methodological implementation of the Bangalore Project is consistent with this view. Brumfit (1984) and Greenwood (1985) both suggest that the pre-task activities which were completed prior to the task-based phase of the methodology contained a surrogate language teaching focus, and so prepared learners for the less structured situation to come. This interpretation, though, has been disputed by Prabhu himself (1987) who downplays the importance of the pre-task activities, and who claims that it was the tasks themselves which were all-important. Whatever the position in this specific situation, though, the more important point is that tasks could take their place in a wider teacher progression, and that learners in such circumstances would not come to them 'cold' but would have been prepared with relevant language, with the transaction of the task enabling the newly acquired language to be used communicatively and meaningfully.

Task-control approaches

The actual way in which a task is implemented can also lead to pedagogic alternatives. First of all, the task can be eased to reduce the cognitive burden on the learner and so, presumably, allow a greater capacity to attend to both meaning and means of expression. In terms of the task difficulty characteristics discussed in the previous section, this could be in relation to cognitive processing or to cognitive familiarity. In either case, the goal would be to provide learners with the opportunity to prepare themselves for the demand of the task. The simplest way in which this might be done is for the learners to practise the task, or elements from it, so that the task itself progressively draws upon more familiar elements.

But they could also make progress without practice. The study by Crookes (1989) is relevant in this regard, demonstrating that planning time is associated with a wider range of lexis and more varied syntax. The additional time available, in other words, had an impact on task performance. In this case, though, learners were simply given time to dispose of in their own ways. It would be interesting to explore whether there are systematic relationships between pre-task time of this sort and the type of activity that learners engage in during that time. They might be led, for example, to engage in linguistic planning, to 'foreground' relevant language. Alternatively, they might engage in cognitive preparation, focusing more on the organisation of the meanings they want to express. In either case, the assumption would be that one wants to go beyond an undifferentiated view of pre-task planning time, and to explore the specific impact of different activities on the nature of a restructuring–accuracy–fluency balance.

It is also possible to manipulate the communicative stress variable. On some occasions learners may be given more or, alternatively, less time to complete a task. This may be linked to modality changes, as in the Ellis study (1987), where the written version of the task enabled more time to be spent planning, monitoring and focusing on accuracy while the task was being done. Alternatively, time pressure may be controlled explicitly, with learners being told how quickly they have to perform.

'Retrospective' approaches to task implementation

Surprisingly, it is also important to consider the impact on doing a task of what happens afterwards. In this respect, two recent approaches to language teaching methodology have in common the fact that they build in a concern with a *post*-task public performance. It is likely that the learner's knowledge of what is still required may influence the nature of actual task performance.

The Cobuild Course (Willis and Willis, 1988) gives students tasks to do, following a version of the deep-end strategy. However, students know that, subsequent to doing the task privately in pairs or groups, they may be asked to do the same task as a public performance in front of other students. Similarly, the approach to project work used at the Bell School, Bath (Carter and Thomas, 1986) gives students considerable latitude in choosing what to do projects on, and how they will do the projects; but the students do have the constraint that there will be a product which 'records' the project, and which is likely to be public, in the shape of, for example, a videotape, which may be seen by others.

So in both cases the deep-end strategy is qualified by the way in which the potential 'anything goes' stage of first doing the task is influenced by the constraint of what is to come. In other words, both methodologies have neatly contrived to make learners think about more than one thing at a time. On the one hand, they can attend primarily to doing the task itself, at any one time. On the other, there is likely to be some concern with pedagogic norms and correctness because of the public performance and the greater attention to speech which is to come (Labov, 1970). In this way, a retrospective methodology for task-based learning achieves balance between the different forces within language development: it enables the acquisition of fluency, integration and synthesis without compromising the way in which restructuring may occur, and learners also attend to accuracy.

5. Summary and conclusions

There was a time when the goal of language teaching was seen as the inculcation of a grammatical system, and the methods available to achieve this were mainly teacher-centred. Now, the goals of language teaching are far more extensive than simply the learning of grammar, and the directive role of the teacher is widely questioned. This means that although grammar is central to the development of communicative competence and performance, the teaching/learning of grammar now has to be balanced by the teaching/learning of other domains, including the capacity to use language in real time, and to be context-sensitive and appropriate in language use. As a result, the scope for the successful direct and focused teaching of grammar must now be regarded as limited, and the challenge for pedagogy is to devise methods by which several goals can be achieved simultaneously, without one being at the expense of the others.

This article has tried to explore ways in which such a balanced language development can be achieved. We have seen that older language learners are (a) interested primarily in communication and (b) remarkably effective at conveying their meanings. This means that the potential ways in which the need to communicate will drive interlanguage change are severely qualified. In addition, a view of language and learning which recognises the importance of memory operations accounts for the way in which language users and learners by-pass syntax and use lexical strategies to enable them to keep up with communication in real time when constrained by a limited-capacity information-processing system. We then saw that a task-based approach to language teaching runs the risk of consolidating these pressures for lexicalised communication, and as a result will underplay the role of accuracy and of interlanguage restructuring.

When we turned to pedagogy, the position was advanced that instruction must achieve a balance between syntactic and lexical processing, to enable system change and correctness, on the one hand, and fluent language use, on the other. Four areas were discussed as relevant to achieving this. Individual differences in language learning mean that teaching should take account of the ways learners may have predispositions to processing language at some point on a syntax–lexis continuum, and should perhaps offset any undesirable processing predisposition on the part of the learner. Instruction, at a global level, makes salient pedagogic norms, and signals to learners that further restructuring of their interlanguage system is desirable; that is, it makes fossilisation less likely (Long, 1988). Even though its direct effects are not obvious at a general level, it works against excessively lexical approaches to language.

Turning to more specific intervention techniques, at a syllabus level task sequencing was identified as crucial if learners are to be presented with reasonable challenges which do not overload their processing capacities and push them into a fossilisation-prone lexical processing mode. A tentative framework for task sequencing was proposed, although this will have to be the basis for much future research. Finally, in terms of methodology, several proposals were made, assuming the use of task-based approaches which foster balance in language development. These included pre-task, while-task and post-task activities. Once again, the framework proposed, although of potential utility in making decisions about how to implement task-based methodologies, must be the focus for further research to explore the language development consequences of choosing different instructional procedures.

References

Anderson, A. and Lynch, T. 1987, *Listening*, OUP, Oxford.

Bachman, L. 1990, *Fundamental Considerations in Language Testing*, OUP, Oxford.

Bialystok, E. 1990, *Communication Strategies*, Blackwell, Oxford.

Bolinger, D. 1975, 'Meaning and memory', *Forum Linguisticum*, vol. 1, 2–14.

Brown, G. and Yule, G. 1983, *Teaching the Spoken Language*, CUP, Cambridge.

Brumfit, C.J. 1984, 'The Bangalore Procedural Syllabus', *English Language Teaching Journal*, vol. 38, 4.

Canale, M. and Swain, M. 1980, 'Theoretical bases of communicative approaches to second language teaching and testing', *Applied Linguistics*, vol. 1, 1–47.

Candlin, C. 1987, 'Towards task based language learning', in Candlin, C. and Murphy, D. (eds.), *Language Learning Tasks*, Prentice Hall, Englewood Cliffs, NJ.

Carter, G. and Thomas, H. 1986, '"Dear brown eyes": experiential learning and a task-based approach', *English Language Teaching Journal*, vol. 40, 196–204.

Clark, H.H. and Clark, E. 1977, *Psychology and Language, An Introduction to Psycholinguistics*, Harcourt, Brace, Jovanovich, New York.

Crookes, G. 1986. *Task classification: a cross-disciplinary review*, Technical report 4, University of Hawaii at Manoa.

Crookes, G. 1989, 'Planning and interlanguage variation', *Studies in Second Language Acquisition*, vol. 11, 367–83.

d'Anglejan, A. 1978, 'Language learning in and out of classrooms', in Richards, J.C. (ed.), *Understanding Second and Foreign Language Learning*, Newbury House, Rowley, Mass.

Ellis, R. 1987, 'Interlanguage variability in narrative discourse: style shifting in the use of the past tense', *Studies in Second Language Acquisition*, vol. 9, 12–20.

Faerch, C. and Kasper, G. 1983, *Strategies in Interlanguage Communication*, Longman, Harlow.

Greenwood, J. 1985, 'Bangalore revisited: a reluctant complaint', *English Language Teaching Journal*, vol. 39, 4.

Gregg, K. 1984, 'Krashen's monitor and Occam's razor', *Applied Linguistics*, vol. 5, 79–100.

Higgs, T. and Clifford, R. 1982, 'The push towards communication', in Higgs, T. (ed.), *Curriculum, Competence, and the Foreign Language Teacher*, National Textbook Co, Skokie, Ill.

Kellerman, E. 1985, 'If at first you do succeed', in Gass, S. and Madden, C. (eds.), *Input and Second Language Acquisition*, Newbury House, Rowley, Mass.

Kellerman, E. 1991, 'Compensatory strategies in second language research: a critique, a revision, and some (non) implications for the classroom', in Phillipson, R., Kellerman, E., Selinker, L., Sharwood Smith, M., and Swain, M. (eds.), *Foreign/Second Language Pedagogy Research: A Commemorative Volume for Claus Faerch*, Multilingual Matters, Clevedon.

Krashen, S.D. 1985, *The Input Hypothesis: Issues and Implications*, Longman, Harlow.

Labov, W. 1970, 'The study of language in its social context', *Studium Generale*, vol. 23, 30–87.

Lightbown, P. 1983, 'Exploring relationships between developmental and instructional sequences in L2 acquisition', in Seliger, H. and Long, M. (eds.), *Classroom Oriented Research in Second Language Acquisition*, Newbury House, Rowley, Mass.

Long, M. 1983, 'Does second language instruction make a difference: a review of the research', *TESOL Quarterly*, vol. 17, 359–82.

Long, M. 1985, 'Input and second language acquisition theory', in Gass, S. and Madden, C. (eds.), *Input in Second Language Acquisition*, Newbury House, Rowley, Mass.

Long, M. 1988, 'Instructed interlanguage development', in Beebe, L. (ed.), *Issues in Second Language Acquisition: Multiple Perspectives*, Newbury House, Rowley, Mass.

Loschky, L. and Bley-Vroman, R. 1990, 'Creating structure-based communication tasks for second language development', *University of Hawaii Working Papers in English as a Second Language*, vol. 9, no. 1, 161–212.

McLaughlin, B. 1987, *Theories of Second Language Learning*, Edward Arnold, London.

Paribakht, T. 1985, 'Strategic competence and language proficiency', *Applied Linguistics*, vol. 6, 132–46.

Pawley, A. and Syder, F. 1983, 'Two puzzles for linguistic theory: native-like selection and native-like fluency', in Richards, J.C. and Schmidt, R. (eds.), *Language and Communication*, Longman, Harlow.

Peters, A. 1983, *The Units of Language Acquisition*, CUP, Cambridge.

Pica, T. 1983, 'Adult acquisition of English as a second language under different conditions of exposure', *Language Learning*, vol. 33, 465–97.

Prabhu, N.S. 1987, *Second Language Pedagogy*, OUP, Oxford.

Schmidt, R. 1983, 'Interaction, acculturation, and the acquisition of communicative competence', in Wolfson, N. and Judd, E. (eds.), *Sociolinguistics and Second Language Acquisition*, Newbury House, Rowley, Mass.

Schmidt, R. 1990, 'The role of consciousness in second language learning', *Applied Linguistics*, vol. 11, 17–46.

Schmidt, R. and Frota, S. 1986, 'Developing basic conversational ability in a second language: a case study of an adult learner of Portuguese', in Day, R. (ed.), *Talking to Learn: Conversation in Second Language Acquisition*, Newbury House, Rowley, Mass.

Skehan, P. 1986, 'Cluster analysis and the identification of learner types', in Cook, V. (ed.), *Experimental Approaches to Second Language Acquisition*, Pergamon, Oxford.

Skehan, P. 1989, *Individual Differences in Second Language Learning*, Edward Arnold, London.

Skehan, P. (forthcoming), *Language Learners and Language Learning*.

Swain, M. 1985, 'Communicative competence: some roles of comprehensible input and comprehensible output in its development', in Gass, S. and Madden, C. (eds.), *Input in Second Language Acquisition*, Newbury House, Rowley, Mass.

Swain, M. and Lapkin, S. 1982, *Evaluating Bilingual Education: A Canadian Case Study*, Multilingual Matters, Clevedon.

Tarone, E. 1977, 'Conscious communication strategies in interlanguage', in Brown, H.D., Yorio, C.A., and Crymes, R.C. (eds.), *On TESOL '77*, TESOL, Washington, DC.

Underwood, M. 1990, *Task Related Variability in Past Tense Morphology: a Longitudinal Study*, unpublished MA dissertation, Institute of Education, University of London.

Wesche, M. 1981, 'Language aptitude measures in streaming, matching students with methods, and diagnosis of learning problems', in Diller, K.C. (ed.), *Individual Differences and Universals in Language Learning Aptitude*, Newbury House, Rowley, Mass.

White, L. 1987, 'Against comprehensible input: The Input Hypothesis and the development of second language competence', *Applied Linguistics*, vol. 8, 95–110.

White, R. 1988, *The ELT Curriculum*, Blackwell, Oxford.

Widdowson, H.G. 1979, 'The significance of simplification', in *Explorations in Applied Linguistics*, OUP, Oxford.

Widdowson, H.G. 1989, 'Knowledge of language and ability for use', *Applied Linguistics*, vol. 10, 2.

Willis, D. and Willis, J. 1988, *Cobuild Book 1*, Collins, London.

Section 4

GRAMMAR AND TEACHING

Explaining Grammar to its Learners

CARL JAMES

1. Explanation in linguistics and language teaching

Adequacy of grammars

Mention of explanation in language teaching calls to mind related notions in linguistics. Teachers are expected to explain. Grammars have to 'explicate' or be explicit. Teachers and grammars are evaluated on their ability to do these things: they are rated for 'adequacy'.

Chomsky (see Radford, 1988) proposed three levels of adequacy: observational, descriptive and explanatory. The first two are for grammars of particular languages and the third is for linguistic theories. It is strange that there is no suggestion of explanatory power being a requirement for a grammar, though perhaps this is because most theoretical linguists have no interest in language teaching. Explanatory power is a measure of theories of grammar, not grammars: in other words, explanation transcends the particular language one is explaining, drawing on more general notions. This article will suggest what those more general notions might be.

Observational adequacy

For *observational adequacy*, a grammar has to specify correctly 'which sentences are (and are not) syntactically, semantically, morphologically and phonologically well-formed in the language' (Radford, 1988: 28). A lot depends here on the meaning of 'specify', but on a minimalist interpretation it need mean no more than simply to mention, inventorise or exemplify. To exemplify the foreign language (FL) is the teacher's main task: doing this adequately means giving correct examples in revealing contexts, so that learners will be able to induce rules.

A slightly richer interpretation is the idea of the classroom as an acquisition-rich linguistic environment providing evidence of two sorts: positive, revealing which sentences do occur in the language, and negative, revealing which don't. Such a classroom will be presided over by a teacher who either is a native speaker of the FL or at least speaks the FL with native-speaker accuracy and fluency – we return to the contentious issue of 'native speakerism' below. He or she will be active and imaginative, well able to promote naturalistic, semantically rich, communicative immersion, with plenty of authentic spoken and written text for learners to interact with. But there will be no recourse to the sorts of grammatical formulations that we recognise as explanations.

Descriptive adequacy

A higher level of adequacy for a grammar is *descriptive adequacy*, which is achieved when the grammar has observational adequacy '*and also* properly describes the syntactic, semantic, morphological, and phonological structure . . . in such a way as to provide a principled account of the native speaker's intuition about this structure' (Radford, 1988). The two key terms here are 'native speaker's' and 'principled'. We shall address the former more closely presently, but we could just touch here on the issue of the relevance, to learners, of native speakers' intuitions. It is arguable that native speakers' mental grammars are irrelevant to learners, being beyond their reach, and that to make the FL grammar relevant and accessible to learners you have to provide them with the opportunity to see it from their own perspective. The requirement that the account be 'principled' is clarified by Littlewood (1975: 92), in terms of 'How it relates to other structures in the overall system'. In the teaching context it is the function of the syllabus to do this: every item introduced is selected according to a number of criteria, among which grading by incremental complexity and sequencing to maximise coherence and positive transfer are paramount (Mackey, 1965). But here again there is no place for explanation.

Explanatory adequacy

We have seen that linguists' grammars and any pedagogic practices that might claim to derive from them do not make provision for explanations. Let us proceed to consider what a pedagogic grammar would look like if it still aspired to *explanatory adequacy*, bearing in mind that a theory of grammar must have such aspirations while linguists' grammars need not.

The constituent features of explanatory adequacy are three: the grammar in question

- must be universally valid
- must have psychological reality
- must be maximally constrained.

However, none of these is wanted in a teaching grammar! Indeed their inclusion would be detrimental to its teaching functions. First, it need not be 'universally valid' because the learner knows the universals already and is exclusively concerned with the idiosyncrasies of the FL. For purely commercial reasons, publishers of FL (particularly EFL) textbooks pretend that these materials are 'universally valid' in the trivial sense of being usable globally, without any adjustment to local conditions (e.g. the learners' L1). Nor is the second ingredient of explanatory adequacy –

'psychological reality' – a requirement for a pedagogic grammar, because we want to equip learners with linguistic resources, not to programme their language behaviour.

As to the third requirement, 'maximally constraining' a grammar means not formulating *ad hoc* rules, or rules that cater only for the particular case in point but distort the wider picture. Avoiding this *ad hoc*ism involves making grammars comply with broad principles such as the autonomous syntax principle or ASP (what used to be called 'No mixing of levels!') formulated as: 'No syntactic rule can make reference to pragmatic, phonological, or semantic information' (Radford, 1988: 31). This restriction, if insisted upon, would seriously impair the utility of a teaching grammar as it would deny access to those crucial associations of grammatical rules that teachers rely on when giving explanations.

This is made clear by Furey (1977: 47), who stresses the need to refer to semantic and pragmatic information in grammar teaching: 'The functional explication gives those conditions which must prevail in the "real world" at large, and in the context of the communicative situation in particular in order for certain forms to be selected'. Similarly, Levenston (1974) sees potential bonuses for FLT in grammars that do mix levels, and so flout the ASP. For example, the grammar of indirect object constructions in English can usefully introduce and highlight the contrast between phonologically strong and weak forms of prepositions, as in the following exchanges:

1. *Who did you give the book to [tu] {NP}? To [tə] John.*
2. *Who did you bake a cake for [fɔ:] {NP}? For [fə] John.*

Here we see that prepositions which are 'stranded' in front of empty noun phrase (NP) positions cannot be reduced to weak forms: these two facts, one syntactic the other phonological, are systematically related, and to treat them separately for the sake of the ASP would incur loss of an opportunity to draw something important to the learner's attention, that is, to begin to explain the FL to him.

Positive and negative evidence

In the context of 'natural' or grammar-free approaches, we mentioned positive and negative evidence. Immersionists have been encouraged by Chomsky's claim (Chomsky, 1986: 55) that 'There is good reason to believe that children learn language from positive evidence only'. He clearly has in mind *indirect* (or incidental) positive evidence, by way of exposure to semantically rich discourse, and would presumably not discount the value to the learner of indirect negative evidence either – that is, of noticing what is *not* said. However, there is now some grudging concession that *direct* negative evidence, in the form of 'corrections by the speech community' (Cook, 1988: 60) can be useful too, though Chomsky had dismissed this years earlier ('There is good reason to believe that direct negative evidence is not necessary for language acquisition', Chomsky, 1981: 9). In FL teaching circles the usefulness of both sorts of negative evidence is more widely accepted, as the following testify:

> Evidence from studies in concept formation shows the importance of negative instances. A concept is achieved ... partly through the illustration of what is *not* an example of the concept, that is through *negative instances*. (Corder, 1973: 293)

> The 'correction' of error provides precisely the sort of negative evidence which is necessary for discovery of the correct concept or rule. (Corder, 1971: 70)

Not everyone agrees with Corder, however. Alter (1986: 426), in her critical review of Clausing's *German Grammar*, disagrees, referring to 'the pedagogically unsound practice of printing sentences full of mistakes in the target language'. But there is little doubt that the provision of direct negative evidence, in the form of pedagogic proscriptions, is the basis for much explanation in FL classrooms. In the growing storm – alluded to above in passing – over the status of native speakers (NSs), both in linguistics (Coulmas, 1981) and in FL teaching (Davies, 1991), the mere use of the term results in getting categorised with sexists and racists. We might say that the NS teacher will tend to provide both direct and indirect negative evidence while the NNS teacher will reliably provide only direct negative evidence. The 'avoidance' of some forms will not necessarily be interpreted by learners as evidence for the non-existence of those forms, which might be the learner's conclusion if they were noticeably absent from the speech of a NS.

Oddly enough, I have seen no reference to *direct positive* evidence. This would take the form of prescription, and the teacher would say 'Look, this is what it's like in this FL', drawing attention explicitly to the formal features and semantic associations of FL signs. Such attention drawing is exactly what is being done more and more in FL classrooms under the label of 'language awareness' work (James and Garrett, 1991), to which we shall return presently. At last we have a first approximation to a definition of explanation: it is the provision of direct evidence, positive as well as negative.

Pedagogic functions of explanation

Let us pause to ask what it is in a given teaching–learning situation that prompts the provision of direct negative evidence. It is response to error. By this I mean stating (explaining) why something is wrong, over and above simply saying that it is wrong: this is the diagnostic face of explanation. It is done as a matter of routine in other types of classroom: for example, Wheeler (1977) advocates remedial mathematics work done through the 'anatomy of a failure'. In his account of how to do grammatical consciousness-raising (C-R) in a FL, Rutherford (1987: 161) advises us that 'it is obviously best if what is to be judged emanates ... from learner production itself'. Likewise, Prabhu (1987: 76) insists that classroom attention to linguistic form must be 'self-initiated ... not planned, predicted or controlled by the teacher'. This means that one important requirement of grammar explanation is that it have a remedial objective. It also implies that the really authentic texts are those that are pedagogically authentic, which means they should have been produced by learners themselves and not by native speakers – even though they might have been produced *for* native speakers.

The other face of explanation is that catered for through the provision of direct *positive* evidence: it is the prophylactic face. The learner has no experience of trying to learn this item and failing to, but the teacher has reason to believe that she or he will have difficulties. This belief might be based on experience and observation of failure, or on the teacher's own experience of difficulties encountered when learning that particular item in the FL. It might also testify to the teacher's conviction that there is a relationship between what is describable and what is learnable. This intuition has been confirmed by research, to which we briefly turn.

2. Explicit teaching of language

Explanation and teachability

Pica (1984) reports work showing that learning of the English indefinite article is not helped by explicit teaching, whereas learning of third person -*s* is. Pica concludes that some forms are inherently more teachable than others, and teachable items are those that are functionally non-complex, show little variability in form and have a neat form-to-function relationship. Similarly, van Baalen (1983) found that the less complex forms, S+V+O word order and third singular -*s*, benefit from formal teaching with explanation, whereas the complex structures such as *do*-support and -*ing* structures do not. Zhou (1991) shows the same: explicit formal instruction accelerated Chinese children's learning of the English passive but not of the more complex features of tense/aspect morphology and *do*-support. These findings are depressing in showing that precisely those forms that perhaps do not need to be explained because they are so obvious can be taught, whereas, conversely, those that are hard and need to be taught are not easy to describe. Alternatively, one can take them as a challenge: the key to improved instruction is 'better' description of those items that are difficult to describe.

The issue, therefore, is: what *can* teachers usefully explain? Chomsky was fully aware of this problem:

> One does not learn the grammatical structure of a second language through 'explanation and instruction' beyond the most elementary rudiments, for the simple reason that no-one has enough explicit knowledge about this structure to provide explanation and instruction. (Chomsky, 1972: 174–5)

So are FL teachers to wait for better descriptions to be delivered to them by linguists? They will have to wait a very long time, perhaps forever, if linguists insist on imposing constraints like the autonomous syntax principle. Teachers will have to look elsewhere. 'Good' explanations will have to be won by teachers from their own action research. In this enterprise the willing collaboration of learners will be indispensable.

Self-help in developing 'good' explanations

The new can best be described – and hence explained – in terms of the already familiar: this is perhaps the most important message we have from psychologists. Of course, what FL learners know – as well as knowing that they know it – is their native language (NL). Observation of language learners shows us repeatedly how they struggle to assimilate the new into the framework of the old, to make sense of the structure and apparent arbitrariness of the FL by associating it with their NL; not only behaviouristically – transferring old habits of speech – but cognitively too – gaining a foothold in the unfamiliar by 'restructuring' it in terms of the familiar, just as some eminent cognitive educationalists (e.g. Ausubel and Piaget) have stressed. This is an additional reason, which we could add to those enumerated by Zhou (1991), why her Chinese learners were able to exploit her explanation of the English passive. Chinese is a topic-prominent language and so its speakers are familiar with fronting in their sentences the assumed–known part of the message; which is exactly what the passive does, but more rarely, in English (Prince, 1981). We used to dare to call this sort of facilitation 'positive transfer'!

> English: *The casualty list was read by the general.* [passive]
> Chinese: *(as for) casualty list, read general.* [topic first]

Good explanations, then, must be at least compatible with, and preferably integrated with, the learner's prior knowledge.

It is fashionable to try to account for FL learning in terms of learner strategies. Oxford (1990: 84–5) describes a whole battery of cognitive strategies used by FL learners and no fewer than 60 per cent of those making up her 'analysing and reasoning metastrategy' are interlingual strategies: they rely on reference to prior and concurrent linguistic knowledge. She claims that learners resort to translation to make FL input comprehensible; they analyse contrastively; and they transfer from NL to FL. Other research shows how badly learners want to be shown the FL in terms of their NL: Raabe analysed over 1800 'interrogative reactions' of learners of French recorded in 400 lessons. Their questions are metalinguistic discourse on material which has been teacher-initiated; but they are NL-centred: 'beginners base their "subjective" questions primarily on their native language or a foreign language previously learnt' (Raabe, 1988: 94). Gass (1983) cites two features of FL learners' behaviour – avoidance and psychotypology – as evidence of their propensity to make cross-linguistic comparisons, to be their own contrastive analysts.

It was Reibel (1969), no apologist for contrastive linguistics, who last drew our attention to the futility of using native-speaker models of the FL in teaching. Native speakers' grammars are, in the old parlance of structural linguistics and the new jargon of artificial intelligence, –etic or 'externally grounded' whereas they ought to be –emic or 'congruent with the point of view of the individual being investigated' (Benfer *et al.*, 1991: 38). Now, learners are not exactly being 'investigated' in classrooms in quite the same way as for example indigenous agroforestry practices might be in a savannah: they are being taught. But being taught is not totally dissimilar from being investigated and the analogy is not so far-fetched. Learners need to be taught grammar from their own perspective. This essentially was Reibel's argument too: since learners are by definition not knowers, they can benefit very little from being told what knowers know.

That Reibel went on to contradict himself by advocating the use of 'authentic' (native-speaker) texts in FL teaching need not detain us: how can one reconcile the rejection of native speakers' grammars with the simultaneous endorsement of NSs' texts in FL teaching? What we really need is text produced by learners alongside parallel text produced by natives, these being used in tandem with similarly paired and juxtaposed grammars of NL and FL. We want it, and I suggest that learners want it too. Learners want some sort of bridge linking NL and FL – an interface, if you like.

3. Learning, acquisition and consciousness- and awareness-raising

The role of consciousness and awareness

There has been a long and inconclusive debate about whether conscious learning can be converted into unconscious acquisition (Krashen, 1985). But why should we expect this convertibility? We could be dealing, after all, with two different modes of knowing, different species. Acquisition is tacit and reflected in skills, while learning is conscious and is reflected in metacognition. It could be argued that we need an interface to link them: they are not in themselves an interface.

To forge the interface required, a common denominator has to be found. This common factor is metacognition and it lends itself to the purpose we have in mind because one can have metacognition both of NL and of a FL. It is useful to distinguish between *language awareness* (LA) of the NL and *consciousness* of the FL. Awareness is an ability to contemplate metacognitively a language over which one has a high degree of control and about which one has therefore developed a coherent and relatively stable set of intuitions: 'implicit knowledge that has become explicit' (Levelt *et al.*, 1978: 5). Consciousness, on the other hand, as in the collocation 'consciousness-raising' (C-R) favoured by Rutherford (1987) is what learners of a language have as opposed to knowers: it is insight into what one does not know in the FL. LA is brought about by explication, which is the function of grammars, the implication being that grammars are intended to be used by knowers. C-R is different: it is the function of teaching, teachers and 'materials' and is realised and activated by explanation. Note that the LA versus C-R distinction runs parallel to the distinction we introduced earlier between explanation and explication. The explication/explanation doublet is the interface we have been looking for.

The next step forward would now be to show that conscious FL knowledge can be related to and integrated with conscious NL knowledge as a first step towards the ultimate automatisation of FL knowledge. Prospects are good. For example,

Ringbom (1987) has shown how Swedish-speaking Finns' high levels of comprehension of a language cognate with English (Swedish) give them a head-start for productive control of English. C-R, even of an unrelated FL, should offer similar advantages to the learner.

Interfacing first and foreign language

What I want to call 'interface theory' has been developing for some time, but uptake has been somewhat reluctant. However, the British Language Awareness Movement, associated with names like Hawkins (1984) and Donmall (1985), is concerned with teaching about language across the curriculum, and that includes the unification of NL and FL teaching. This is exactly what the interface offers: a new coherence in the school curriculum which unites L1 and FL study under a common purpose. Such unified and unifying work would, as Hawkins shows, form a new 'trivium' (not to be confused with 'trivia'!) in the language curriculum:

---

mother tongue + language awareness + foreign language
INTERFACE

In a parallel development this interface has recently found some resonance at the Department of Education, where the *Kingman Report* (DES, 1988) for the teaching of English and the *Harris Report* (DES, 1990) for FL teaching share the term 'knowledge about language' – or KAL for short.

Yet we seem to be lagging behind our European colleagues in such developments. The French government, for example, called for the integration of NL and FL teaching in its *Instructions ministérielles pour le collège* as early as October 1985. The French research and development in this field of *l'enseignement grammatical intégré* is documented in several papers emanating notably from the Centre de Didactique des Langues at Grenoble III (Bourguignon and Dabène, 1983; Bourguignon and Candelier, 1984). Unlike classical contrastive analysts, with their morbid preoccupation with NL interference, these scholars have been looking for ways to build bridges between NL knowledge and FL ignorance. The point of contact between NL and FL they see as metalanguage, which I would prefer to expand into explication/explanation: the function of metalanguage anyway is to describe, to compare and to explain.

Awareness in practice

The clearest demonstrations of how NL awareness can solve problems in learning a FL are to be found in Roulet (1980). He recounts how his daughter was having problems with Latin *cum* ('with'), problems which could not be explained wholly in terms of her ignorance of Latin, but had to be referred ultimately to her low level of awareness of the preposition *avec* in her NL, French. Gomes da Torre (1985) makes a similar point independently about certain fossilised errors in the FL English of advanced Portuguese learners, errors which they would not have made if they had known Portuguese 'better' – or, in this case, if they had known 'better' (i.e. standard) Portuguese. The following English error reflects directly the learner's non-standard NL grammar:

> ** Just now [why not thinking] of visiting London?*
> ** Já agora [porque não pensando] em visitar Londres?*

Here, the bracketed segment (*porque não pensando*) is non-standard Portuguese, and its participial structure gets transferred to the FL English, resulting in the error also bracketed. We are not saying that people ought not to speak non-standard dialects: that is not the point. Here the point is rather that they should be aware of their dialect and how it relates to the standard: this would not only contribute to their NL awareness, but also to their skill in monitoring unwanted transfer in FL learning. This would be an exemplary case of the interface in action.

The most extensive example of how access can be gained to a problematic FL form through analysis of the NL is Ducrot (1978). It concerns the French learner's meeting with 'problem pairs' corresponding to French *mais* ('but'); for example, Spanish *sino/pero*, Portuguese *senão/mas*, and German *sondern/aber*. The English speaker has the same problem as the French with these cases of divergent polysemy, as in the pair of sentences:

> *He is not Portuguese but$_a$ Brazilian.*
> *He is not Portuguese; but$_b$ he IS Brazilian.*

Here *but$_a$* corresponds to *sino/senão/sondern*, while *but$_b$* corresponds to *pero/mas/aber*. The point is that the contrast that is overt in German, Portuguese and Spanish exists also in the NL English, but there it is covert; or if not quite covert, it has other manifestations than the obviously lexical. First, the two *buts* are pragmatically different: *but$_a$* substantiates the refutation made in the antecedent clause:

> *Eddie is not English but$_a$ Welsh.*

whereas *but$_b$* is concessive and makes an independent assertion about Eddie:

> *Eddie is not English; but$_b$ he IS Welsh (and can prove it).*

Second, VP ellipsis is licensed by *but$_a$* but not by *but$_b$* in the following instances:

> *It's not for sale, but$_a$ free to take away.*
> ** He won't sell it; but$_b$ [ellipsis] give it away.*
> *He won't sell it, but$_b$ he'll [no ellipsis] gladly GIVE it away.*

Thus we see how ellipsis provides a useful test for explicitly diagnosing the sense of any *but* we encounter in use. The point again is that this syntactic and pragmatic knowledge is tacit and latent in the NL and needs to be explicated for the benefit of the English or French learner of Spanish or German. This LA operation will then in turn have the effect of achieving for the learner a C-R of what it is that is proving difficult in French. The learner will gain insight into what is intuitively known (the NL) and what is needed to be known in the FL. With this knowledge, the mystery of there being two words in the FL, where the learner's NL had appeared to manage well with one, will disappear.

Other examples spring to mind. Consider the problems that arise in trying to teach the grammar of reported speech in English to German learners of English, for instance. They usually have trouble with tense shifting in English reported speech. The problem is essentially that of distinguishing between sentences (a) and (b):

(a) *He said that he likes coffee.*
(b) *He said that he liked coffee.*

Both derive from: *He said, 'I like coffee'* in just the same way as *Er sagte: 'Ich trinke gern Kaffee'* is the source of (c) and (d), the German equivalents of (a) and (b) respectively:

(c) *Er sagte, daß er gern Kaffee trinkt.*
(d) *Er sagte, daß er gern Kaffee trinke.*

In other words, English uses the past tense where German uses the Konjunktiv I, which, according to Durrell (1991: 311) 'shows a statement to be "merely reported" without any commitment as to whether it is true or not'. Informal enquiry among NSs of English reveals that the German 'explication' for selection of Konjunktiv I is plausibly applicable also to the English form. More importantly, this explanation of English in terms of the NL is a key that unlocks the German learner's mind to this grammatical maze.

4. Teaching implications

In the first place, I have shown that what initially looks like a local lexical confusion (*sondern/aber*) is far from simple when we begin to see all the syntactic, semantic and pragmatic factors governing and resulting from the 'right' choice. Second, we should remind ourselves that a language is *'un système où tout se tient'* and that linguists are again now starting to show how true this is. It has been shown how the setting of one parameter can determine a whole range of syntactic options which would not have been associated ten years ago; for example, the PRO-Drop parameter sets up not just empty subject pronoun slots, but also licenses subject–verb inversion, violation of the that-trace filter and inflected modals, and excludes expletives. Third, the use being made of the L1 is an essentially cognitive use: interlingual associations, as we have said, provide a 'key' to the mysteries of the FL.

In this respect it is interesting perhaps to compare the present cognition-based case for the exploitation of L1:L2 isomorphisms with the function-based proposal which I elaborated (James, 1980: 160 ff.) for developing an 'interlingua' or a facilitating bridge between the two languages. Whereas I advocated the interlingua in that earlier work as an error-avoiding facilitator of communication, my present argument is more concerned with giving learners insight – showing them that they know already something which superficially might appear to be quite exotic in the L2, but has parallels in the L1. To echo my title, we have to show learners that large parts of the FL grammar are already theirs, and they its.

Fourth, people are now beginning to write contrastive analyses in which the contrasts are not seen as separate and unconnected linguistic accidents, but as related by implication: two surface contrasts are related to and shown to be reflexes of the same underlying contrast. For example, Hawkins (1986) convincingly argues that a large number of English–German contrasts, hitherto not seen as connected, are reflexes of the following general tendency: 'The morphological and syntactic structures of German are regularly in closer correspondence with their associated semantic representations than those of English' (Hawkins, 1986: 215). What this means is that every little detail explained and consequently learned is going to have a multiplier effect.

Finally, there is another sort of bonus to be taken: explaining grammar in this perspective is likely not only to assist in the learning of the particular FL one happens to be learning now, but also to equip learners for future learning of any other foreign languages they might need to learn: to contribute to the individual's L2 learning know-how.

References

Alter, M.P. 1986, 'Review of S. Clausing: *German Grammar: A Contrastive Approach*', in *Modern Language Journal*, vol. 70, no. 4, 426.

Benfer, R.A., Brent, E.E. and Furbee, L. 1991, *Expert Systems*, Sage Publications, London.

Bourguignon, C. and Candelier, M. 1984, 'Réflexion guidée sur la langue maternelle et l'apprentissage d'une langue étrangère', *Les Langues Etrangères*, vol. 2, no. 3, 103–35.

Bourguignon, C. and Dabène, L. 1983, 'Le metalangage: un point de rencontre obligé entre enseignants de langue maternelle et de langue étrangère', *Le français dans le monde*, vol. 177, 45–59.

Chomsky, N. 1972, *Language and Mind*, Harcourt, Brace, Jovanovich, New York.

Chomsky, N. 1981, *Lectures on Government and Binding*, Foris Publishers, Dordrecht.

Chomsky, N. 1986, *Knowledge of Language: Its Nature, Origin and Use*, Praeger, New York.

Cook, V.J. 1988, *Chomsky's Universal Grammar: An Introduction*, Blackwell, Oxford.

Corder, S.Pit. 1971, 'Idiosyncratic dialects and error analysis', *IRAL*, vol. 9, no. 2, 149–59.

Corder, S.Pit. 1973, *Introducing Applied Linguistics*, Penguin, Harmondsworth.

Coulmas, F. (ed.) 1981, 'A Festschrift for the Native Speaker', *Janua Linguarum Series Minor*, no. 97, Mouton, The Hague.

Davies, A. 1991, *The Native Speaker in Applied Linguistics*, Edinburgh University Press, Edinburgh.

Donmall, G. (ed.) 1985, *Language Awareness: NCLE Papers and Reports*, Centre for Information on Language Teaching, London.

Ducrot, O. 1978, 'Deux *mais*', *Cahiers de linguistique*, vol. 8, 109–20.

Durrell, M. 1991, *Hammer's German Grammar and Usage*, 2nd edition, Edward Arnold, London.

Furey, P. 1977, 'The preparation of grammar explanations in the teaching of English as a second language', in Brown, H.D., Yorio, C.A. and Crymes, R.H. (eds.), *ON TESOL '77*, TESOL, Washington, DC, 46–56.

Gass, S. 1983, 'The development of L2 intuitions', *TESOL Quarterly*, vol. 17, no. 2, 273–91.

Gomes da Torre, M. 1985, *Uma Analise de Erros: Contribuição para o Ensino da Lingua Inglesa*, unpublished Ph.D thesis, University of Oporto.

Harris, M. (Chairman) 1990, *Initial Advice: Report of the National Curriculum Modern Foreign Languages Working Group*, Department of Education and Science and Welsh Office.

Hawkins, E. 1984, *Awareness of Language: An Introduction*, CUP, Cambridge.

Hawkins, J. 1986, *A Comparative Typology of English and German: Unifying the Contrasts*, Croom Helm, London.

James, C. 1980, *Contrastive Analysis*, Longman, Harlow.

James, C. and Garrett, P. (eds.) 1991, *Language Awareness in the Classroom*, Longman, Harlow.

Kingman, J. (Chairman) 1988, *Report of the Committee of Enquiry into the Teaching of English*, HMSO, London.

Krashen, S.D. 1985, *The Input Hypothesis: Issues and Implications*, Longman, Harlow.

Levelt, W.J.M., Sinclair, A. and Jarvella, R.J. 1978, 'Causes and functions of linguistic awareness in language acquisition: some introductory remarks', in Sinclair, A., Jarvella, R.J. and Levelt, W.J.M. (eds.), *The Child's Conception of Language*, Springer, Berlin and New York.

Levenston, E.A. 1974, 'Teaching indirect object structures in English – a case study in applied linguistics', *English Language Teaching*, vol. 28, no. 4, 299–305.

Littlewood, W.T. 1975, 'Grammatical explanations', *Audio-Visual Language Journal*, vol. 13, no. 2, 91–4.

Mackey, W.F. 1965, *Language Teaching Analysis*, Longman, London.

Oxford, R.L. 1990, *Language Learning Strategies: What Every Teacher Should Know*, Newbury House, Rowley, Mass.

Pica, T. 1984, 'L1 transfer and L2 complexity as factors in syllabus design', *TESOL Quarterly*, vol. 18, no. 4, 639–704.

Prabhu, N.S. 1987, *Second Language Pedagogy*, OUP, Oxford.

Prince, E.F. 1981, 'Toward a taxonomy of given-new information', in Cole, P. (ed.), *Radical Pragmatics*, Academic Press, New York.

Raabe, H. 1988, 'The analysis of learners' questions and questions-guided grammar instruction', *AILA Review*, vol. 5, 89–98.

Radford, A. 1988, *Transformational Grammar: A First Course*, CUP, Cambridge.

Reibel, D.A. 1969, 'Language learning analysis', *IRAL*, vol. 7, no. 4, 284–94.

Ringbom, H. 1987, *The Role of the First Language in Foreign Language Learning*, Multilingual Matters, Clevedon.

Roulet, E. 1980, *Langue maternelle et langues secondes: vers une pédagogie integrée*, Hatier-Credif, Paris.

Rutherford, W.E. 1987, *Second Language Grammar: Learning and Teaching*, Longman, Harlow.

van Baalen, T. 1983, 'Giving learners rules: a study into the effect of grammatical instruction with varying degrees of explicitness', *Interlanguage Studies Bulletin*, vol. 7, no. 1, 71–101.

Wheeler, D.H. 1977, *Notes on Mathematics for Children*, CUP, Cambridge.

Zhou, Y. 1991, 'The effect of explicit instruction on the acquisition of English grammatical structures by Chinese learners', in James, C. and Garrett, P. (eds.), *Language Awareness in the Classroom*, Longman, Harlow.

Foreign Language Teachers and the Teaching of Grammar

ROSAMOND MITCHELL

1. Introduction

The earlier article ('Grammar, Syllabuses and Teachers') in Section 2 of this volume reviews the nature and quality of the advice available to language teachers in one particular context (British secondary schooling in the late 1980s/early 1990s) regarding the teaching of grammar. A range of teaching syllabuses and of government-sponsored policy and advisory documents was scrutinised, and the view was taken that the advice available was generally characterised by a lack of clarity and consistency on two key points:

1. the kind of grammatical models most relevant to pedagogy
2. the relationship between grammar study and language learning/development.

This lack of coherence was found both for the teaching of English as a mother tongue, and for foreign language teaching.

In this article, attention shifts from the kind of information and advice on offer to teachers regarding the nature of grammar, and its place in language instruction, to the teachers themselves, and ways in which they are currently interpreting and using this advice. In the first part of the chapter, a brief account is given of a study exploring the present state of British teachers' knowledge about grammar, and their beliefs about its role in the classroom. In the later part of the chapter, the limited available evidence on how grammar gets talked about in contemporary second/foreign language classrooms will be reviewed. The article is thus mainly descriptive; however, it concludes with some tentative proposals regarding the kinds of grammatical knowledge which teachers seem to need, and productive ways of exploiting this knowledge in the classroom.

2. What teachers think of the role of grammar

In autumn 1988, the present writer conducted an investigation into the thinking of English and foreign languages teachers in Hampshire schools on the topic of 'knowledge about language' (KAL) and its role in language teaching and learning. (A fuller account of the study is given in Mitchell and Hooper, 1992.) This study was timed (fortuitously) to pick up the views of foreign languages teachers just after the point of the highest public profile for 1980s 'language awareness' ideas in debates on L2 education (Donmall (ed.), 1985), and on the other hand, just prior to the impact on the thinking of English mother-tongue teachers of the Cox Report (DES/WO, 1989), the Language in the National Curriculum (LINC) project (LINC, n.d.; Carter, ed., 1990), and other National Curriculum documentation, reviewed earlier in this volume. While, for the purposes of the study, we did not equate 'knowledge about language' solely with 'knowledge about grammar', inevitably grammar and the teaching of grammar were a major focus of the research.

In this study, we conducted lengthy semi-structured interviews with 13 Heads of Modern Languages and 14 Heads of English in Hampshire secondary schools, exploring the teachers' academic background and training as well as their current knowledge of language and views on the place of explicit talk about language in the classroom.

The Heads of Modern Languages all had first degrees in one or more foreign languages, but it was clear that their language studies at university had had a primarily literary orientation. Six mentioned having studied some historical linguistics for their first degree; only one recalled a substantial linguistics component other than this. None recalled any further KAL work during their initial professional training (which was for most via the route most usual in Britain, the one-year Postgraduate Certificate in Education, which involves a combination of university-based study and school-based teaching practice). There was little evidence in their comments of any major subsequent influences on their understanding of grammar or grammar pedagogy; thus, for example, references to the 'language awareness' movement were rare.

At the time of the interview, this group of teachers interpreted KAL very similarly, and primarily in terms of grammatical topics, such as parts of speech, sentence patterns, verb tenses, gender and number. There was a striking bias towards morphology, in the examples teachers offered in their accounts of what 'grammar' was, and an absence of reference to any textual features above the level of the clause or sentence. Generally, points in the target language system which contrasted most strikingly with the grammar of English were most likely to be mentioned.

Moving on to discuss pedagogy, the foreign language teachers generally claimed to teach in a 'communicative' way, with a pupil-centred, topic-based approach. However, almost all were following coursebooks with a syllabus based on a systematic grammatical progression, though it appeared that the structures of the syllabus were generally taught inductively, using a traditional three-part cycle of presentation – practice – exploitation.

Such explicit discussion of grammar as the foreign language teachers reported entering into in the classroom, sometimes prompted by pupils' questions, was grounded in this framework. Typically, such discussion took place through the medium of English, and was thus a cause of anxiety on other grounds (given the contemporary orthodoxy that foreign language classroom interaction should take place exclusively through the medium of the target language); it was reported always to follow, not precede, the presentation and practice of 'new structures'.

These teachers welcomed what they perceived to be a shift away from the explicit teaching of target language grammar, in the contemporary orthodoxy of 'communicative language teaching'. They seemed to share the view that pupils could effectively assimilate new structures through active practice and use. However, some feeling was also expressed that 'more able' and/or 'older' pupils wanted, and could benefit from, systematic and explicit presentation of grammatical rules and explanations, and also that grammatical expositions could assist pupils in shifting from rote learning to a more creative use of the target language.

The Heads of English (as a mother tongue) also interviewed in this Hampshire study shared with the foreign language teachers a primarily literary orientation in their initial academic and professional studies. However, their concepts of KAL had typically been more affected, subsequently, by a range of influences entering mainstream English teaching debates in the 1970s and 1980s from the academic study of language use in schools (e.g. Barnes *et al.*, 1971) and from sociolinguistics more generally (e.g. Trudgill, 1975; Stubbs, 1976). Thus the English teachers talked about developing familiarity in the course of their teaching career with notions such as 'register' and 'awareness of audience', as well as a growing awareness of the nature and social significance of language variation.

Regarding 'grammar' itself, however, no such ongoing growth in understanding had taken place. For example, the Halliday-inspired interest in text structure above the level of the sentence which is apparent in materials produced in the early 1990s by the Language in the National Curriculum project (LINC, n.d.; Carter, 1990), but which had been promoted spasmodically from considerably earlier by initiatives such as the 'Language in Use' project of the 1970s (Doughty *et al.*, 1971), had not yet worked its way through into the English teachers' current thinking. Thus at the time of the survey, the English teachers appeared generally lacking in knowledge, confidence and interest as far as grammar was concerned. (That this finding reflects a general tendency among English teachers is suggested by Chandler's 1988 study of a similar sample of English teachers in Oxfordshire. On the basis of a questionnaire survey, he reports that it was only the older teachers in his sample who in general perceived themselves as possessing secure grammatical knowledge.)

As for the study of grammar in class, this was talked about generally negatively by the Hampshire sample (though there was a small minority who held a well-developed opposing view). It was narrowly defined as the teaching of the parts of speech, and perhaps traditional clause analysis. Most of the teachers favoured a 'responsive' approach to such discussion about the language system as took place – that is to say, they claimed it arose most often, and was most useful, in the context of commentary and discussion of pupils' ongoing (written) work.

This wariness of grammar, evident among English teachers in particular in our 1988 study, continued to be apparent even in subsequent efforts to promote KAL-related activities in line with the requirements of the first statutory version of the National Curriculum for English (DES/WO, 1990). Texts produced by teachers or teacher advisers as a basis for knowledge about language work, such as the publications of Bain (1991) or the Oxford Special Diploma English group (OSDE, n.d.), typically deal sketchily or not at all with grammar, while encouraging discussion and activities on sociolinguistic topics. Thus, for example, suggestions made in both these texts for pupil investigations into local varieties of English encourage exploration of lexical variety and of accent, but effectively ignore the possibility of syntactic variation (e.g. Bain, 1991: 31–5; OSDE, n.d.: 2). In this respect, despite all intervening debates, they represent no advance on materials produced ten years earlier (e.g. Raleigh, 1981). It remains to be seen whether the offerings of academic linguists focusing more centrally on grammar, such as Carter's previously mentioned work (1990), or Hudson's *Teaching Grammar* (1992), will have an impact on this key group.

3. Talk about grammar in the language classroom

In this section of the article, attention will be concentrated on the second/foreign language classroom, as there does not appear to be any recent published evidence on how L1 teachers talk about grammar with their students. Indeed, there is also relatively little direct evidence available on how teachers talk about grammar with their students in the foreign language classroom, despite some decades of active research into classroom interaction, including more than ten years of great activity in L2 classroom research. This activity is comprehensively documented by Chaudron (1988: 86); he notes that 'explanation, in the sense of providing information about grammatical rules, meanings of words, social uses of expressions and so on', has been 'surprisingly little investigated'.

A partial explanation may be that this upsurge of classroom research interest coincided with (and partly drew its vigour from) an upsurge in theories of teaching and learning which downplayed the role of explicit instruction in general, and grammatical explanation in particular. Thus, for example, the 'communicative language teaching' movement, with its central concern to increase the proportion of meaning-oriented 'fluency work' in the L2 classroom (Brumfit, 1984), naturally generated both descriptive and process–product research which focused its attention on the extent to which 'fluency work' was occurring, and its apparent effects. While this research tradition documented to some extent the occurrence of classroom talk which concerned itself with language form, the detail of such meta-talk was not generally explored. (For a review of research on communicative language teaching, see Mitchell, 1988.)

A somewhat different, more psycholinguistically oriented classroom research tradition, deriving from Krashen's 'comprehensible input' hypothesis (Krashen, 1985), has focused on the narrower question of how such input is negotiated in classroom conditions, and has similarly marginalised the issue of 'talk about grammar'. Notable figures here are Long (1981) and Pica and her collaborators (Pica and Doughty, 1985).

There has, however, been a recent revival of interest in the role of 'instruction' in bringing about L2 learning, again initiated by Long (1983). Somewhat surprisingly, though, researchers in this tradition have generally not documented comprehensively exactly what it is that teachers do when 'instructing' their learners, and have continued to pay little detailed attention to talk about grammar. In several studies in this tradition, 'instruction' is simply equated with class attendance, and not analysed further, as a review by Ellis shows (1990, Ch. 6). Ellis himself, in his review of studies of teachers' classroom talk in Chapter 4 of the same book, confines himself to three topics: error treatment, 'input features' (such as rate of speech, range of vocabulary, etc.) and 'interactional features' (such as use of open/ closed questions); again, teacher talk about grammar is not considered. Lightbown and her Canadian colleagues, currently working on a longitudinal study of 'instructed language learning' involving classroom observation as well as process–product studies, have not yet reported in any full descriptive detail on the nature of teachers' talk when engaged in 'form-focused instruction' (see Lightbown and Spada, 1990; Lightbown, 1991). Similarly, the currently active strand of research on learners' 'learning strategies' (e.g. O'Malley and Chamot, 1990), while showing considerable interest in the state of learners' metalinguistic awareness, has not typically attended to the detail of classroom interaction or to instructional processes by which that awareness may have been developed.

Only a few isolated studies have been published, then, which focus centrally on how teachers talk about grammar in the L2 classroom. The main example is Faerch's avowedly exploratory study of the 'rules of thumb' produced by Danish high school teachers in English lessons (1986). Here, Faerch reports frequent occurrence of a four-part sequence of activities, as follows:

1. Problem-formulation. The sequence leading up to the formulation of the rule may be initiated by

- the teacher
- the pupil who is presently having a turn at speech
- a pupil who is not having a turn, and who formulates a problem located either in a fellow student's contribution or – more rarely – in the teacher's contribution . . .

2. Induction. Typically, the teacher steers the conversation from the point of problem-formulation to rule-formulation through a process of 'induction' – inducing the students themselves to formulate the rule.

3. Rule-formulation. If the teacher manages to make a student formulate the desired rule, she will generally repeat it. But often the teacher will have to formulate the rule herself.

4. Exemplification. Sometimes the teacher exemplifies a rule after she has formulated it . . . The obvious function of the exemplification is to make sure that the pupils have understood the implications of the rule . . ., but exemplification probably also serves the purpose of providing learners with an implicit representation of the rule. (Faerch, 1986: 132)

This 'typical sequence' is illustrated with a number of quoted examples, centring on the formulation in Step 3 of 'rules of thumb' such as the following:

You can make an adjective out of a substantive. (e.g. *wood/wooden*)

When you use 'do' and 'did' . . . you use the infinitive.
You can't end a sentence with a preposition like that.

Most of the examples discussed (like those above) have to do with morphology or sentence structure; there are no examples of 'rule giving' about the structure of larger units. Faerch's study also supports the claims made by teachers interviewed in the very different Hampshire context, that grammar gets talked about explicitly mostly in response to student problems, rather than as a pre-planned teacher initiative (Mitchell and Hooper, 1992). However, Faerch also discusses more briefly the mnemonic rules which he claims are more systematically taught, typically in intensive periods of pre-examination revision!

Faerch was very conscious of the limitations of purely descriptive/observational studies on this topic, and suggested a research agenda which would not only document more fully how grammar gets talked about, but also (a) seek teachers' retrospective reflections and comments on their own observed rule-giving behaviour, and their motivations for it, and (b) seek to document 'learners' *explicit* knowledge of the foreign language and the interaction between this and [grammatical] input in the classroom' (p. 138). Here, he recognised that he was repeating a call made much earlier by Seliger (1979); both writers also suggest the obvious final step in such an agenda, which would explore relationships between developments in learners' explicit knowledge and their language performance.

It is difficult to improve on this agenda for research, once it is accepted that classroom talk about matters of language form, including grammar, is actually of theoretical interest. Firstly, we badly need some richly descriptive ethnographic studies, which will document instances of classroom talk about grammar, both teacher- and student-initiated, and hopefully back this up with participants' accounts of why they asked for/provided particular kinds of grammatical explanation, and what the perceived value of the observed incidents was for them. Secondly, we need explorations of learners' explicit knowledge of target language systems, and the extent to which these derive from classroom experiences, and/or from other sources. And thirdly, we need continuing explorations of the links between this explicit knowledge and the state of learners' 'procedural competence' in the relevant language(s) (as in Kadia, 1988; and Green and Hecht, 1992).

4. Conclusion: why do teachers need grammar?

The final topic to be considered in this chapter concerns the kinds of explicit linguistic (and especially grammatical) knowledge which the effective language teacher actually needs; in the light of the inadequacies and disagreements in the theoretical/research base available (outlined above) this concluding section will be brief and programmatic.

It is possible, however, to clarify a range of pedagogic purposes for which teachers may require a knowledge of grammar. These possible purposes include:

• to make sense of the advice they are given, in syllabus documents, examination syllabuses, etc., and if necessary to provide the basis for an independent critical perspective on these documents, partial and sometimes internally contradictory as they are;

- to transform such policy documents and syllabuses into actual lesson plans and schemes of work;
- to diagnose and monitor the developmental stages through which their learners pass;
- to correct and/or provide feedback on their learners' language production;
- to talk about the target language system with their learners, and assist them in developing a conception of it as a system.

The first three items on this list have to do essentially with the planning and shaping of the linguistic 'input' and language-using activities most appropriate for a particular group of learners in a specific educational context. A knowledge of grammar is by no means the only, or perhaps the most important, kind of knowledge a teacher needs here, but there will be little dispute that it remains an important dimension, especially in the light of the evidence offered in the article on 'Grammar, Syllabuses and Teachers' in Section 2 of this volume, regarding the indifferent quality of much official advice.

However, the last two items on the list are different in character. Here, the degree of importance given to the provision of form-focused feedback, and/or grammatical explanations, will depend on the view taken of the language learning process itself.

As Ellis points out (1990: Ch. 7), the most solid theoretical rationale for grammatical explanations in the L2 classroom can be derived from cognitive theories of second language learning. An example of this line of argument is advanced by Johnson in this volume; the general position is summarised by Ellis:

> According to cognitive theory, formal instruction can help to increase the learner's analysed knowledge. Focusing on specific linguistic forms and encouraging the learner to manipulate these with varying degrees of awareness facilitates restructuring and also builds propositional representations of L2 knowledge. This enables the learner to participate in the kinds of decontextualised language use which require analysed knowledge. (Ellis, 1990: 181)

There is no clear agreement as yet among cognitive theorists on the details of this hypothesised process, however; Ellis goes on to say that views of the precise role of explicit knowledge about language are still 'rather vague' (p. 182). Unlike many of Krashen's critics, Ellis himself accepts the Krashen argument that 'explicit knowledge does not turn into implicit knowledge' (p. 193), but sees a much wider role for 'explicit knowledge' in the learning process than does Krashen. Ellis summarises his own position as follows:

> Briefly, it is claimed that conscious knowledge functions as an acquisition facilitator, enabling the learner to 'notice' L2 features in meaning-focused input which would otherwise be ignored. The features themselves, however, are acquired from this input in accordance with the learner's internal cognitive and linguistic processing facilities. (Ellis, 1990: 193)

This is in fact a similar argument to that made by Rutherford (1987) in favour of 'consciousness-raising'. Whatever the details of the disputes between cognitive theorists, the broad pedagogic conclusion remains the same: that helping the learner to build an explicit reference model of the target language, without any immediate expectations that this will lead directly and mechanically to improved performance, will be useful (if in ways not yet understood in detail), in illuminating problematic features of the system, providing contrastive evidence with the learner's L1 as well as negative evidence on how the system does *not* function, and in general constraining the learner's hypotheses about the workings of the system.

We thus need teachers who can work with their students in a responsive, text-based way, reacting to errors some of the time, but also capable of providing a systematic linguistic commentary on written and spoken texts, whether previously produced or in process of production. Such teachers need an understanding of grammar as offering a tool either for prescription or description; they need a set of concepts, and a metalanguage, which will allow them to deal with pragmatic, discoursal and rhetorical features of texts, as well as with sentence-level features. Teachers of both L1 and L2 need a comparative orientation; teachers of English as a mother tongue need to be able to draw pupils' attention to key points of contrast between the grammar of formal and colloquial speech, or between Standard and non-Standard English (Cheshire and Trudgill, 1989), just as foreign language teachers need to be ready to comment on key points of contrast between mother tongue and target language.

At present, as the earlier evidence of this paper shows, we are some way from having teachers who themselves are both confident in their grammatical knowledge and confident that they know how to share their conceptual map of language as a system with their pupils in productive ways. To develop the number of such teachers, much more systematic attention to descriptive linguistics and to applied linguistics will be needed, both in all kinds of language-linked first degrees and in inservice education. There is a continuing teacher education agenda, as well as a research agenda, if we are finally to make better sense across the board of the question of grammar. Our teachers deserve it, and so do our students.

References

Bain, R. 1991, *Reflections: Talking about Language*, Hodder and Stoughton, Sevenoaks.
Barnes, D., Britton, J. and Rosen, H. 1971, *Language, the Learner and the School*, Penguin, Harmondsworth.
Breen, M. 1991, 'Understanding the language teacher', in Phillipson, R. *et al.* (eds.), *Foreign/Second Language Pedagogy Research*, Multilingual Matters, Clevedon.
Brumfit, C.J. 1984, *Communicative Methodology in Language Teaching*, CUP, Cambridge.
Carter, R. (ed.) 1990, *Knowledge about Language and the Curriculum*, Hodder & Stoughton, London.
Carter, R. 1990, 'The new grammar teaching', in Carter, R. (ed.), *Knowledge about Language and the Curriculum*.
Chandler, R. 1988, 'Unproductive busywork', *English in Education*, vol. 22, no. 3, 20–8.
Chaudron, C. 1988, *Second Language Classrooms*, CUP, Cambridge.
Cheshire, J. and Trudgill, P. 1989, 'Dialect and education in the United Kingdom' in Cheshire, J. *et al.* (eds.), *Dialect and Education*, Multilingual Matters, Clevedon.

DES/WO 1989, *English for Ages 5 to 16* (Cox Report), Department of Education and Science and Welsh Office.
DES/WO 1990, *English in the National Curriculum (No. 2)*, HMSO, London.
Donmall, B.G. (ed.) 1985. *Language Awareness*, NCLE Reports and Papers 6, CILT, London.
Doughty, P., Pearce, J. and Thornton, G. 1971, *Language in Use*, Edward Arnold, London.
Ellis, R. 1990, *Instructed Second Language Acquisition*, Blackwell, Oxford.
Faerch, C. 1985, 'Meta talk in FL classroom discourse', *Studies in Second Language Acquisition*, vol. 7, no. 2, 184–99.
Faerch, C. 1986, 'Rules of thumb and other teacher-formulated rules in the foreign language classroom', in Kasper, G. (ed.), *Learning, Teaching and Communication in the Foreign Language Classroom*, Aarhus University Press, Aarhus.
Green, P.S. and Hecht, K. 1992, 'Implicit and explicit grammar – an empirical study', *Applied Linguistics*, vol. 13, no. 2, 168–84.
Hudson, R. 1992, *Teaching Grammar*, Blackwell, Oxford.
Kadia, K. 1988, 'The effect of formal instruction on monitored and spontaneous naturalistic interlanguage performance', *TESOL Quarterly*, vol. 22, no. 3, 509–15.
Krashen, S.D. 1985, *The Input Hypothesis: Issues and Implications*, Longman, Harlow.
Lightbown, P. 1991, 'What have we here? Some observations on the influence of instruction on L2 learning', in Phillipson, R. *et al.* (eds.), *Foreign/Second Language Pedagogy Research*, Multilingual Matters, Clevedon.
Lightbown, P. and Spada, N. 1990, 'Focus-on-form and corrective feedback in communicative language teaching: effects on second language learning', *Studies in Second Language Acquisition*, vol. 12, no. 4, 429–48.
LINC (n.d.), unpublished, Language in the National Curriculum: Materials for Professional Development, University of Nottingham.
Long, M. 1981, 'Input, interaction and second language acquisition', in Winitz, H. (ed.), *Native Language and Foreign Language Acquisition*, Annals of the New York Academy of Sciences, 379.
Long, M. 1983, 'Does second language instruction make a difference? A review of the research', *TESOL Quarterly*, vol. 17, no. 3, 359–82.
Mitchell, R. 1988, 'Researching into communicative language teaching', *Annual Review of Applied Linguistics*, vol. 8, 109–25.
Mitchell, R. and Hooper, J. 1992, 'Teachers' views of language knowledge', in James, C. and Garrett, P. (eds.), *Language Awareness in the Classroom*, Longman, Harlow.
O'Malley, J.M. and Chamot, A.U. 1990, *Learning Strategies in Second Language Acquisition*, CUP, Cambridge.
Oxford Special Diploma English Group (n.d.), *Knowledge About Language*, Department of Educational Studies, University of Oxford.
Pica, T. and Doughty, C. 1985, 'The role of group work in second language acquisition', *Studies in Second Language Acquisition*, vol. 7, no. 2, 737–58.
Raleigh, M. 1981, *The Languages Book*, ILEA English Centre, London.
Rutherford, W. 1987, *Second Language Grammar: Learning and Teaching*, Longman, Harlow.
Seliger, H.W. 1979, 'On the nature and function of language rules in language teaching', *TESOL Quarterly*, vol. 13, no. 3, 359–69.
Stephens, C. 1989, *Metalanguage Set in Context*, MA (Ed) dissertation, University of Southampton.
Stubbs, M. 1976, *Language Schools and Classrooms*, Methuen, London.
Trudgill, P. 1975, *Accent, Dialect and the School*, Edward Arnold, London.

Product and Process: Grammar in the Second Language Classroom

ROB BATSTONE

This article considers different ways of exploiting grammar in the classroom, including the teaching of grammar as product (as tightly controlled target language) and as process (as part of dynamic language use). Drawing on research in second language acquisition and in cognitive psychology, it is suggested that we need to aim for a measure of control over learner language together with regular opportunities for work which is meaning-focused. In this light, an approach to grammar teaching is suggested which involves a repositioning of grammar, so that it evolves as the product of learners' own processes of working with words. This approach to teaching grammar is known as 'grammaticisation'.

1. Approaches to the teaching of grammar: product and process

One of the most striking characteristics of grammar is that it is multi-dimensional: we can choose to regard it from any of a wide range of possible viewpoints. Each viewpoint conjures up a different set of priorities, and each involves a different set of assumptions about grammar and its relationships with meaning, with language use, and with language learning.

We can, for example, regard grammar as essentially a formal framework: a set of categories and forms which help us to see language as structured and systematic. Or we can emphasise the myriad ways in which grammatical forms relate to meaning. But these two viewpoints have something in common. They both involve a prior analysis of language into discrete parts, whether these parts are labelled formally (noun phrase, finite clause) or functionally (past tense, reported speech). This fundamentally analytic way of looking at grammar has been enormously influential in language teaching, where it is often called a 'product' perspective.

But of course there are other ways of looking at grammar. Instead of thinking in terms of an analytic display of separate forms, we can think of grammar as a dynamic; as a resource which language users exploit as they navigate their way through discourse. Looked at this way, we can observe how grammar impinges on the choices language users make, how it is called upon in different ways at different points through the flow of language use, and how grammar helps us to make our developing meanings more precise. This, clearly, is a very different viewpoint, one which has to do with movement, with change, and with the numerous factors which condition the ongoing deployment of grammar in action. I refer to this as a 'process' perspective.

Both process and product perspectives are influential in language teaching. The distinction, in brief, is between the careful control of language *for* the learner (as product), and the creative use of language *by* the learner (as process). Yet this seemingly straightforward distinction requires some further investigation. Effective grammar teaching presupposes a clear view on how this teaching can advance the learning process. We need, then, to scrutinise process and product approaches to teaching in this light.

2. Product approaches

Noticing and structuring

Critics of product teaching (and there are many) argue that if teaching is to be in the service of learning, then a product approach is seriously flawed. It is said, for example, that the obsession with the prior analysis of target language into structures, notions and functions takes precedence, quite erroneously, over considerations of how these items might eventually find their way into the learner's own learning mechanisms. As one recent (and very critical) account puts it: '[product] syllabuses consistently leave the learner out of the equation' (Crookes and Long, 1992). Such pointed criticism merits further consideration, not least because product teaching is by far the most widespread approach to language teaching worldwide.

SLA research demonstrates beyond any doubt that learners do not move in one super-efficient leap from 'zero' knowledge of a particular grammatical structure to full native-like proficiency. Rather, learning grammatical forms involves a gradual shift towards the full target form. The learner who is grappling with the past tense, for example, might pass through a series of 'stages': *she go office* might become *she goed office* before (with luck) the appropriate form finally begins to manifest itself. What is happening here, in brief, is that the learner is formulating working models of how the target grammar is structured: a series of interim hypotheses, each of which represents the learner's 'best bet so far' and which may periodically be 'restructured' in closer alignment with the target form. Of course the processes of restructuring hypotheses are considerably more complex than this (see, for example, Kellerman, 1985; McLaughlin, 1990). In essence, though, the point is this: when we teach grammar as product, we are said to be confronting the learner with a conveyor belt of target forms which *cannot*, on first encounter, be concisely 'structured' into the learners' working models.

But this does not mean that teaching grammar as product is without value. There are two ways of justifying product teaching. One, the 'strong version', says that there is indeed a direct equation between what is taught and what is learned, and that learners can somehow take on board the items which we teach as and when they are taught. It is this view which critics of product approaches so often address, and which they rightly reject out of hand. As Long puts it, there is no evidence that: 'structures, notions, functions, etc., can be acquired separately, singly, in linear additive fashion' (Long, 1989: 6).

But there is another, more moderate version, which runs as follows. Teaching grammar as product can give the learner a clear and explicit framework: most product courses come with a clear sense of structure, with an outline provided, step by step, of the material to be covered. Such a structured and systematic approach can provide the learner with a strong sense of position and direction, and this in itself can generate a much needed feeling of security and purpose which can have a motivating effect. In this regard, Brumfit notes that 'what can be made systematic by the learner is more likely to be learned than random elements' (Brumfit, 1984: 98).

Indeed, it is argued that before learners can begin to structure language into working hypotheses, they will need explicitly to notice particular features of the grammar (Schmidt, 1990), so that noticing grammar may be a necessary preliminary stage in the learning process.[1] Through product teaching, teachers can help to make grammatical items as salient and noticeable as possible (see, for example, the argument in Ellis, 1993). As for the learners' processes of structuring and restructuring, this too is something which product teaching can (in principle) facilitate, provided that learners are afforded repeated opportunities to structure and restructure target forms, giving them every chance to compare their current 'best bet' with the target models available in the input. In such circumstances they can continue to renotice (and hence to restructure) their own mental models. Very often, product approaches are criticised for not providing sufficient input of this 'rich' variety. There is some truth in this, but in actual classrooms learners may get considerable exposure to target forms from a whole range of sources: from teacher talk, from 'incidental' discussions about classroom activities, from the wide diversity of language which product textbooks contain (well beyond a mere formulation of the 'target items'), from recycling and revision activities in textbooks, and so on.

Learning mechanisms: memory and analysis

It is often claimed that some or all product syllabuses will lead to a superficial mode of learning, in which learners will merely 'accumulate' language items (Widdowson, 1979: 248; Rutherford, 1987: 154–5). If true, this would be a damning criticism which would undermine much of the argument already made in favour of a product approach. Fundamentally, effective learning requires the activation of two key mechanisms: memory and analysis. Memory is central, for example, in the early 'lexical' phase of learning where 'chunks' of language are initially perceived by the learner as wholes, without awareness of their internal structure (see Peters, 1983). This, presumably, equates with the notion of 'accumulation'. But if this is the only mechanism activated by a product approach, then teaching and learning will be severely handicapped.[2] Of equal importance is the capacity to analyse language, segmenting it into its component parts so that they can then be combined creatively in the generation of new utterances. In this sense, the capacity to analyse language is a prerequisite to continued restructuring.[3]

But the view that a product approach is largely oriented to memory/accumulation unfairly minimises the role played by methodology. It is up to teachers and materials designers to decide how the various syllabus items will be exploited and extrapolated in actual activities, and textbook writers have for many years constructed activities which key in with both learning mechanisms. Some activities will encourage the accumulation of memorised wholes, as when the learner rehearses fixed target expressions – *what did you do at the weekend?*, *could you open the window?*, etc. Others will facilitate encounters with language of a more analytic kind, requiring a manipulation of language forms.

There is insufficient space here to do full justice to the scope and flexibility of a product approach (see Batstone, 1994, for a more extended discussion). However, very generally, I am suggesting that a product approach has its place. It can facilitate the learning of grammar by providing a clear framework within which targeted grammatical forms can be made salient for two key elements in the learning process: noticing and structuring.

3. Process teaching and a product/process continuum

Meaning focus and proceduralisation

And yet there are dangers in relying too inflexibly on teaching grammar as product, since it disregards the factor of language use. Noticing and structuring are necessary components of the learning process, but they are not sufficient on their own for the effective learning of grammar. Instructed purely through a form-focused product approach, learners may not retain what they have been taught for very long. Instead, certain carefully practised forms can soon disappear from their working systems once the period of instruction is over (see Lightbown, 1983). If learners are to learn grammar to the point where they have effectively internalised it, then they will need considerable practice in language use, involving a genuine focus on meaning and on self-expression. Such an emphasis on language use can help learners to reorganise their knowledge of language, storing it mentally as a large network of routines – fixed or semi-fixed expressions which can be activated at speed, thereby equipping the learner to handle the communicative stress typical of much real-time communication (see Pawley and Syder, 1983). As language is reorganised into this 'user-friendly' mode, it is said to become *proceduralised* (see Anderson, 1985, and the discussion in O'Malley and Chamot, 1989).[4] In short, proceduralisation constitutes a vital 'third stage' in the process of language learning, which operates in approximately the way shown in Figure 1.

Figure 1: Stages of proceduralisation

NOTICE $\rightarrow$ STRUCTURE $\rightarrow$ PROCEDURALISE

It is through process work in classrooms that proceduralisation can be developed. Process teaching aims to encourage learners to use language effectively and with a focus on meaning. Competent language users take this highly complex activity for granted: they converse, debate and introspect without paying much attention to the grammar which they decode and deploy with such apparent ease. Their primary attention is, for the most part, on meaning. It is a major objective in process teaching to develop this skill, and to this end teachers are urged to use tasks which engage learners in 'meaning-focused' activity.

But we should not underrate the objectives which process teaching sets itself. For learners, competent language use is a highly complex skill – or, more accurately, a complex of skills – which can prove immensely difficult to accomplish. Learners will need to make sense of language (receptively) and to make sense with language (productively) under the considerable pressure of everyday communication. They may have to extract the 'gist' of language used at speed, to formulate and express their meanings appropriately, to interact and turn-take sensitively and without undue hesitation, and so on. Beyond this, there may lie the additional requirement that they should use language with a reasonable degree of accuracy.

Let us consider, then, a fictional classroom where a group of intermediate learners are given a task which requires a focus on meaning through language use. The task is shown in Figure 2.

Figure 2: Picture story

These eight pictures tell the story of what happened to Mrs Brewin and her cat last week. Tell the story to your partner using your own words:

(The pictures are from Soars, J. and Soars, L. 1986: 14. The task is mine.)

The class gets down to the task in hand, and the following is typical of the language they produce:

Well erm . . . she work his garden that cat it lie . . . it lie grass it go tree . . . and she she say 'puss puss' up tree there . . . yes . . . after this then she telephone is . . . erm . . . she take any food for try get down his cat . . . after this come the black car . . . is a man he take down cat and ... so everybody sits drink the tea then ... the car kill the cat under ... is very sad I think.

While by no means chaotic, we would be hard-pressed to make sense of much of this learner's language if we did not have the pictures in front of us. It lacks any clear focus: features of the narrative come and go without clear expression, and there is precious little grammatical elaboration of any kind.

This brings us to an important issue for grammar teaching. Unless we are very careful with the tasks we design, we can all too easily proliferate this kind of qualitatively poor language. But if learners repeatedly fail to elaborate their grammar, they will never properly proceduralise language which has been temporarily structured through product work. Instead, they will proceduralise a body of knowledge which is (to all intents and purposes) grammatically fossilised.

Manipulation, regulation and abdication

In many product classrooms, a great deal of pedagogical contrivance is devoted to the manipulation of target language, thereby providing a framework for the learner to facilitate the noticing and structuring of grammar. But in the very act of constructing such a framework we inevitably exclude much of the dynamism and unpredictability of actual language use. In process work such manipulation is rejected in favour of a focus on meaning and self-expression by the learner. But a focus on process, if it is not handled with some care, may suffer from a corresponding absence of control, leading ultimately to the proceduralisation of language which is grammatically impoverished. So a focus on ill-conceived process activity – where the learner's responses are not properly anticipated – constitutes a surrender of control to the point of abdication, and such process activities are not unheard-of in current teaching materials.

So at first sight, we have something of a pedagogic conundrum here: excessive manipulation of learner language on the one hand, and an effective abdication of any principled control on the other. What would seem desirable is a degree of balance between what are (as I have represented them) two extremes. A conception of grammar teaching which provides a measure of regulation over learner activity, but which does not jettison the need to harness the processes of language use. With this in mind, I believe that we should think of process and product not as polarities, but as points on a pedagogic continuum, with the kind of regulation I am suggesting located somewhere towards the centre (as shown in Figure 3).

Figure 3: A pedagogic continuum

MANIPULATION	REGULATION	ABDICATION
PRODUCT --- PROCESS		
language pre-selected *for* the learner	creating conditions for the learner to foster a capacity to use language and to deploy grammar by the learner	language generated *by* the learner

Regulating learner choice

The notion that learner language requires some form of regulation is not new, and the past ten years in particular have seen a number of proposals which aim for precisely this objective. One of the most notable is task-based language teaching (TBLT) as conceived by Crookes and Long (1987a, 1987b, 1992). In TBLT there is a firm emphasis on language use through interaction, and on the argument that interactional tasks can generate language which is rich both quantitatively and qualitatively. With the right kind of regulation and design, such tasks can encourage learners to 'stretch' their language (Long, 1985, 1989). This interlanguage stretching means that learners will 'operate at the outer limits of their current abilities, especially to use a) as linguistically complex speech as possible, and b) as much optional syntax as possible' (Long, 1989: 13).

To this end, a number of interactional patterns have been identified which can be generated through task design. Long (1989) argues that two-way tasks (where a two-way exchange of information between interlocutors is essential for the task to be completed) generate more negotiation than one-way tasks. Similarly, he suggests that 'closed' tasks (where learners know they must reach a pre-determined correct solution) should lead to greater quantity and quality of negotiation than 'open' tasks (where there is no such pre-determined outcome). It is also suggested that 'diverging' tasks – in which learners take up divergent views on a particular issue, as with a debate – may lead to the production of language which is grammatically quite complex and elaborate (see Duff, 1986).

Such proposals offer interesting insights into how learner language might be subtly regulated. But of course we cannot assume that such tasks will automatically lead to grammatically rich learner language, or that interlanguage stretching will thereby occur. The more initiative is given to learners, the more responsible they inevitably become for the quality of their own production. We need to give learners practice in the complex of skills involved in language use, yet at the same time we have to recognise that teachers are 'partners, not masters, in a joint enterprise' (Long, 1988: 118). This is not an argument against task-based teaching, but a call for additional measures to guide learners carefully in the skill of using grammar for communicative purposes, encouraging them to become more aware of the value of grammar within their own language production. In the next section we will consider one such measure: an approach to grammar teaching which focuses on the processes of *grammaticisation*.

4. Teaching grammar as grammaticisation

From lexis to grammar: learner choice

What I am proposing here is an approach in which learners begin with words, which they combine and modify through the application of grammar (this approach owes its origins to work by Rutherford, 1987, and Widdowson, 1990: 79–98).

In teaching which is firmly product-based, learners are repeatedly exposed to target language which is, of course, already grammatical. The direction of flow is very often from grammar to lexis, with learners presented with grammatical target language which they then manipulate through the application of different lexical items. Yet there is a strong case for reversing this trend, and for proceeding instead from lexis to grammar. Many studies of first and second language acquisition indicate that this is just what learners do. Early on, learner language is typically lexical: words are put together with minimal grammar in order to convey basic meanings (see, for example, Peters, 1983; Nattinger and DeCarrico, 1992). Starting from a basis in words, learners learn grammar gradually, as words are put together with greater sensitivity through the processes of restructuring: *man clean car* might become *man cleaned car*, and so on. Learners, then, are gradually structuring a more sensitive working model of grammar, as they become increasingly aware of the grammatical constituents which go to make up the language system. Some researchers maintain that the entire process of interlanguage development can be seen as a gradual movement from lexis to grammar, involving a progressive shift towards a more 'syntactic mode' (Givón, 1979).

One of the principal motivations for this shift towards grammar is a communicative one: it is the motivation to make meanings clear in relation to context. As Widdowson puts it:

> The greater the contribution of context in the sense of shared knowledge and experience the less need there is for grammar to augment the association of words. ... The less effective words are in identifying relevant features of context ... the more dependent they become on grammatical modification of one sort or another ... grammar is not a constraining imposition but a liberating force: it frees us from a dependency on context. (Widdowson, 1990: 86)

This explains one of the problems with the task in Figure 2. The narrative was set in the past, but the learners failed to use the past tense. One good reason for this 'failure' is simply that it was made clear to everyone from the outset that the story took place in the past – it is spelled out in the very rubric of the task. Why, then, trouble to devote scarce resources to using the past tense when such an effort would be communicatively redundant? In effect, there was no regulation of 'context gap': the gap in knowledge between what is shared (and known to be shared) between learners at the outset of a task, and the knowledge which they have clearly to signal through language to complete the task successfully. The wider the context gap, the more language becomes (to borrow Widdowson's words) 'dependent . . . on grammatical modification of one sort or another' (ibid.). Figure 4 illustrates one way in which this principle can be utilised in pedagogy. The learners are presented with words and pictures, which together form an incomplete narrative, an unfocused context. Their task is to combine and add to these words – calling on grammar in the process – to formulate clearly their own versions of events.

The pictures and the words together convey a kind of partial scenario: here is a story involving a cat, a woman, a ladder, a tree, and all these brought together through some possibly bizarre sequence of events. But exactly how these elements combine is not clear, and it is up to the learners to signal their own individual

Figure 4: Materials encouraging grammaticisation

Use all the words in Table A and at least 8 of the words in Table B to make a story. You can add any other words you like. The pictures may help you, but they do not tell the whole story. Write your final version in Table C:

Table A

She
It
Her cat
They
The firemen
Mrs. Brewin

Table B

die bite save run over arrive
leave   put up   thank   work   lie
telephone   climb   garden   tree
ladder   grass   fire-engine

Table C:

Decide in which order your events took place. When two of your events happened at the same time, put one in column A and the other in column B:

	A	B
1	*Mrs. Brewin was working in the garden.*	*Her cat lay on the grass.*
2	*The cat climbed a tree and …*	
3		
4		
5		
6		
7		
8		

interpretation and to make this interpretation clear through grammatical elaboration. Merely rearranging the words provided should not be sufficient. There is thus a built-in context gap between the initial unfocused context (provided for the learner) and the grammaticised outcome (fashioned by the learner). It is a conception of grammar as *grammaticisation* which is central here, because learners are asked to combine and add to words through the deployment of grammar for a communicative purpose. Given the degree of context gap, each learner's final formulation is likely to be different. It is important that learners are encouraged to make their particular formulations as clear as possible, perhaps by requiring them to tell their version to each other, and to note the ways in which each is distinct through a public performance. In so doing, they will be elaborating grammar to the extent that they need to for the sake of communicative clarity, and because they cannot assume that their choices will have been reproduced by others in the class.

But although it is important that each individual's version should be different, there are certain aspects of grammar which they are likely to deploy. One is the use of reference words – *she*, *it*, *they* – which (in order to be clear) need to be selected and distributed with some care. The other is the signalling of simultaneity: through Table C learners are encouraged to consider not only the sequencing of events, but also which events might have occurred simultaneously. Thus they might produce something like 'She was climbing the tree when the firemen arrived' or 'As the firemen were leaving the cat climbed the tree again'.

The objective is to allow a measure of choice in what the learner produces, while at the same time regulating or guiding these choices down particular pathways. Too often, perhaps, learners work with language which is fully grammaticised in advance, as typically happens in much product teaching. They are given, for instance, a dialogue to practise, or a series of sentences to manipulate or grammatically transform (e.g. from active to passive). Grammaticisation tasks, in contrast, aim to present grammar not as the pre-formulated product of someone else's choice, but as the outcome of the choices made by the learners themselves. This is, after all, how grammar is called upon in normal language use: as a resource for choice, and as an integral part of the construction of a wider discourse. With the task in Figure 4, then, the learner's selection and elaboration of grammar should emerge as the consequence of wider decisions made about the discourse as a whole: 'Who did what to whom?' 'When?' and 'How can I make these factors clear?'. It is precisely this conception of grammar which Rutherford argues for. He notes that grammar should be seen as the 'on-line processing component of discourse, and not the set of syntactic building blocks with which discourse is, as it were, constructed' (Rutherford, 1987: 104).

Grammaticisation and the process/product continuum

Central to the whole enterprise, then, is the issue of learner choice, and the grammatical consequences of the choices the learner makes. In principle, we can vary the degree of regulation depending on how strongly we wish to direct learners towards particular forms. We could shift the whole framework towards a greater emphasis on product, controlling the learner's choices more rigorously by supplying certain obligatory grammar words and inflections to cue the use of a particular progressive structure: *when* and *-ing*, for example, might feature as elements which the learner is required to use. Equally, the teacher may wish to stress the process element more strongly, by regulating the available choices less tightly. We might, then, give the learners fewer 'cue' words than in Figure 4, or remove one of the pictures. Words and pictures could then be distributed between a group of learners, who then have to collaborate to achieve an agreed oral version. Such a procedure would effectively widen the context gap, providing greater scope for learners to signal their own meanings, and in so doing to fashion the development of their own grammar-in-discourse. Grammaticisation tasks allow teachers to alter the degree and type of regulation from time to time in tune with learner responses. Some learners, for example, may require very careful guidance towards a point where process is emphasised more strongly.

But the very fact that the learners have a degree of choice in the language they use will mean, of course, that their language is unlikely to be completely accurate. So we might get utterances like 'she was climb the tree' or 'as they were left the cat climbing the tree', where the progressive form is wrongly or inappropriately used. Where, then, does the grammar come from for learners to use in grammaticisation tasks? There are two answers to this question. The first is that this approach to grammar teaching cannot be exclusive. The learners will continue to need the more careful focus on form which product teaching provides, and they will still need opportunities for less restrained language use through process teaching. Grammaticisation tasks might be used, then, alongside more controlled product teaching, where grammatical forms can be carefully practised. Clearly we cannot expect learners to grammaticise out of thin air, and concurrent product teaching can help them to notice and structure language which they then seek to use in grammaticisation tasks (see the argument in Batstone, 1994).

The second answer to this question has more to do with the way grammaticisation tasks are followed up. When the learner produces an utterance such as 'she was climb the tree', she is revealing what she is presently capable of, something of her existing hypothesis about language structure. Having guided her this far, the teacher can re-fashion some of her language, demonstrating how 'she was climb' can be re-shaped into 'she was climbing'. Alternatively, the teacher could play a less explicit role, asking learners to reflect for themselves on the quality of their language, perhaps by discussing it and improving it through collaborative effort (for further ideas on learner reflection on grammar, see Ellis and Sinclair, 1989). But whether the grammaticisation task is followed up with more or less teacher involvement, the learners are here considering accuracy and appropriacy from a firm basis in their own language production. They are considering how their own choices might be improved, and thus there should be a greater sense of involvement in the whole procedure.

5. Conclusions

Proposals for the regulation of learner language (including task-based teaching and – on a more modest scale – grammaticisation) may have much to recommend them, though the effectiveness of any approach can only be properly appraised by particular teachers and learners.[5] Meanwhile, there remains a strong argument in favour of a mixed methodology, where a range of teaching devices are utilised, and where process work co-exists with more product-oriented activities which can give learners repeated opportunities to notice native-like target norms. The process/ product continuum is best thought of as a continuum of pedagogic choice, a framework which represents the options available to teachers who do not locate their teaching solely within the confines of a single inflexible 'method'.

The effective teaching of grammar has never been an easy task, since the learning of grammar (like the beast itself) is multi-dimensional. It requires both a well-structured knowledge of the language system, and an ability to act on this knowledge in language use. What counts is that, whatever is done in classrooms, we continue to aim for achievement in both these critical areas.

Notes

1. The term 'noticing' suggests a degree of consciousness which is particularly pertinent to product teaching, but we should allow for the intake of data which is not achieved through conscious noticing, so the broader term 'intake' might be more generally applicable.
2. Learners will vary, though, in the degree to which they utilise memory and analysis as mechanisms for learning (see Skehan, 1989).
3. Widdowson's claims about accumulation are restricted to criticism of the notional/functional syllabus, and therefore (perhaps) to syllabuses which present language expressions as 'items for accumulation and storage' (Widdowson, 1979: 248). It is arguable whether or not this qualification can be maintained alongside Widdowson's own insistence on the independence of syllabus design from methodology.
4. Skehan, in this volume, refers to the cognitive processing by which knowledge becomes proceduralised as 'relexicalisation'.
5. These claims for teaching grammaticisation are as yet largely untested.

References

Anderson, J.R. 1985, *Cognitive Psychology and its Implications* (2nd edition), Freeman, New York.
Batstone, R. 1994, *Grammar*, OUP, Oxford.
Beebe, L. (ed.) 1988, *Issues in Second Language Acquisition: Multiple Perspectives*, Newbury House, Rowley, Mass.
Brumfit, C.J. 1984, *Communicative Methodology in Language Teaching*, CUP, Cambridge.
Crookes, G. and Long, M.H. 1987a, 'Task-based second language teaching: a brief report' (Pt. One), *Modern English Teacher*, vol. 24, no. 5, 26–8.
Crookes, G. and Long, M.H. 1987b, 'Task-based second language teaching: a brief report' (Pt. Two), *Modern English Teacher*, vol. 24, no. 6, 20–3.
Crookes, G. and Long, M.H. 1992, 'Three approaches to task-based syllabus design', *TESOL Quarterly*, vol. 26, no. 1, 27–56.
Day, R.R. (ed.) 1986, *Talking to Learn: Conversation in Second Language Acquisition*, Newbury House, Rowley, Mass.
Duff, P. 1986, 'Another look at interlanguage talk: taking task to task', in Day, R.R. (ed.), *Talking to Learn*.
Ellis, G. and Sinclair, B. 1989, *Learning to Learn English: A Course in Learner Training*, CUP, Cambridge.
Ellis, R. 1993, 'The structural syllabus and second language acquisition', *TESOL Quarterly*, vol. 27, 1.
Gass, S. and Madden, C. (eds.) 1985, *Input in Second Language Acquisition*, Newbury House, Rowley, Mass.
Givón, T. 1979, 'From discourse to syntax: grammar as a processing strategy', in *Syntax and Semantics, Vol. 12*, Academic Press, New York.
Givón, T. 1984, *Syntax: a Functional Typological Introduction*, John Benjamin, Amsterdam.

Kellerman, E. 1985, 'If at first you do succeed', in Gass, S. and Madden, C. (eds.), *Input in Second Language Acquisition*.

Lightbown, P. 1983, 'Exploring relationships between developmental and instructional sequences in L2 acquisition', in Seliger, H. and Long, M.H. (eds.), *Classroom Oriented Research in Second Language Acquisition*, Newbury House, Rowley, Mass.

Long, M.H. 1985, 'Input and second language acquisition theory', in Gass, S. and Madden, C. (eds.), *Input in Second Language Acquisition*.

Long, M.H. 1988, 'Instructed interlanguage development', in Beebe, L. (ed.), *Issues in Second Language Acquisition*.

Long, M.H. 1989, 'Task, group, and task-group interactions', *University of Hawaii Working Papers in ESL*, vol. 8, no. 2, 1–26.

McLaughlin, B. 1990, 'Restructuring', *Applied Linguistics*, vol. 11, no. 2, 113–28.

Nattinger, J.R. and DeCarrico, J.S. 1992, *Lexical Phrases and Language Teaching*, OUP, Oxford.

O'Malley, J.M. and Chamot, A.U. 1989, *Learning Strategies in Second Language Acquisition*, CUP, Cambridge.

Pawley, A. and Syder, F. 1983, 'Two puzzles for linguistic theory: nativelike selection and nativelike fluency', in Richards, J.C. and Schmidt, R. (eds.), *Language and Communication*.

Peters, A. 1983, *The Units of Language Acquisition*, CUP, Cambridge.

Richards, J.C. and Schmidt, R. (eds.) 1983, *Language and Communication*, Longman, Harlow.

Rutherford, W.E. 1987, *Second Language Grammar: Learning and Teaching*, Longman, Harlow.

Schmidt, R. 1990, 'The role of consciousness in second language learning', *Applied Linguistics*, vol. 11, no. 2, 17–46.

Skehan, P. 1989, *Individual Differences in Second Language Learning*, Edward Arnold, London.

Soars, J. and Soars, L. 1986, *Headway Intermediate*, OUP, Oxford.

Widdowson, H.G. 1979, *Explorations in Applied Linguistics*, OUP, Oxford.

Widdowson, H.G. 1984, *Explorations in Applied Linguistics 2*, OUP, Oxford.

Widdowson, H.G. 1990, *Aspects of Language Teaching*, OUP, Oxford.

Adjusting the Focus: Teacher Roles in Task-based Learning of Grammar

MARTIN BYGATE

1. Introduction

The purpose of this article is to explore some of the ways in which the learning of grammar in classrooms can be promoted through the use of communicative tasks, and to argue that, within a task-based approach, which centres work heavily on the involvement of the learners, there is a crucial role for the teacher.

There are two dimensions which can be stressed in any kind of learning. The first concerns the relative emphasis on the presentation of information, including exposure and input, as opposed to practice and exploration. The second dimension concerns the means of structuring the learning process – whether by the teacher or by the task. In one case, the learning is structured by the direct mediation of the teacher, which is typical of much institutional learning. In the second case, the structuring is mediated by the task, whether decontextualised and controlled, or contextualised and unscripted. This offers the range of options shown in Figure 1.

Figure 1: Pedagogy intervention through teacher or task

	Teacher-based	Task-based
presentation	1	2
practice	3	4

Much of the discussion of the methodology of the teaching of grammar has in the past tended to concentrate on cells 1 and 3. More recent discussion of learner-centred process syllabuses (e.g. Allwright, 1984; Breen, 1989; Prabhu, 1987) has tended to locate the focus of the discussion in cell 2. The argument is that a syllabus consists of a selection of tasks chosen in the light of the language input that learners judge they need. The work of Long and colleagues (e.g. Long and Porter, 1985) on the role of group work in generating negotiated input similarly locates the major issues primarily in cell 2. For Long, tasks provide a context for learners to negotiate their input at the micro-level of learner–learner interaction. Breen (1989) argues

237

that tasks provide a context for the learning of all aspects of language, but stresses the issue of providing an effective procedure for promoting input and intake.

In contrast, a separate line of argument has been gradually emerging for attention to be paid to the kind of learning that might occur in cell 4 (e.g. Brumfit, 1984a; Swain, 1985; Johnson, this volume). The use of unscripted tasks, in particular, has often been advocated to satisfy the need for learner-centred *practice* in classrooms. Two major aspects of learning engaged here are those of integrated practice of grammar within language processing, and the restructuring of language knowledge (see Skehan, this volume).

These concerns underlie two particular methodological issues which this paper aims to discuss. Firstly, is it possible for teachers to select unscripted tasks with particular linguistic aims in mind? This simple question involves the interesting issue of whether learner-centred tasks should fall within the domain of the overall responsibility of the teacher, and if so, in what ways. The second issue concerns the extent to which task-based learning should be essentially 'creative' in Brumfit's sense (1984b), or whether the successful learning of the communicative use of language might not, quite importantly, depend upon the opportunity learners have to generalise from one communicative situation to another, and to re-use or refine familiar solutions to familiar problems, rather than be continually inventing new responses (cf. Cameron, 1991, for a similar point regarding mother-tongue development).

This paper will provide evidence for suggesting that some predictions, albeit in varying degrees of probability, can be made about the grammar that will be practised on certain language tasks. It will also argue for the systematic manipulation by teachers of unscripted tasks with a view to developing learners' grammatical proficiency. Both these views are at odds with some of the stronger positions regarding the role of the teacher in communicative language teaching. However, there are various reasons for believing that language teachers should not abdicate from intervention even in unscripted classroom learning. This position also argues for a closer alignment between applied language research and language pedagogy.

2. Background

There are – inevitably – a number of assumptions which underlie such discussions. First of all, and most fundamentally, I assume that articles such as those appearing in this volume are written in order to make generalisations about the nature of language learning, and about the nature of teachers' possible contributions to or interventions in language learning. In addition, these generalisations will describe common patterns in the nature of language ability and language development, though they will not exhaust all possible patterns or be entirely predictive for any given learner. Hence this article considers the task-based learning of grammar from the perspective of the teacher (see also Batstone, this volume). What kinds of language outcome can teachers expect to derive from the use of particular activities, and how can they adjust tasks to promote development?

There is also the question of what is referred to by the term 'grammar'. Grammar can be defined as the conventions according to which lexical items, phrases and clauses are combined, their roles and relations are identified, in the communication of meanings. This is carried out through devices such as sequencing and morphemic marking. The term 'convention' is preferred to 'rule', since conventions emerge through custom, whereas rules are formulated and applied. Furthermore, conventions, like grammar, gradually evolve.

Grammatical phenomena tend to be distinguished from lexical phenomena because:

(a) they involve sequencing conventions;
(b) where morphemes are concerned, either they depend on the presence of lexical items (as with inflections, determiners), or they make up closed sets, such as pronominal items, prepositions or conjunctions.

Grammatical features have meaningful functions. They interrelate elements at three levels of analysis: lexical items at group level; groups at clause level; and clauses at sentence level. Grammatical features are also used above sentence level to mark relations between sentences, or between lower level units within or across different sentences. These functions help to disambiguate meanings, sometimes signalling the role of units (e.g. with markers such as *to* with the infinitive), sometimes contributing contrastively to the meaning of units (such as plural *-s*, tense markers or determiners). Grammar, in other words, contributes in different ways to communicative success, and consists of a range of different phenomena.

A further assumption concerns the nature of grammatical ability and the nature of grammatical development. Issues underlying this are discussed in greater detail in other papers in this volume, particularly those by Johnson, Skehan and Willis. I will briefly outline them here.

Grammar within language use

One set of issues concerns the relationship between grammar and other aspects of language. Speakers have to apply grammatical rules in and for the construction of utterances. Some grammer is always necessary for the deployment of lexis, however elementary the speaker. Grammar has therefore been described as a set of procedures (Johnson, this volume) involving decisions at various points in the assembly of utterances. Various issues arise in connection with this. One key question concerns the point at which grammatical decisions are taken in relation to the selection of lexical items. Grammatical decisions involve choosing:

● which sequence to put words in
● which word or phrase should follow a previously selected word or phrase
● which groups and clauses need marking, and how to mark them
● what kinds of cohesive relations need to be marked, and how to mark them

- what tense, aspect or number information to select from amongst the options available in the language, and how to mark it.

Because of the different kinds of function of grammatical features, meanings to be encoded grammatically will often only be selected after the lexical items. Hence, grammar needs to be practised around the selection of vocabulary (cf. Sinclair, 1991, for a similar view).

In any case, grammatical decisions will often (though not always) depend on lexical choices. For example, consider the following example:

1(a) We'd better catch the bus
 (b) The bus had better be caught (??)

The sentence is uncomfortable in the passive. This may be due to the phrase *catch the bus*, which resists passivisation because of its semantics (i.e. the bus is a part of a process, not the subject or theme of a process), rather than because of the modal structure. This can be seen once the lexical items are changed:

2(a) Someone had better phone the security guards
 (b) The guards had better be phoned

In the following example we have a slightly different case:

3(a) We finally got the hang of it
 (b) The hang of it was finally got (?)

This sentence seems even more abnormal in the passive – the meaning is lost altogether by passivisation. There seems to be a semantic constraint in which nouns forming part of a process are unlikely to be passivised. In both examples 1 and 3 we have phrases which have particular grammatical qualities reflecting different degrees of 'formulaicity'. Pawley and Syder (1983) list large numbers of such phrases which are more or less tightly bound together and which cannot be used with all the potential grammatical options for the word classes they represent. This then is one way in which grammar can be used; that is, systematically to relate prefabricated phrases to other lexical units. In language production, then, grammatical decisions need to be taken as lexical items or formulaic phrases are accessed.

Let us look at a further example of grammatical decisions following the use of the verb with an indirect object. The indirect object position (and presence or absence of the preposition *to*) varies according to the specific verb which has been selected, for example *tell* or *explain*:

4(a) Nick told me how to get to the school
 (b) Nick explained to me how to get to the school

We know that the choice of lexical verb signifies certain semantic distinctions, one of which may involve a suggestion of difficulty in the content where the verb *explain* is used. A speaker producing this utterance, having chosen a particular lexical verb, will have to structure its completion according to the grammar of the verb. Note that the semantic value of the verb is not what influences the syntactic pattern. Selection of the verb *say* has different semantic implications, the verb *describe* has possibly more, but both involve the same forms of indirect object complementation as *explain* and *tell*. So we can remind ourselves once again that syntactic patterns are often semantically largely arbitrary, arising as a result of the conventional ways in which users of English deploy verbs (one group requiring the preposition *to*, the other group allowing a choice).

The selection of a syntactic pattern in a given utterance can then arise out of the choice of lexical item. The implication of this discussion is that the kind of practice which foreign language speakers need at some point is in both choosing their lexical items and selecting appropriate grammatical structures to weave the lexis into their utterances. Seen from this perspective, learning is, in part, likely to take the form of gradual improvement in the accuracy and fluency of grammatical processing around learners' use of lexical items.

This leads us to recognise the crucial importance in language learning of practising the processing of grammar within the context of unscripted communication. In other words, cell 4 in Figure 1 above takes on particular importance. So what kind of grammar learning can this aspect of classroom work be expected to promote? This question is considered in the following section.

The learning of grammar

There must be a second set of assumptions concerning our views of how grammar is learnt. Johnson and Batstone (both this volume) suggest two major ways of learning grammar – firstly from initially 'acquired' language, and secondly through conscious attention to patterns. In the first case, grammar is viewed as an inexplicit awareness of the combinatory patterns with which different types of words occur. In the other case, grammar is viewed initially as a procedure to be applied to the use of lexical items. In the case of the learning of grammar from previously acquired language, grammar is learnt rather in the way other patterns of behaviour are learnt. Generalisations are made intuitively across utterances. On the other hand, in the case of learning through conscious attention to patterns or to rules, what tends to happen is that conventions need to be learnt independently, and then associated with relevant lexical items in relevant contexts, in order to be appropriately applied. In this mode, rules are learnt as separate bits of language knowledge, and thus have to be 'accessed' from memory, rather in the way individual vocabulary items have to be recalled. Task-based learning can be defined so as to fit equally well into either pattern.

There are two particular types of language learning that task-based practice can be expected to promote. In the first place, task-based practice can be expected to promote fluency in the accessing of given types of grammatical structure in relation to the deployment of different lexical units. For instance, tasks can be selected because they pose problems for speakers in specifying reference (as in descriptions or narrations), time sequence (as in narrations), position (as in descriptions of scenes), or other characteristics, such as appearance. They can be selected because they can be expected to provide practice in the use of specific verb forms, such as tenses, aspects or expressions of modality. Ur (1988) provides a wide range of unscripted tasks intended to give rise to the communicative use of specific grammatical features. Thus the teacher's choice of exercise may be intended to engage learners in specific grammatical decisions along with the meaningful selection of lexical items for the communication of information (see Bygate, 1992, for other ways in which task can influence language). The intention is also likely to be that these decisions will be gradually routinised.

A second aspect of grammar learning that tasks can be expected to promote is what McLaughlin (1990) and Skehan (this volume) term 'restructuring'. 'Restructuring' refers to the internal process whereby learners generalise from specific learning experiences to reorganise their knowledge into a more efficient storage pattern. One recent study aiming to explore this kind of effect is Doughty (1991). The form this process takes will depend partly on the learner's previous experiences. In addition, efficiency will inevitably be judged partly in terms of the external demands placed upon a learner. Bruner (1966) refers to the need for learners to store their knowledge in a way which corresponds to the demands of the environment, and hence effective restructuring can be thought of as arising both from the perception of similarities (and contrasts) between comparable events (presumably the only basis upon which generalisations can be made), and from the pressures of subsequent situations.

The relevance of this view to the use of unscripted learning tasks (by 'unscripted' is meant tasks in which learners have to decide on both the content and form of messages) is the implication that helpful pedagogy might provide learners with a basis for making useful generalisations through the systematic use of tasks. Systematic use of, say, 'prioritising tasks' (such as selecting equipment for a journey, or prioritising candidates for a job) could enable learners to work out ways of handling such tasks, and to begin to develop a facility for the kinds of utterances that turn out to be useful in carrying them out. This is a neglected perspective on the use of communicative tasks in a discussion which has revolved around the need to promote creativity in language learning (e.g. Brumfit, 1984b). The danger, it would seem, from emphasising too great a reliance on learners' creativity would be that it would sanction a random use of tasks, giving rise to random creative solutions. This could make it difficult for learners to generate useful generalisations about the grammar, vocabulary or discourse structures used on different tasks. Restructuring might then occur only at a very simple level, possibly encouraging the emergence of uninflected (i.e. 'stem-form') English, and possible fossilisation.

What is needed, rather, is the systematic use of unscripted tasks, so as to encourage learners to look either explicitly or implicitly for generalisations about different aspects of their use of language. Thus creativity would be exploited along with a constructively systematic exploitation of unscripted activities. This approach leads to the need to examine the language produced by learners working on such tasks, in order to pick out typically occurring features. The following section provides an initial sketch of how this might work. Although the term 'task' can be used to refer to any language practice activity, in the following discussion the term refers to unscripted communication activities.

3. Tasks, grammar and teacher intervention

There are four main areas where a teacher may intervene in task-based learning: pre-task preparation; task selection; manipulation of on-task conditions; and post-task follow-up (see also Bygate, 1988; Skehan, this volume). All four areas provide opportunities for the teacher to influence learning by varying different aspects of the learning tasks. This outline is sketched out in the belief that although there are a number of other factors that teachers need to take into account in the classroom (such as learner motivation, learner independence and the quality of interaction), focus on these four areas could permit a systematic implementation of tasks which could then be accessible to regular evaluation.

Long and Porter (1985) suggested that pedagogical decisions might be justified both on psycholinguistic and on pedagogical grounds. Long and Porter were discussing group work, but their point can presumably apply to other aspects of classroom methodology and I would like to suggest that there are pedagogical and psycholinguistic reasons for believing in the importance of these four dimensions of tasks.

The psycholinguistic reasons are the following:

1. Student preparation for a task may have an effect on both fluency and accuracy: pre-task preparation may help to reduce the amount of on-line planning, either of form or message, hence releasing capacity for last minute selections of forms and monitoring of self or others (Ochs, 1979). This may also encourage students to focus on forms in unscripted tasks.
2. Selection of tasks with a particular language focus is likely to encourage repeated exposure to particular clusters of forms and meanings (Brown and Yule, 1983; Bygate, 1992).
3. Manipulation of conditions is likely to influence the proportional amounts of attention that can be devoted to form and to meaning (Johnson, this volume).
4. Post-task follow-up is likely to provide the opportunity for both repetition and formal feedback on students' use of linguistic features (Willis and Willis, 1987), as well as to help focus attention on form and meaning (Skehan, this volume).

From the pedagogic perspective, these four dimensions can be expected to influence learning largely by promoting motivation in the students, through raising awareness about the pedagogical coherence of the course, in the following ways:

1. by providing the students with a motivation for the use of learning activities prior to doing them;

2. by enabling explicit connections to be made between activities carried out on different occasions;
3. by enabling students to understand aspects of the rationale underlying the selection of tasks and the ways they are used;
4. by indicating how the teacher and the learners themselves may be made to account for their work (the teacher in terms of being answerable to the learners for the use of learners' time in the selection of tasks and their implementation; and the learners in terms of how they meet agreed evaluation criteria).

We now look in detail at the parameters along which communicative grammar practice can be varied in classroom activities.

4. Aspects of task variation

This section outlines ways in which the four intervention points can be exploited in order to vary the focus and difficulty of unscripted tasks. The section is largely programmatic, since relatively little research has been carried out into this aspect of learners' language.

(a) Pre-task preparation

Prior to doing a task, the teacher has the option of preparing the students or not. In some cases, the teacher will want to allow the learners to work on their own and explore their own possible ways of carrying out the task, and the kinds of language they think will work. On other occasions, however, the teacher will want to cue learners in advance to the purpose of the task. This will often be desirable in order to focus the learners' attention so that they know what they are working towards, which may help to integrate a focus on form into a communicative use of language. It can also have the effect of helping students to relate the coming task to previous comparable language tasks. Preparatory focusing can also provide a useful framework for the provision and understanding of post-task feedback.

Student preparation involves two major types of decision on the part of the teacher regarding grammatical features:

1. how far learners' attention should be drawn to grammatical forms and patterns, as opposed to their meanings;
2. how far focus on form should involve explicit grammatical commentary.

Meaning-focused or form-focused exposure may be provided through listening to or reading native speakers modelling the task and providing useful language. Alternatively, it might be provided through the teacher modelling the task with the whole class. This could be thought of as procedural if it does not invite explicit discussion.

Explicit description can be provided in conjunction with exposure, or it can be provided separately. And as Wilkins (1976) noted, there are different types of provision – synthetic, where the learner proceeds from the rules to their application; or analytic, where the learner deduces the rules from sample data. Matching rules to samples of language presented in data would be an example of the analytic approach. This could be done to exemplify grammatical or, indeed, discourse features likely to be useful on the task.

(b) Task selection

The topic of task selection raises the question of what linguistic reasons there may be for the selection of a given task. This may involve the issue of determining what features of language are practised by different tasks; and whether the main task should be principally receptive or productive. Task selection is likely to be made bearing these opportunities in mind. This area of decision making may often be taken for granted in courses where the coursebook provides most of the learning activities. However, the issue of task selection is central in teachers' planning and monitoring of their work. Without a clear perception of the reasons for selecting one task rather than another, particularly where oral work is concerned, the development of learners will be hard to monitor or assess.

Furthermore, once teachers are aware of the linguistic purpose for a given task, the option is open to explain the purpose of tasks to the learners, as we have already mentioned. A recent institution-based study by Young (1992) found that learners are frequently unaware of the reasons for doing classroom tasks. While this may be less important for some learners and for some tasks than for others, the issue is one which deserves attention.

(c) Manipulation of on-task conditions

Different practice conditions will facilitate learning to different degrees. One basic but much neglected topic is that of repetition – to what extent, and in what ways, can repetition of the same or similar tasks promote learning? The question raised here is not what language will be practised through the task, but rather whether familiarity with the task is worth exploiting for promoting further development. Skill theory would predict that repetition would be useful in one way or another – either to improve selection and accuracy of key language features, or to improve fluency of those or other parts of the discourse.

There are a number of possible ways of varying the task. One is to vary processing time (cf. Johnson, 1986 and this volume), so that learners are forced to do the task faster than they would if left alone, and so increase automation. Another way of varying task conditions is to alter preparation time, so that learners have less time to think about what they are going to say or how they are going to say it. It may also make a difference to vary the presence or absence of visual support (such as linguistic prompts, diagrams or pictures) so as to force learners to work from memory. Group size may itself increase the pressure on speakers. And by having students monitor each other (for example, by including one or more observers in each group), it is possible to increase the focus on form, since the presence of an observer provides the possibility of on-line feedback or delayed feedback. A final variant involves the simple choice between doing a given task orally or in writing. Once again, in either case varying the conditions is likely to affect the processing load; that is, the difficulty of carrying out the task.

(d) Post-task follow-up (implicit or explicit)

Follow-up can be related to learners' awareness of the reasons for doing a given task. If a task is to be done for a purpose, and learners know the purpose, then it makes sense for them to be able to assess the outcome. Indeed, a major frustration within communicative language teaching (CLT) may be that students can be required to carry out tasks without being provided with constructive feedback. Study under these circumstances can be demotivating. Why carry out a task if the teacher is not interested in the linguistic outcome, or if the teacher doesn't report back on the outcome?

Focus on form was discouraged in the strong version of CLT (e.g. Brumfit, 1984b; Prabhu, 1987; Ur, 1981), according to which focus on meaning would on its own entail a gradual improvement in accuracy, as well as providing its own re-inforcement for further use of the language. In particular, correction was seen as problematic where learners were supposed to be concentrating on the communi-cation of meaning: firstly, it would frustrate them, and secondly, it would not be effective, because of the cognitive load of incorporating feedback while struggling to convey meaning. In addition, oral communication activities would in any case be virtually impossible to monitor where carried out in group work.

With respect to the problem of coping with feedback while engaged on a com-municative task, ultimately skilled performance involves integrating fluency and accuracy (Levelt, 1978). Hence, although it is true that learners can easily be overloaded, a refusal on the part of the teacher to confront the integration of fluency and accuracy can be seen as a dereliction of duty. After all, any form of learning involves reconciling precisely this conflict. Willis and Willis (1987) suggest a solution to the logistical difficulty of monitoring group work through using some group work as a rehearsal stage for an ensuing 'performance'. The 'performance stage' would then be available for monitoring by the teacher. Within this stage, there are then a number of ways in which the teachers can monitor learners' ability to handle tasks, either individually or in groups.

We will now illustrate this framework by considering how these options of preparation, task selection, variation of on-task conditions and post-task follow-up might be applied to the use of a particular oral communication task.

5. Learner data

This section reports on the range of grammatical features used by groups of non-native speakers while carrying out a communication task. These features are discussed, and the discussion is followed by an enumeration of a range of different procedures in which teachers could embed the task in order to increase learners' attention to the features in question.

The data referred to are part of a larger study (Bygate, 1988) and were recorded from ten groups of non-native speakers working on a small number of well-known oral tasks. In general terms it is worth remarking that many aspects of the data collected are consistent with a skills interpretation of language production. For instance, although all the ten groups who were recorded knew the basic grammatical features of the language (such as simple clause structure using present tense verbs, *there is*, prepositional phrases, simple (first) conditional structures, subordinate clauses with *when*, expressions such as *kind of* and *sort of*) nonetheless there are very clear differences in the students' selection of grammatical exponents. This would be broadly explained within skill theory by the lack of proceduralisation of basic grammatical knowledge.

Grammar in task performance

The task discussed here is a 'picture differences' task. It involves learners in communicating with each other about two pictures in order to identify differences between them. This is a simple and well-known CLT task. Elsewhere (Bygate, 1992) I have suggested that one of the characteristic features of this task is that learners of different levels may carry it out in different ways. More elementary students will tend to break the task down into a question-and-answer routine, one of the students asking about specific aspects of the other's picture and, on receiving information, then drawing the conclusion explicitly that there is a similarity or difference. Students may remain in one role throughout the activity, which is likely if one is weaker than the other, or else they may exchange the questioning and answering roles. More advanced students will tend to provide a full oral report of their picture in one go, and rely on the listener to extract key differences from that oral report. In this case, roles are assumed at the outset and have little chance of being exchanged.

Given the nature of the task, much of the language used involves the identification and description of elements in the pictures. The grammar then typically involves use of present tense verbs, simple present involving descriptive use of the copula:

S.2: *there is a clock on – on top – of the door that is open* (Group D)

and the present progressive to describe a posture or movement of people in the picture:

S.2: *and a man is getting away – through the door – he's running* (Group D)
S.14: *the old lady is looking at the man who is leaving* (Group E)

Relative clauses (as in this last example) are often used to introduce descriptions of the people. Objects are located using adverbial phrases and *there is*. Objects and people are identified generally with the use of the indefinite article. Some second reference to objects and people occurs and in those cases the definite article is usually used, sometimes with a supporting adjective.

A further feature of verb use arises from the fact that the exercise requires the students to identify differences. They tend to do this in one of two ways. They might produce negative clauses to contrast with preceding affirmative clauses, for example:

S.3: *it isn't eh he isn't eh a man who is sitting on a chair – it's a – a woman* (Group A)
S.1: *we don't have flowers we have er a kind of plant* (Group C)
S.3: *I have a lamp on the table which you don't have* (Group D)
S.17: *there's not a small – t'erm a high table there is a very l low one* (Group F)

Alternatively speakers may produce directly contrasting parallel affirmative structures:

S.3: *in mine she's sitting on a table*
S.4: *in mine she's sitting in the stairs* (Group D)

Sometimes differences are conveyed more implicitly:

S.17: *some differences in between yours and my mine picture there instead of a five year old girl there is erm I think maybe a fifteen years old girl [. . .] there is no basket there is a teddy bear instead* (Group F)

At times this may be occurring for strategic reasons, such as to avoid using the negative, or to use a more common L1 structure:

S.3: *the girl is without shoes and your little girl is with shoes; there's a man only [. . .] while in mine there's a man with a boy*
S1: *and in my picture the lady is missing one button [. . .] and in yours*
S2: *has all the buttons* (Group D)

These different ways of communicating the information may well reflect differences in levels of proficiency, since Groups D and F had considerably higher TOEFL scores than Group C. Finally, there is use of the modal *can*, particularly to introduce new items of information:

S.2: *and then I can see a buffet* (Group D)

A third area of verb group use arises out of the need for students to produce language to monitor their progress on the task. Speakers may need to use the present perfect in order to assess where they have got to in the task:

S.1: *I think that if we start comparing . no our pictures because we have already established the differences* (Group A)

More often they tend to use the simple present, however:

S.1: *so you have three differences the first one is a man [. . .]* (Group D)
S.13: *so that is the difference [. . .]; so that's another difference [. . .]; so there is the first difference* (Group E).

The data provide evidence that the task can require some use of adjectives, although in many cases this seems redundant. It may be a stylistic feature (the speakers were Peruvian speakers of Spanish), a possibility suggested by Tannen's 1980 study of the oral narrative strategies of Greek and American English speakers, and Dart's 1992 study of a child's narrative styles in English and French. There are however other possible explanations, such as the intention to produce additional means of distinguishing verbally between the referents:

1.66 S.14: *behi behind him is a young lady [. . .]* (Group E)
1.73 S.14: *just . the old lady* (Group E)

the use of adjectives as a way of trawling for further possible differences:

so I have just – two three men a child and a lady an old lady (Group E)

or the desire on the part of the speakers to perform to the tape recorder:

S1: *this little girl – this nice little girl is wearing [. . .]* (Group A)

(In the last case, 'nice' is unlikely to be of much help in completing the task. This type of occurrence is, however, more rare.) It is quite conceivable that carrying out a picture differences task will naturally encourage speakers to encode more information than is strictly necessary for the task to be completed, since at least one of the speakers will not know what is relevant and what is not. There may also be a natural tendency to use redundancy in order to help memory processes.

As noted above, a final feature of the language deserving mention is the strategic use of questions on the part of one of the speakers in order to direct the interlocutor to provide information. This is not a necessary product of working on this task (indeed several of the more advanced groups complete the task without using questions at all). However, questions may be employed as a way of lightening the processing load of the task. This may be because questions can be used to get a colleague to share some of the load of accessing relevant language. Alternatively it may be that questions are used as a way of regulating the flow of information from a stronger to a weaker member of the group. Examples include the following:

S.2: *how about the rug – on the floor – do you have it*
S.1: *no we have a carpet*
S.2: *carpet – I mean carpet*

S.2: *how about the lamp*
S.1: *we don't have a lamp*

S.2: *how about the picture*
S.1: *we we have instead a picture*
S.2: *on the wall*

S.1: *we have a clock*
S.2: *oh no I got here a picture hanging on the wall*
S.1: *and near there is a picture* (Group C)

These extracts indicate how a single question can be used routinely to obtain information – both content and language information – from the interlocutor. It is worth noting that these exchanges may also have the function of negotiating new input attributed to the 'negotiation of meaning' routines studied for instance by Long (1981), Pica (1987), and discussed in Long and Porter (1985). Questions are asked in order to elicit information about what appears in the colleague's picture, and at the same time to obtain relevant language items to carry out the task. Responses tend to take the simple form of affirmative or negative statements. The questioners may then use their partners' language to build further utterances. A summary of the features occurring in the task appears in Figure 2.

Figure 2: Grammatical features in a *Picture Differences* task

---

(a) **Functions – description: identification, characteristics, position, disposition**
simple present, present progressive
noun groups
prepositional phrases
descriptive relative clauses of place, of action, of attribute
adjectives
questions: yes/no; *wh-*

(b) **Functions – interpretation**
  • identity and characteristics: modals, present copulas (*seems*; *looks like*), subordinate *because*, adverbs of probability
  • position and disposition (linked to narrative potential): modals, present copulas (*seems*; *looks like*), present perfect, subordinate *because*, adverbs of probability

(c) **Functions – similarities/differences**
  • implicit: contrasting descriptions (using above exponents)
  • explicit descriptions: use of negatives;
      interpretations: lexical verbs and modals expressing opinions and
      (dis)agreement; nominal clauses

Evidence of the need for task-based practice

While an analysis of the occurrence of grammatical features is essential to form an impression of the type of practice learners are likely to derive from using a particular task, the question may nonetheless arise whether the occurrence of a given number of grammatical features is only due to the fact that they were already learnt. What is the point of using an activity, a critic might ask, if the students already know how to deploy the relevant grammatical features? One response might be to show ways in which even quite proficient students are often not able to produce forms fluently while working on tasks. There are many examples of this type of deviant language use. By 'deviant language use' is meant language which deviates from target language norms.

Students at post-intermediate level produced frequent instances of deviant utterances of varying degrees of importance in relation to standard British English. Examples include the following:

Group A

it has a brown colour
it has – – – – waste basket – it has a basket – who probably serves buy *er for buying some things in the market*
this is a man running away of *the room*
and then I can see . out of the room – a little child that it's *by the window*
and there is also a woman – that is er stand *– and is looking at the man . that is running away – out of the room*
there is also a mirror who *is – er which is used to – to – er – – to keep – some brushes – – that . probably they are* using *the for – for – – – for – – – – keeping their clothes . without dust*
– – erm the stairs are also with *rugs*
in my picture I have twelve at *sharp*

Group B

I have a man that is leaving out
[a man] with a handbag in her in her *in his left hand*
an er passengers who is *hurrying*
and I can see another erm behi *eh under the under the> . window*

Group C

a boy is erm – – – is / ? / is erm – is at *the wall*
in the cafeteria is a man drinking coffee
on the floor after *– outside of the front of the restaurant*
the> rich girl doesn't have shoes – his *shoes off*

Group D

in *my clock it is ten o'clock and* in *yours it's twelve*
in mine's just a> the seven seven or eight y years years

S3: then another difference is er> the teddy bear – on *mine is just* on *the steps by – – alone – and in yours the teddy bear is* carried by

S4: she's she's holding the teddy bear

and the girl is <u>without</u> *shoes and your little girl is* <u>with</u> *shoes and* <u>with</u> *socks in my picture the lady is* <u>missing</u> *one button*

Group E

he has er – . he has his . his hands – <u>in the</u> *back*
his head is <u>down</u> *so it seems that he is punished*
you feel he is <u>in a stress</u>

Group J

there is a . flower pot with – six . white flowers <u>on</u> *it*

Thus, relatively proficient speakers make a range of errors even when working on what appear to be fairly simple communication tasks. Such tasks then provide an important context both for diagnosing and practising grammatical performance.

It should be said that none of these forms caused a breakdown in communication. On the other hand, they are fairly commonly described and frequently taught aspects of standard AE or BE grammar. The students were well aware of the standard forms – indeed self-correction sometimes indicates such awareness. The point is that practised speakers working with a stable grasp of the L2 grammar could be expected to manage these features without too much variation. This is not to deny that there will always be certain aspects of the L2 grammar which will be used so rarely that they remain particularly susceptible to variation. At the same time, one interpretation must be that despite the simplicity of the task and of the pictures, speakers have difficulty in encoding a number of aspects of the content according to native-speaker (NS) norms. This may be due less to ignorance of the normal forms than to a lack of capacity on the part of the speakers to select the appropriate forms, when under pressure to perform in the context of a given task. In other words, task-based practice, and indeed task-related teacher intervention, might well help learners to increase their ability to deploy what they know in accordance with NS norms. To paraphrase Clark (1974), task-based practice may help learners to perform their competence. How then can teachers intervene to promote this development? This is the topic of the next section.

Task-based grammar learning and teacher intervention

We have seen that there are a number of linguistic criteria for the selection of a given task, to the extent that it will be likely to provide practice in the use of a range of language features, for example verb groups such as simple, perfect, progressive, passive or modal. The task may place stress on the importance of adequate referential precision which might influence the use of determiners, pronouns or lexical items, particularly adjectives (cf. Brown and Yule, 1983). The referential load may also influence the use of relative clauses, one function of which can be to insert information related to one time frame into a clause with a different time frame (Perdue and Klein, 1992). Other features of a task may place stress on the use of prepositions to mark place or time.

Nonetheless, task-based language use may not of itself necessarily lead to adequate integration of fluency and accuracy, as has been frequently pointed out (e.g. Batstone, Johnson and Skehan, this volume). Apart from the fact that learners do not always do what they are expected to do, clearly teaching does not end with task selection. What opportunities for teacher intervention are there around an exercise such as the one which we have been examining? Using the framework outlined in Section 3 of this paper, the next section provides a brief outline of a number of ways in which aspects of a picture differences task can be varied, many of them susceptible to systematic research and evaluation.

(a) Preparation

Preparation can take at least four different guises:

- general purpose review
- preparing the language
- rehearsing the language
- rehearsing the actual activity

A general purpose review of the activity can serve to remind the learners of the nature of the activity from the point of view of speaker and hearer; the kinds of interactive work they are likely to be doing in the two roles; and the purpose of combining fluency and accuracy work. In a picture differences task, this could take the form of reviewing the ways in which the interaction can be organised, and the likely stages of the task. This can have the general effect of helping concentration, and providing an appropriate mental set, akin to 'visualisation', whereby athletes think through the activity they are about to perform, a procedure thought to enhance performance (e.g. Terry, 1989).

Language preview on the other hand involves more specific previewing of potentially useful language features before the task is begun, under the direction of the teacher. In the case of a picture differences task, this may involve practising negative structures, *there is/are*, prepositional phrases, relevant phrases or vocabulary. This may be done without implying that these forms have to be used: rather as musicians might practise one or two scales and arpeggios in the key of the piece they are about to play, a learner might try out useful structures before trying a language task.

Language rehearsal, in contrast, would involve encouraging learners to anticipate for themselves the kinds of language they would use before embarking on the task – possibly the first in a series of rehearsals enabling learners to work on their control of language in use. Rehearsal of this kind is something second language users will often use as a strategy prior to real-life communication. Planning ahead can be one way of taking some of the load off the performers and may even enable them to mobilise more language than they might otherwise be able to access when engaged in the task.

Finally, *whole task rehearsal* may well be used, involving the teacher in doing another example of the same task with the whole class. This might consist of a teacher–class dialogue involving picture differences, or else large groups of the class sharing the same picture so as to enable the teacher to demonstrate ways of doing the task. This stage can focus on all levels of performance of the task – the language, the interaction, the stages, or more detailed features such as clarification routines. This can enable pair or small group work to be opened up to public view before a task is undertaken, and can be of help to weaker students.

The point behind this phase is that, rather like work in the science laboratory, the art class or the sports field, various types of preparation can be helpful to heighten attention and improve performance.

(b) Conditions

Task conditions can be varied in order to ensure repetition of valuable tasks under different guises, particularly under differing conditions of difficulty. The value of this is that similar discourse problems can be experienced on more than one occasion, and learners are able to perceive improvements in their understanding and performance of the tasks. In the picture differences task, a number of variations can be used on the basic task type.

Distribution of information: Two students can be asked to share a picture, with the likely effect that they will help each other to produce aspects of the language such as vocabulary, or help to structure or complete each others' utterances. To complicate the task, there might be more than two similar pictures, requiring identification of similarities and differences between all of them. This might be expected to have the effect of increasing the amount of reference to previously identified features, increasing the frequency of use of articles and pronouns.

Information content: Varying the amount of information content can also affect the difficulty of a task (Brown and Yule, 1983). A set of pictures packed with details is likely to require more specific use of language (such as lexical selection and noun modification) than pictures with few details. Variation in the proportion of features carrying differences could also have an effect on the language: a high proportion would imply that most nominations of features will reveal differences. This would be more likely to produce contrasting structures, such as affirmative/ negative utterances and utterances involving contrastive substitution of lexical items.

A further point is that, as Brown and Yule point out, the language work involved in comparing pictures will be influenced by the similarity of the features in the picture. With pictures of a bowl of fruit, we would expect differences mainly at the level of numbers and types of fruit, so that most language work would involve the naming and counting of objects. On the other hand, pictures of a football match would involve two teams of ten identically dressed players, leading to relevant differences occurring in the details of the players' appearance, posture or position. Before being able to establish these differences, however, speakers would have to be quite precise in establishing common reference.

Finally, the information load could have an effect on the interaction pattern. Tasks involving communication of large amounts of detail and careful reference are also likely to have the effect of producing a higher number of shorter turns whereby speakers would negotiate precise information. It would be much harder (though not impossible) under these circumstances for one speaker to produce lengthy turns which the listener can confidently follow without interrupting.

Performance constraints: Carrying out the task under different conditions can influence the way a task is performed, and may affect the extent to which the speakers focus on form or meaning. This can be done, for instance, by imposing a time limit, or doing the task as a race between groups. It can also be done by requiring the activity to be carried out before an audience (who would need to be provided with their own purpose for listening). A further constraint can be to require speakers to monitor themselves or each other for accuracy. A peer observer can be added to the group to do this. Variations of these kinds may of course influence the students' listening as well as their speaking.

Other variations: Other variations can be introduced, such as not revealing in advance the number of differences in the pictures. This can be expected to influence the amount of checking that the students will engage in. If the pictures are easy, speakers can be asked to turn the pictures over once they have looked at them, and then carry out the task from memory. Once again, the purpose of this set of variations is not simply to provide the students with an amusing task: it is to vary the stress they are under as they integrate their use of language into a wide range of communication processes.

(c) Follow-up

The follow-up can be divided into two areas: first, the direct outcome from the activity itself, enabling teacher and students to evaluate their performance on the task; and secondly, further activities which would enable various aspects of the language to be re-used. The purpose of focusing on an outcome is to see how students do the task, and to provide added motivation for them to concentrate on it in their groups: students should know before starting group work what kind of follow-up activity will be required. The intention is not to make this aspect of the class unpleasantly inquisitorial, but simply to demonstrate the pedagogic importance of being able to do the activity, and to review ways of doing it. A desirable secondary effect might be to make the whole-class interaction more like cooperative group work, rather than to deform the activity into some kind of arcane ritual.

Outcome: The basic outcome on a task such as this is obviously to check the number of differences identified. The underlying point, however, is to ensure that the students are able to describe the differences orally in appropriate, accurate and fluent language, so the class can usefully focus on some aspect of their performance. For example, they might check on the accuracy and appropriacy of grammatical features, such as article or pronoun use, relative clauses or verb forms, and the precision of prepositional phrases. Alternatively, they can be concerned with the fluency of performance. One key issue needs stressing here: simplicity of focus is very important. Any corrective feedback from peers or from the teacher must be limited to what the student can remember, and preferably to what can be useful to other students.

In order for teacher and class to check differences together, a number of possible oral performance tasks can be used. Students might sometimes be required to report the differences orally, working directly from their pictures. With many groups it might be done from memory. To provide support, the teacher could supply a list of features from the pictures on a master list which students could work from. Alternatively, the students could be given oral prompts for them to describe the differences. A further possibility for teacher/class monitoring is to use a similar pair of pictures containing the same components but in a different configuration, and have the students carry out this task while being observed.

Checking could be done in plenary mode. However, the teacher could equally well listen to a sample of the students individually or in small groups. Teachers might record students for evaluation purposes, although delayed feedback is likely to be less helpful than immediate modelling of the target behaviour, unless the feedback is limited to one or two key points.

Further task activities: A wide range of follow-up activities are possible, such as reading exercises requiring students to match text and pictures; and writing exercises reporting differences, or writing a story on the basis of the picture(s). Alternatively, students might design their own pairs of pictures using elements present in the pair they were working with before. Activities of these kinds have long been described elsewhere. The purpose of mentioning them here is to reinforce the point that carrying out tasks without consolidating the work done wastes invested effort, misses the need to provide opportunities for revision and reworking, and sends the implicit message that students' investment of effort in the activity is not as worthwhile as it could be. Students who sense the existence of 'task-dependency' (Morrow and Johnson, 1981) are likely to take any given task more seriously than students who perceive tasks as 'one-off'.

To conclude this section, the manipulation of tasks outlined here can have two main purposes:

1. pedagogic: to raise awareness of the main purpose or purposes of a given task, to ensure that the students carry out this and future versions of the task with this in mind, and to provide a way of ensuring that students get a stimulating variety of activities in the classroom;

2. psycholinguistic: to vary the amount and focus of pressure students are placed under in carrying out the task, providing the basis for evaluation of student performance and of task effect.

In the light of the work of Schmidt (1990) and the importance he gives to conscious awareness of aspects of language in the learning process, the pedagogic purpose may well be seen as closely related to the psycholinguistic factors which ultimately constitute the major reason for using learning tasks in a given way.

6. Conclusion

This paper has attempted to contribute to an understanding of the linguistic value of pedagogic tasks. In particular, the paper has suggested that it is possible to make reasonable predictions regarding the likely grammatical features produced by students working on unscripted activities, and has provided a highly specific illustration of this. It raises the question of how students of different levels of proficiency can be expected to perform on such a task, and of how they might be able to benefit from working on such tasks under different conditions.

Taking a broader perspective, systematic studies of this kind might be relatable to the notion of novice–expert shifts in understanding and processing, discussed in the literature of cognitive psychology (e.g. Bechtel and Abrahamsen, 1990; McLaughlin, 1990). These studies suggest that an important aspect of learning concerns major qualitative changes in the way knowledge is organised, and in the speed with which it is accessed. Learners develop from taking local one-off decisions in early learning towards a point where they are able to generalise across contexts about what they know. This can in turn be expected to give way to the exploration of new resources in the handling of tasks, and to increase the range of options available for carrying them out.

Through the systematic use of unscripted tasks, learners and teachers may be able to move beyond the stage of seeing each activity as a unique communication task, consisting of a series of unique and creative decisions, to the point where the language demands – and the ways in which they can be met – can be generalised from one occasion to the next. In addition, as learners become familiar with given types of task, they are likely to improve in the speed with which they prepare, formulate and articulate their messages. Routines may be developed at discourse and utterance levels as familiarity increases, so promoting improved fluency. From this perspective, teachers and their learners may be better able to exploit the potential of systematic task-based practice so as to promote a type of learning that other kinds of course cannot offer.

The argument developed in this paper suggests a substantial coincidence of interest between researchers and practising teachers, as well as between those interested in promoting development and those interested in testing proficiency. It may be that evaluative studies in this area could contribute to developing a more carefully researched pedagogy of second language grammar than we have been able to assemble hitherto, by documenting how learners use grammar in given communicative contexts, and how their use of grammar changes and improves under different conditions. For the second language teacher, what is at issue is an understanding of how systematic use of teaching techniques can promote proficiency over time. Research could also contribute to developing documented profiles of task-based learner development which could provide a frame of reference for teachers and for materials development. Overall, the hope might be that, given a long-term programme of research and evaluation, approaches to language teaching methodology might develop a more discriminating perspective on the range of outcomes that can be expected from the systematic use of a wide range of language teaching materials. This would constitute a professionally responsible and questioning basis to the development of task-based language teaching and its impact on the learning of grammar.

References

Allwright, R.L. 1984, 'The importance of interaction in classroom language learning', *Applied Linguistics*, vol. 5, no. 2, 156–71.

Bechtel, W. and Abrahamsen, A. 1990, *Connectionism and the Mind*, Blackwell, Oxford.

Bolinger, D. 1975, 'Meaning and memory', *Folia Linguisticum*, vol. 1, 2–14.

Breen, M. 1989, 'The evaluation cycle for language learning tasks', in Johnson, R.K. (ed.), *The Second Language Curriculum*, CUP, Cambridge.

Brown, G. and Yule, G. 1983, *Teaching the Spoken Language*, CUP, Cambridge.

Brumfit, C.J. 1984a, *Communicative Methodology in Language Teaching*, CUP, Cambridge.

Brumfit, C.J. 1984b, 'Creativity and constraint in the language classroom', in Davies, A. *et al.* (eds.), *Interlanguage*, Edinburgh University Press, Edinburgh.

Brumfit, C.J. and Johnson, K. (eds.) 1979, *The Communicative Approach to Language Teaching*, OUP, Oxford.

Bruner, J.S. 1966, *Toward a Theory of Instruction*, Harvard University Press, Harvard.

Bygate, M. 1988, *Linguistic and Strategic Features of the Language of Learners on Oral Communication Exercises*, unpublished Ph.D thesis, Institute of Education, University of London.

Bygate, M. 1992, 'Neither chaos nor magic: on the systematic influence of task type on the language of learners', *Working Papers*. Department of Linguistic Science, University of Reading.

Bygate, M. 1993, 'Supporting frames or collapsing hierarchies: the role of tasks in the second language syllabus', keynote talk given at the conference of the Catalan Association for Teachers of English, Barcelona, Spain.

Cameron, L.J. 1991, 'Off the beaten track', *English in Education*, vol. 25, no. 2, 4–15.

Clark, R. 1974, 'Performing without competence', *Journal of Child Language*, vol. 1, no. 1, 1–10.

Crookes, G. 1986, *Task classification: a cross-disciplinary review*, Technical report no. 4, University of Hawaii, Manoa.

Dart, S.N. 1992, 'Narrative style in the two languages of a bilingual child', *Journal of Child Language*, vol. 19, 367–87.

Doughty, C. 1991, 'Second language instruction *can* make a difference', *Studies in Second Language Acquisition*, vol. 14, 3.

Downing, A. and Locke, P. 1992, *A University Course in English Grammar*, Prentice Hall, Hemel Hempstead.

Ellis, R. 1990, *Instructed Second Language Acquisition*, Blackwell, Oxford.

Fotos, S. and Ellis, R. 1991, 'Communicating about grammar: a task-based approach', *TESOL Quarterly*, vol. 25, no. 4, 605–27.

Johnson, K. 1986, 'Language teaching as skill training', Centre for Applied Language Studies, University of Reading, colloquium paper.

Levelt, W.J.M. 1978, 'Skill theory in language teaching', *Studies in Second Language Acquisition*, vol. 1, 1.

Littlewood, W.J. 1984, *Second and Foreign Language Learning*, CUP, Cambridge.

Long, M.H. 1981, 'Input, interaction and second language acquisition', *Annals of New York Academy of Sciences*, 259–78.

Long, M.H. and Porter, P.A. 1985, 'Group work, interlanguage talk and second language acquisition', *TESOL Quarterly*, vol. 19, no. 2, 207–28.

McLaughlin, B. 1990, 'Restructuring', *Applied Linguistics*, vol. 11, no. 2, 113–28.

Morrow, K. and Johnson, K. (eds.) 1981, *Communication in the Classroom*, Longman, Harlow.

Nunan, D. 1989, *Designing Tasks for the Communicative Curriculum*, CUP, Cambridge.

Ochs, E. 1979, 'Planned and unplanned discourse', in Givón, T. (ed.), *Discourse & Syntax*, Academic Press, New York.

Pawley, A. and Syder, F.H. 1983, 'Two puzzles for linguistic theory: native-like selection and native-like fluency', in Richards, J.C. and Schmidt, R.W. (eds.), *Language and Communication*, Longman, Harlow.

Perdue, C. and Klein, W. 1992, 'Why does the production of some learners not grammaticalize?', *Studies in Second Language Acquisition*, vol. 14, no. 3, 259–72.

Pica, T. 1987, 'Second language acquisition, social interaction and the classroom', *Applied Linguistics*, vol. 8, no. 1, 3–21.

Prabhu, N.S. 1987, *Second Language Pedagogy*, OUP, Oxford.

Schmidt, R.W. 1990, 'The role of consciousness in second language learning', *Applied Linguistics*, vol. 11, 2.

Sinclair, J.McH. 1991, *Corpus, Concordance, Collocation*, OUP, Oxford.

Swain, M. 1985, 'Communicative competence: some roles of comprehensible input and comprehensible output in its development', in Gass, S. and Madden, C. (eds.), *Input in Second Language Acquisition*, Newbury House, Rowley, Mass.

Tannen, D. 1980, 'A comparative analysis of oral narrative strategies', in Chafe, W.L. (ed.), *The Pear Stories: Cognitive, Cultural and Linguistic Aspects of Narrative Production*, Ablex, Norwood, NJ.

Tannen, D. 1984, *Conversational Style*, Academic Press, New York.

Tarone, E. and Yule, G. 1989, *Focus on the Learner*, OUP, Oxford.

Terry, P. 1989, *The Winning Mind*, Thorsons Publishing Group, Wellingborough.

Ur, P. 1981, *Discussions That Work*, CUP, Cambridge.

Ur, P. 1988, *Grammar Practice Activities*, CUP, Cambridge.

Widdowson, H.G. 1978, *Teaching Language as Communication*, OUP, Oxford.

Wilkins, D.A. 1976, *Notional Syllabuses*, OUP, Oxford.

Willis, D. and Willis, J. 1987, 'Varied activities for variable language', *ELT Journal*, vol. 41, no. 1, 12–18.

Young, J. 1992, *Do They Know What They Are Doing? A Study of the Extent to which Teachers Explain Methodology*, unpublished MA dissertation, Centre for Applied Language Studies, University of Reading.

Yule, G., Powers, M. and Macdonald, D. 1992, 'The variable effects of some task-based procedures on L2 communicative effectiveness', *Language Learning*, vol. 42, no. 2, 249–77.